FORENSIC GROUP
PSYCHOTHERAPY

NEW INTERNATIONAL LIBRARY OF GROUP ANALYSIS

Series Editor: Earl Hopper

Contributions of Self Psychology to Group Psychotherapy
  Walter N. Stone

Difficult Topics in Group Psychotherapy: My Journey from Shame to Courage
  Jerome S. Gans

Resistance, Rebellion and Refusal in Groups: The 3 Rs
  Richard M. Billow

The Social Nature of Persons: One Person is No Person
  A. P. Tom Ormay

The Social Unconscious in Persons, Groups, and Societies.
Volume 1: Mainly Theory
  edited by Earl Hopper and Haim Weinberg

Trauma and Organizations
  edited by Earl Hopper

Small, Large, and Median Groups: The Work of Patrick de Maré
  edited by Rachel Lenn and Karen Stefano

The Dialogues In and Of the Group:
Lacanian Perspectives on the Psychoanalytic Group
  Macario Giraldo

From Psychoanalysis to Group Analysis:
The Pioneering Work of Trigant Burrow
  edited by Edi Gatti Pertegato and Giorgio Orghe Pertegato

Nationalism and the Body Politic:
Psychoanalysis and the Rise of Ethnocentrism and Xenophobia
  edited by Lene Auestad

Listening with the Fourth Ear:
Unconscious Dynamics in Analytic Group Therapy
  Leonard Horwitz

The One and the Many: Relational Psychoanalysis and Group Analysis
  Juan Tubert-Oklander

THE PORTMAN PAPERS SERIES

Series Editor: Stanley Ruszczynski

Lectures on Violence, Perversion, and Delinquency
  edited by David Morgan and Stanley Ruszczynski

Containment in the Community: Supportive Frameworks for Thinking about Antisocial Behaviour and Mental Health
  edited by Alla Rubitel and David Reiss

FORENSIC GROUP PSYCHOTHERAPY

The Portman Clinic Approach

Edited by

*John Woods and
Andrew Williams*

A joint publication between
New International Library of Group Analysis
and
The Portman Papers

Routledge
Taylor & Francis Group
LONDON AND NEW YORK

First published 2014 by Karnac Books Ltd.

Published 2018 by Routledge
2 Park Square, Milton Park, Abingdon, Oxon OX14 4RN
711 Third Avenue, New York, NY 10017, USA

Routledge is an imprint of the Taylor & Francis Group, an informa business

Copyright © 2014 to John Woods and Andrew Williams for the edited collection, and to the individual authors for their contributions.

The rights of the editors and contributors to be identified as the authors of this work have been asserted in accordance with §§ 77 and 78 of the Copyright Design and Patents Act 1988.

All rights reserved. No part of this book may be reprinted or reproduced or utilised in any form or by any electronic, mechanical, or other means, now known or hereafter invented, including photocopying and recording, or in any information storage or retrieval system, without permission in writing from the publishers.

Notice:
Product or corporate names may be trademarks or registered trademarks, and are used only for identification and explanation without intent to infringe.

British Library Cataloguing in Publication Data

A C.I.P. for this book is available from the British Library

ISBN 9781780490496 (pbk)

Edited, designed and produced by The Studio Publishing Services Ltd
www.publishingservicesuk.co.uk
e-mail: studio@publishingservicesuk.co.uk

CONTENTS

ABOUT THE EDITORS AND CONTRIBUTORS — vii

NEW INTERNATIONAL LIBRARY OF GROUP
ANALYSIS FOREWORD by Earl Hopper — ix

THE PORTMAN PAPERS FOREWORD by Stanley Ruszczynski — xiii

INTRODUCTION by John Woods and Andrew Williams — xix

PART I: PRINCIPLES

CHAPTER ONE
Principles of forensic group therapy — 3
John Woods

CHAPTER TWO
On the containing structures required by
forensic group psychotherapy — 33
Andrew Williams and Anne Zachary

CHAPTER THREE
Acting out, the repetition compulsion, and
forensic group therapy — 53
Andrew Williams

PART II: THEMES AND APPLICATIONS

CHAPTER FOUR
My first year as a forensic group therapist 69
Aikaterini Papaspirou

CHAPTER FIVE
Therapist as "perverse female": the implications of 79
therapist gender for working with perverse and
violent patients
Jessica Yakeley

CHAPTER SIX
Paedophilia, child abuse, and group analysis 107
John Woods

CHAPTER SEVEN
The abused, the abuser, and the confusion of tongues 129
Alla Rubitel

CHAPTER EIGHT
Mentalization-based group treatment for antisocial 151
personality disorder
Jessica Yakeley

CHAPTER NINE
The invisible men: forensic group therapy with people 183
with intellectual disabilities
Alan Corbett

INDEX 203

ABOUT THE EDITORS AND CONTRIBUTORS

Alan Corbett is a psychotherapist and supervisor in private practice who specialises in the forensic treatment of patients with intellectual disabilities. His previous organisational roles include that of Clinical Director of Respond, The CARI Foundation, and ICAP. He is Chair of the Training Committee of the Institute of Psychotherapy and Disability, is a psychotherapist with the School of Life, consultant psychotherapist with the Clinic for Dissociative Studies, and lectures on a number of psychoanalytic training courses in London and Dublin.

Aikaterini Papaspirou is a specialist registrar in forensic psychotherapy at the Portman Clinic. She has published a book review on *The Murderess*, a novella by Alexandros Papadiamantis, in the *Journal of Forensic Psychiatry and Psychology*.

Alla Rubitel, is a member of the Institute of Psychoanalysis, and a consultant psychiatrist in psychotherapy in the NHS and in private practice. She is co-editor and author of a chapter in *Containment in the Community*, Volume II in the Portman papers series, published by Karnac.

Andrew Williams is a consultant psychiatrist in forensic psychotherapy at the Portman Clinic, previously at the Maudsley and Bethlem Royal Hospitals, and Broadmoor Hospital. He offers teaching and consultation to probation services, secure inpatient units, and prisons. He is currently training at the Institute of Psychoanalysis.

John Woods is a consultant psychotherapist at the Portman Clinic, Member of the British Association of Psychotherapists, the Association of Child Psychotherapists, and the Institute of Group Analysis. He has published articles on various clinical topics, and is the author of *Boys Who Have Abused; Psychoanalytic Psychotherapy with Young Victims/Perpetrators of Sexual Abuse*. He has also written dramatic monologues, and full-length plays, two of which, dealing with psychotherapeutic engagement with trauma and abuse, have been performed and published.

Jessica Yakeley is a consultant psychiatrist in forensic psychotherapy at the Portman Clinic, Director of Medical Education and Associate Medical Director, Tavistock and Portman NHS Foundation Trust, Fellow of the British Psychoanalytic Society, and Editor of the journal *Psychoanalytic Psychotherapy*. She has published research into psychodynamic methods of teaching medical students, papers on risk assessment, MAPPA (The Multi Agency Public Protection Arrangement), prison health, antisocial personality disorder, and is the author of *Working with Violence: A Contemporary Psychoanalytic Approach* (Palgrave MacMillan, 2010).

Anne Zachary qualified in medicine and then psychiatry at the Royal Free Hospital. She is a member of the British Psychoanalytic Society and for more than twenty years, until 2010, was Consultant Psychotherapist at the Portman Clinic. During that time, she also consulted to medium secure units, and Broadmoor Hospital. Currently, she works in private psychoanalytic practice in Kew. She has published journal papers on puerperal breakdown, the menopause, and on firesetting. She has contributed chapters to several books on such subjects as murderousness and the assessment of sexual offenders.

New International Library of Group Analysis Foreword

In the fields of psychoanalysis, psychoanalytical psychotherapy, psychoanalytical group therapy, and group analysis, "perversion" rarely means turning away from the true, biologically structured trajectory of human psychosexual development, as was once accepted doctrine. Usually, it now means the preoccupation with, and the enactment of, infant and child "sadomasochistic" sexuality during subsequent phases of the life trajectory within a particular socio-cultural context. It also refers to forms of interpersonal relations that are equivalent to these more explicit sadomasochistic sexual interactions, which are often called "perverse", if not "perverted". I have learnt that although, in this sense, perversions and their vicissitudes are universal, they also have socio-cultural and even political colouration. The social psychological genesis of the many forms of sexuality, involving sexual identity and gender identity, as well as sexual and gender object-choices, is still largely unknown. However, there are many kinds of heterosexuality, homosexuality, and bisexuality, some perverse and some not. Criminality, delinquency, and perversion are rooted in the fear of annihilation and its vicissitudes. What is true of mental life is not necessarily true of actual behaviour.

We must be grateful to those who developed the Portman Clinic, such as Glover, Rubinstein, Limentani, and Glasser, and later Campbell, Hale, and Welldon. It was Estela Welldon who initiated the practice of group analysis for "forensic" patients. This work, which has many special features and parameters, has also contributed to our understanding of these difficult patients, who are often not accepted for treatment in other clinical settings. The Portman Clinic continues to be at the vanguard of the application of psychoanalytical and group analytical ideas to the processes of healing such troubled and extremely troubling people. This can readily be seen in the development of the International Association of Forensic Psychotherapy, and in the representation of the staff of the Portman Clinic in the programmes of international conferences and workshops, in their many publications in leading journals, and now in the chapters of this most interesting and valuable book.

I am especially pleased to be able to include this book in The New International Library of Group Analysis. It is also included in the special series sponsored by the Portman Clinic. The authors convey the complexity of their clinical efforts and their struggle to understand their clinical experience, which is characterised by their patients' compulsions to project their internal worlds into all around them, especially into those who might be able to assist them. Such patients have also introjected the unwanted parts of all of us, which we have tended to project into them. We should be grateful to our colleagues for their willingness and ability to function as buffers between their patients and ourselves. Our colleagues help us to understand how we have collectively contributed to the inability of their patients to manage these projected parts of ourselves. So often, we would prefer to demonise them and make them invisible, which is not to say that we do not sometimes need to protect ourselves from them.

I am most grateful to John Woods and Andrew Williams, the Editors of this book, for their careful and concerned editorial work and for their own writing. John Woods became involved in the adult group work programme at the Portman Clinic as an extension of his work with adolescent sexual offenders, as represented in his (Woods, 2003) *Boys Who Have Abused*. He realised early on in his work that problematic sexual behaviour in adulthood stems from unresolved issues of adolescence. He realised that if the child is father to the man, the infant is father to the child, and, therefore, that therapeutic work in adulthood often supplies another chance to revise some of the wrong choices that have been made at an earlier stage of life. John has developed his clinical role at the Portman Clinic through teaching for the Tavistock and Portman Trust, and lecturing both here and abroad.

Andrew Williams, who is now training as a psychoanalyst, began at the Portman Clinic in 2006 as a Specialist Registrar in forensic psychiatry and psychotherapy, within the forensic psychotherapy dual training scheme. He has been actively involved in developing a service for men with antisocial personality disorder, using mentalization-based treatment. Despite the current challenges within the National Health Service, Andrew remains passionate about maintaining the identity of psychotherapeutic approaches within forensic settings.

I have been deeply influenced by the work of my colleagues at the Portman Clinic, especially while I was a teacher and supervisor on its Diploma Course. I am particularly pleased to have acknowledged the application of my theory of the basic assumption of Incohesion: Aggregation/Massification or (ba) I: A/M to the treatment of these very difficult, traumatised patients. They are so vulnerable to the suction of roles that typify incohesion, which, in turn, reflect and manifest their crustacean and amoeboid internal worlds. It is paradoxical that although this makes work in groups with "Portman patients" extremely difficult, it is also the basis for suggesting that, for them, group analysis supplemented by individual psychotherapy is the treatment of choice (Hopper, 2003).

Earl Hopper, PhD
Series Editor

References

Hopper, E. (2003). *Traumatic Experience in the Unconscious Life of Groups*. London: Jessica Kingsley.
Woods, J. (2003). *Boys Who Have Abused*. London: Jessica Kingsley.

The Portman Papers Foreword

Working therapeutically with patients or offenders who enact their conflicts, disturbance, and distress through acts of delinquency, criminality, and general or sexualised violence is a challenge being increasingly taken up by both mental health and criminal justice services. At the time of writing, growth in this particular service provision for forensic and antisocial personality disordered patients might appear to be in contrast to the general experience of welfare services, which are being threatened and sometimes closed as a result of recent and ongoing financial constraints. However, over the past dozen years or so, there has indeed been, and continues to be, a concern to offer *therapeutic* interventions to such people as well as, when appropriate, continuing to manage and contain them through institutional provision, through monitoring, and/or, when necessary, through the use of medication.

The genesis of this development crystallised in several government documents, among which was one entitled *Personality Disorder: No Longer a Diagnosis of Exclusion* (Department of Health, 2003); this took up the sometimes confused discussion about people with "disorders of the personality", manifested in transgressive behavioural enactments. Previously, to some large degree but not totally, such people had been dismissed as, at best, being "untreatable", and were often referred to with rather moralising and critical language; for example, the "obnoxious patient" (Martin, 1975), the "hateful patient" (Groves, 1978) the "heartsink patient" (O'Dowd, 1988), "patients psychiatrists dislike" (Lewis & Appleby, 1988), and "patients who are hard to like" (Watts & Morgan, 1994) were all phrases used in writings about a particular patient group.

The demonisation and exclusion of these patients is revealed by these terms. An alternative, however, was generated by government initiatives whereby the task was to develop new treatment services, informed by new conceptual thinking, specifically to address the disturbing distress often present, albeit hidden, in the behaviour of people variously known to forensic and antisocial personality disorder services. One of the central factors that needed to be addressed was how to provide settings that could withstand the often intrusive nature of the disturbances aroused by the criminal, violent, or sexually destructive behaviours.

The inevitable distress and disturbance experienced by the victims of this behaviour can be understood as, in part, the desperate and despairing unconscious purpose of much such behaviour on the part of the perpetrator. In an attempt to defend themselves against unmanageable internal states, versions of these states are aroused in others, who then come to carry the pain, fear, terror, confusion, and threat to sanity that would otherwise be felt by the perpetrator. Such projection takes place through behavioural and psychological enactments. Some understanding of this psychodynamic process is central in understanding how such patients and offenders function in the world.

From its inception in 1931, the Portman Clinic developed on the basis that such patients could be helped by the application of psychoanalytic principles to construct a psychotherapeutic treatment adapted to address this central feature of such patients. The lack of an internal psychological space within which such patients can process their conflicts, the external environment, and the mind and body of others, especially, of course, their victims, becomes the arena within which such evacuative expression takes place.

The Portman Clinic has always offered individual assessment and treatment for such patients and, since the early 1970s, mostly through the work of Estella Welldon and others, forensic group psychotherapy has also been offered. As is stated in this book, some clinicians argue that for many forensic and antisocial patients, group treatment is most often the treatment of choice. Although I think that this view warrants an ongoing debate, it is argued in this book that there may be, for some such patients, a dilution of the overwhelming and violent transference when in a group setting compared to that evoked in individual treatment, where it might feel unbearable and unmanageable. I might add that it may also be that the fragmented internal world of such forensic patients are both better expressed in the multiple transferences available in a group treatment and better contained by the interaction of group members. A parallel experience is well known to clinicians who consult to teams in residential mental health settings or to staff on prison landings, who, among themselves, become the recipients of different aspects of the patients' projected internal world and its conflicts and disturbance. Certainly, for some patients, the setting of the group might offer the opportunity of a more accurate reflection of the way in which they function psychically, through the multiple projections of their internal states into their environment.

In its nine chapters, the book offers an overview of various matters requiring sophisticated thinking in the structuring of forensic group psychotherapy. This includes a chapter by a group facilitator who writes about the process of establishing her first forensic treatment group, another chapter by a clinician who took over a group following the retirement of the previous group facilitator, and another chapter addressing the issues of the gender of the female therapist (including her pregnancy) working with perverse and violent men. I think that these are little written about topics, and yet they are probably common matters in most treatment settings.

The book then takes on some of the more difficult specific issues worked with in forensic and antisocial personality disorder services: enactments which are often among the most disturbing to clinicians and to the community at large. I am referring to chapters on group psychotherapy treatment with those suffering from paedophilia, with the victims and perpetrators of child sexual abuse, and with men with histories of very serious violence.

It is often these behaviours that most readily arouse moral and legal condemnation and even demonisation, and yet the clinician writers in this book show, with many clinical illustrations, how it is possible, in the face of these disturbing behaviours, to offer group psychotherapy treatment to these perpetrators as a way of providing containment and treatment. Hinshelwood has offered a very apt and pithy comment when he wrote that such patients are often referred to as "difficult patients" exactly because they arouse difficult feelings in their clinician (Hinshelwood, 1999) as well as in the community.

The final chapter addresses what is evocatively referred to as "invisible patients", people with intellectual disabilities whose group treatment is rarely written about.

Crucially, this book describes very clearly the multi-layered containment offered by group psychotherapy in an institution: the containment offered by the group facilitator, the group members, the administrative team in the clinic, and the clinic itself. This is understood as fundamental to the provision of forensic group psychotherapy. It should also be said that the same containment is required by the group facilitator; as well as having the possibility of supplementary containment offered by the group members to each other, he or she also has the containment offered by the institutional arrangements of the clinic, including a regular workshop within which to discuss the work. The Russian doll metaphor offered in one of the early chapters is very apt in describing this multi-layered container, available to both the patient and group facilitator, and without which forensic group psychotherapy probably could not take place.

By providing a clearly described set of theoretical and technical principles, this book adds a further layer to this multi-layered containment. The ideas in the book contribute further to the meaning-making process offered in psychoanalytically informed forensic group psychotherapy treatment. A setting is made available which can be used developmentally by some forensic patients to address the often compulsive and disturbing acting out which dominates their lives and the lives of those around them. Thus, they may find an opportunity to move from action and reaction of their behaviours towards reflection and thoughtfulness.

Stanley Ruszczynski
Clinical Director, Portman Clinic

References

Department of Health (2003). *Personality Disorder: No Longer a Diagnosis of Exclusion. Policy Implementation Guidance for the Development of Services for People with Personality Disorder*. London: National Institute for Mental Health/Department of Health.

Groves, J. E. (1978). Taking care of the hateful patient. *New England Medical Journal, 298*(16): 883–887.

Hinshelwood, R. D. (1999). The difficult patient. *British Journal of Psychiatry, 174*: 187–190.

Lewis, G., & Appleby, L. (1988). *British Journal of Psychiatry, 153*: 44–49.

Martin, P. A. (1975). The obnoxious patient. In: P. Giovacchini (Ed.), *Tactics and Techniques in Psychoanalytic Psychotherapy: Vol II Countertransference* (pp. 196–204). New York: Jason Aronson.

O'Dowd, T. C. (1988). Five years of heartsink patients. *British Medical Journal, 97*: 528–530.

Watts, D., & Morgan, G. (1994). Malignant alienation: dangers for patients who are hard to like. *British Journal of Psychiatry, 164*: 11–15.

Introduction

John Woods and Andrew Williams

This book is about the practice and underlying theory of psychodynamic group therapy as undertaken in the Portman Clinic. Since its inception in 1931, this outpatient setting within the Tavistock & Portman NHS Foundation Trust, in North London, has provided psychodynamic treatment to people of all ages who have difficulties arising from their criminal, violent, or sexually deviant behaviour. By definition, therefore, our patients are predisposed to action rather than symptoms of distress, and might be excluded or rejected by other services because of their past or present behaviour. The experience of working with such patients has enabled the development of theories about the psychopathology that underlies violence, perversion, and delinquency. (Most notably, Glover, 1960; Limentani, 1989; Rosen, 1964.) There have been many further contributions to this literature in subsequent years, for instance, Welldon (1988), Morgan and Ruszczynski (2007). The broadening out of these findings in consultation to many organisations and agencies has been conveyed in the second of the Karnac series "The Portman Papers", *Containment in the Community*, edited by Alla Rubitel and David Reiss (2011). Much of this work has been based on findings from individual psychotherapy, even though, for more than twenty years, up to half of our patients at any one time are in group treatment. One overall purpose of this book is to redress that balance.

Forensic psychotherapy can be described as the offspring of psychoanalytic psychotherapy and forensic psychiatry (Welldon, 2011, p. 139). From the beginnings of psychoanalysis, there has been intense interest in the understanding of not only the criminal mind, but of the significance of transgression for the human psyche. Indeed, the existence of the Oedipus complex, the forbidden desires to kill the rival and take the object of desire, can be seen as fundamentally breaking the law, whether of the family, "the Father", or society, a modern version, one might say, of original sin. Psychoanalysis has been built on the internal conflicts arising from such forbidden desires and the consequent neurotic symptoms. With "forensic" patients, however, the restraints against antisocial impulses have broken down. Having broken the law, and potentially becoming a threat to society, an individual will also tend to be antagonistic towards any hint of authority in the treatment setting. Thus, a complex therapy is required that has to take into account not only the individual patient's needs, but also the impact of the patient's behaviour upon others. The development of this model has been intricately associated with the work of the International Association of Forensic Psychotherapy (Welldon, 2011, Chapter Eight).

The dual nature of the task has always been a central tenet of forensic psychotherapy, which posits that perpetrators are not born, but created through their experiences of having themselves been victims, even though this is often split off or hidden, (Welldon & Van Velsen, 1997, pp. 1–9). Breaches of normative social boundaries (whether actually illegal or not) affect both the individual and society. For the individual, there is the harm that he or she has done, and in the background, inevitably, also the damage from the trauma, neglect, or actual abuse committed previously against him or her. For society, there is the responsibility for having allowed it. Winnicott's (1956) concept of the antisocial tendency shows how the damaged individual brings attention to the ill he has suffered in the hope (perhaps often futile) of some recompense. A social form of treatment symbolises this lifelong drama and might enable an individual to work through his conflict with other people.

Group work, multi-faceted as it is, is well placed to undertake this complex task. Joining a group of strangers might seem a daunting task, but we are often surprised by the willingness of patients to overcome their sense of shame, fear of exposure, and to begin to take responsibility. A prospective member might feel reassured when he is told that the group comprises people who have similar problems, and are seeking recovery. This may be less threatening than a one-to-one therapy, where the transference might be felt as too intense. There is often a hope that the group will create a new reality, and although a process of disillusion might ensue, nevertheless, each individual gets to understand their personal story better and begins to create, as it were, a new narrative, about their harmful and harmed self, in relation to others. Thus, the group presents for each member the possibility of new norms, new boundaries and expectations. There is an interplay between internal and external reality in this form of therapy. Although the tendency to action is the predominant feature of forensic patients, the group very soon will focus on states of mind that will have driven the individual, often unconsciously, to acts that he comes to regret, even though they might be repeated. "Please help me stop myself," is often the underlying request. The therapist provides the means to think about those states of mind, and begin a process of change.

Foulkes described group analysis as "ego training in action" (Foulkes, 1964, p. 82), but it is at the same time an exploration of unconscious processes. The "forensic patient" has little difficulty in grasping the fact that he has been driven by fears and desires he does not understand. The work of self-exploration is usually intense. There is little point in "luxuriating in stupefaction", as Spoto (2004) described a certain stage of psychoanalysis. Group members know why they are there, and only occasionally have to remind each other that they had better get on with the work. Portman groups tend to be active; there is little silence, little repetition. Group members confront each other's self-deception, though it is part of the therapist's job to ensure that this remains within tolerable limits.

As a leading group analyst has pointed out more recently, the question of technique is central to the work of the group analyst (Behr, 2008, p. 57). The main thrust of the articles published in this collection is in relation to practice, and how that is so bound up with our theory and understanding of our patient's needs. Transference and counter-transference issues mean that the person of the therapist is always involved. It will be seen from the various contributors that there are variations of technique between them, resulting from their own different personalities, orientation, and interests, as well as from the needs of a particular group. What binds the contributors together is a shared commitment to the value of group therapy, and the need to keep on thinking about the interactions that take place between group members and therapist.

As the papers on various aspects of group therapy were written, we realised that our contributors sometimes have rather different views; the classic debate, for instance, between different models represented by Foulkes and Bion are explored in these contributions, as is also the recent development of mentalization-based treatment within a more traditionally psychoanalytic clinic (see the chapter by Jessica Yakeley). It is also clear from our ongoing group therapy workshop that there are also differences in practice. We have come to realise that there is no totally uniform approach to group therapy. Each group is in some ways a reflection of the group conductor. It builds its own culture and, therefore, identity. At an obvious level, this is determined by each therapist's preoccupations and concerns, not only what he or she chooses to take up, which indicates to the group a conception of the task, but also the "how", that is, the quality of the therapist's being in the room; certain non-verbal signals and cues that might be unconscious all have an impact upon the group members' state of mind. The therapist might be anxious, sad, critical, judgemental, or impatient at what he or she is hearing and taking in, and, therefore, needs the opportunity to process this emotional "fallout", which will affect the therapist's relationship with the group. Group work is not without stresses and strains, and the occasional breaking of boundaries. All members will have experienced disrupted attachments at the very least, if not severe trauma arising from neglect and abuse. The emotional and psychological consequences of these childhood experiences will be brought into the treatment setting and will have an impact upon the therapist. As Hinshelwood has put it, "if you work with disturbed people you are likely to feel disturbed" (Hinshelwood, 2011 p. xxiii). For a therapist to grow into the role, and begin to work with a group of forensic patients to produce change, there has to be the continual sharing and learning that can be provided best by a peer group supervision.

The first section of this book takes on the more general questions of principle that underlie the practice of forensic group therapy. After a broadly theoretical overview in the first chapter by John Woods, Chapter Two, by Andrew Williams and Anne Zachary, addresses practical questions of structure and containment. Chapter Three, by Andrew Williams, considers what responses are possible to the ubiquitous problem for our groups of acting out. The second section of the book consists of explorations of specific clinical topics: gender, which is such an important factor in regard to rates of offending, is highlighted by the role of female therapists. Jessica Yakeley very courageously examines the impact of her gender, and pregnancy, on the working relationship with her all male group. We are particularly fortunate in having two presentations by colleagues who, though experienced in related fields, reflect upon their time as beginners at this modality of work in the chapters by Alla Rubitel and Aikaterini Papaspirou. Their enthusiasm in getting to grips with the internal world of the offender as manifest in the group is impressive. The differences between the two groups is noteworthy; whereas the one portrays the group as container of deeply felt trauma in a maternal and ambivalent transference, the other was characterised by open conflict, at perhaps a more oedipal level. Specialised or homogeneous groups have been found to be helpful with certain types of patients, or at least those who present with certain types of problem. We have experienced problems integrating into group those who have overtly abused children, or been convicted of downloading illegal images of child sexual abuse. The questions that arise as to why those patients seem to do better in a more specialised group are discussed in a further chapter by John Woods. Finally, Al Corbett provides us with many insights derived from the treatment of men where their learning disability is intricately bound up with their sexually abusive behaviour.

Despite the many differences between the various contributors, it will be clear that a certain theoretical framework is shared. This consistency provides a holding of its own, which militates against the traumatic material contained by the therapists in their work with these groups. The reader will notice the recurrence of certain concepts, and references to the work, for example, of Glasser, Gilligan, Foulkes, Stoller, Welldon, Perelberg, and others. These might, at times, seem repetitive, but it is intended that each chapter stand on its own, though it may have points of reference in common with the others. The importance of Estela Welldon's contribution to the field of psychoanalytic psychotherapy, not only in the forensic sphere, has been widely cited, the most recent examples being by Baroness Helena Kennedy and Professor James Gilligan in their respective forewords to the recent volume of collected papers (Welldon, 2011). Our particular indebtedness at the Portman Clinic will clearly be seen in the number of references to her work throughout this book. Her influence, especially in the early years of establishing group work at the clinic, has been enormous. She has bequeathed us not only a set of concepts, but also a model of a lively humane interest, so necessary to face the complexities of offending behaviour and access the creative energy needed to produce change.

A clinical service such as that at the Portman Clinic has, unfortunately, not had the capacity to undertake a great deal of empirical research, although some advance in this direction is described in Chapter Eight. While there is little proof in terms of randomised control trials to demonstrate beyond doubt the effectiveness of our methods compared to others, the evidence in these pages is that through careful audit and clinical supervision, we build on our experience of "what works for whom". What we see through our own eyes is that, by and large, slowly but surely, our patients get better. The groups would not survive if this were not so. These papers represent "learning from experience", in Bion's sense, that is, paying careful attention to the meaning of contact with and between patients, being free as far as possible of preconceptions, and enabling new thoughts and meaning to arise. All of this is perhaps difficult to measure, except that reoffending rates while patients are in treatment are low, and "patient satisfaction", in terms of their commitment to therapy, remains very high.

Although the Portman Clinic, as a National Health Service outpatient facility, is a very specific setting, we would hope that the clinical findings presented here will be relevant to group work in different settings. Psychodynamic work is not in competition with cognitive–behavioural therapy, or sex offender treatment programmes, because the task is different. Frequently, we are referred "graduates", as it were, of these programmes, where it is recognised that they have long-term therapeutic needs. On the other hand, some new referrals might be seen as not ready for a psychodynamic approach, but more in need of the structure provided by cognitive–behavioural therapy. A psychodynamic model of treatment can attend to the inner life of the person who has offended and who is in the process of moving on to become more than just his offence. Our aim is that the erstwhile offender uses his experiences, including what he has done, to grow and develop in his humanity, to re-establish his "membership of the human race", as one group member put it, and to be in a position to transform his life into something far more constructive than what it was before.

Acknowledgement to our patients and in relation to confidentiality

It would not have been possible to produce this book without using clinical material from group sessions. However, we have been extremely mindful in the preparation of this book about our duty to protect our patients' right to confidentiality. While this has been a difficult balance to address, we feel that we have managed to change the details of our patients' histories sufficiently so as to make them as minimally recognisable as is possible without taking away the meaning of the clinical vignettes and accounts. We are extremely grateful to our patients for the rich experience that they have given us through sharing their experiences within the context of group psychotherapy.

References

Behr, H. L. (2008). Education about group analysis is as important as research. *Group Analysis, 41*(1): 53–59.

Foulkes, S. H. (1964). *Therapeutic Group Analysis*. London: Allen & Unwin [reprinted London: Karnac, 1984].

Glover, E. (1960). *The Roots of Crime*. London: Imago Publishing [re-issued New York: International Universities Press, 1970].

Hinshelwood, R. D. (2011). Foreword. In: A. Rubitel & D. Reiss (Eds.), *Containment in the Community* (pp. xxiii–xxiv). London: Karnac.

Limentani, A. (1989). *Between Freud and Klein*. London: Karnac 1999.

Morgan, D., & Ruszczynski, S. (Eds.) (2007). *Lectures on Violence, Perversion & Delinquency: The Portman Papers*. London: Karnac.

Rosen, I. (1964). *Sexual Deviation*. Oxford: Oxford University Press.

Rubitel, A., & Reiss, D. (2011). *Containment in the Community: The Portman Papers*. London: Karnac.

Spoto, G. F. (2004). Luxuriating in stupefaction: the analysis of a narcissistic fetish. In: E. Hargreaves & A. Varchevker (Eds.), *Pursuit of Psychic Change: The Betty Joseph Workshop*. London: Brunner-Routledge (New Library of Psychoanalysis).

Welldon, E. (1988). *Mother, Madonna ,Whore: The Idealisation and Denigration of Motherhood*. London: Free Association Books.

Welldon, E. (2011). *Playing with Dynamite*. London: Karnac.

Welldon, E., & Van Velsen, C. (1997). *A Practical Guide to Forensic Psychotherapy*. London: Jessica Kingsley Publishers.

Winnicott, D. W. (1956). The anti-social tendency. In: *Deprivation and Delinquency*. London: Hogarth Press.

PART I
PRINCIPLES

CHAPTER ONE

Principles of forensic group therapy

John Woods

The place of forensic group therapy

In her landmark paper, Estela Welldon states, "Group analytic psychotherapy is frequently the best form of treatment, not only for severely disturbed perverse patients but also for sexual abusers, and sexually abused patients" (Welldon, 1996, p. 63). The experience at the Portman Clinic is that group treatment has been an effective form of psychotherapy, not for all, but perhaps the majority of our patients. The effectiveness of group treatment in general is being substantiated by empirical evidence (Burlingame, Fishman, & Mosier, 2003; Leichsenring & Leibing, 2003; Lorentzen, 2000; Taylor, 2000). In addition, at a time when cost effectiveness is ever more crucial, it is important to note that society also benefits from this treatment (Dolan, Warren, Menzies, & Norton, 1996; Hall & Mullee, 2000). Although there is much evidence for the effectiveness of the group-analytic model (Blackmore, Tantum, Parry, & Chambers, 2012), the majority of group work in many settings is highly structured, using a cognitive approach in order to correct faulty patterns of thinking and provide skills training (Saunders, 2008). This has meant that group process has been largely unexplored (Morgan & Flora, 2002, p. 204). The aim of this publication is to redress that balance by adding a psychodynamic perspective.

Yalom (1972) characterised the benefit of group therapy as representing the universality of experience; the individual no longer feels isolated and, therefore, stuck with his problems, but how does this sit with people who have demonstrated their rejection of social mores? Welldon goes on from the statement quoted above to show that "the group comprises three elements; the therapist, the patient, and a third element that represents society" (Welldon, 1996, p. 63). This last element has various manifestations. It exists outside the room in the form of the criminal justice system, more benignly, perhaps, in the National Health Service (NHS) that provides the treatment, or more viciously in the sometimes unthinking public media: for instance, in the demonisation of child abusers. The therapist has to think about what kind of contact is possible with statutory agencies such as the Multi Agency Public Protection Arrangements Panel, (known as MAPPA). The third point of the triangle is always there, even if only implicitly, in the group's awareness. It is represented concretely by the clinic setting, which is why such work is best undertaken in the public sector. The process of triangulation between fellow patients, therapist, and institution creates a thinking space so that each is free from what, in one-to-one treatment, might become a claustrophobic and hostile dependency. As a social form of treatment, the group provides a new experience for an individual that integrates their inner world of desires, impulses, and emotional conflicts with what before has been so mismatched: the demands of the external world.

The person presenting as a "forensic" patient has come up against society's standards in terms of legal, or morally acceptable, behaviour. They will have broken the law and/or transgressed social norms. They might not be seeking psychotherapy as others might, for some inner reason, depression, anxiety, or need for personal change, though they might admit to a need to understand the meaning of their actions. Their conflicts will have been with others rather than experienced as internal. Typically, they will have been given to action rather than thought. This particular kind of relationship with the social world needs to be accommodated in the treatment. The therapist must pay specific attention to the external world. Indeed, the word "forensic" is derived, according to the *Oxford English Dictionary*, from the Latin "forum", the public place where judgements are made. Legal process, child protection, the risk of harm to self or others—all are very live issues and include various interested parties outside of the treatment setting. Yet, the treatment demands an investigation of a patient's innermost thoughts and feelings. How can the privacy and confidentiality upon which any psychotherapy depends be reconciled with the demands of the external world? Forensic psychotherapy has found that perpetrators are not born, but created through their experiences of having themselves been victims, though this is often split off or hidden (Welldon & Van Velsen, 1997, pp. 1–9). However, the statement "He did it because he was abused" inspires mistrust and hostility in those who expect the law to protect society. Understanding can easily be confused with permissiveness. Forensic psychotherapy, thus, holds an uncomfortable position, balancing the opposing demands of internal and external laws.

Since much group work in prisons, or by agencies such as the Probation Service, aims to manage and correct behaviour, we have to ask whether working on the causes or internal dynamics of offending are relevant, or whether they are distractions from the main task which would, for many, be defined as the prevention of reoffending. For the psychoanalytic practitioner, another question is whether analytic work is possible or even advisable for such a group. An outpatient service such as the Portman Clinic has a wider remit than, say, a Sex Offenders Treatment Programme (Brown, 2010) because our patient population includes not only those who have committed offences, but those who might be in danger of doing so, as well as those who themselves suffer the ill effects of sexual perversion. In the context of a health service setting, rather than part of the criminal justice system, the treatment is voluntary and, thus, requires the active participation of the patient. With this broader perspective comes the possibility of investigating the psychodynamics that might underlie these problematic behaviours. The aim is not only to help certain patients, but also to extend our understanding of their origin and meaning. The challenge is to ensure that this does not happen at the expense of safeguarding against further harm, whether to or by the patient.

A psychodynamic model of group therapy

"I know its no excuse, but I damn well know that if I had not been sexually abused every night in boarding school I would not have this compulsion to use prostitutes every day."

Psychoanalytic psychotherapy has come a long way from the ivory tower it was once seen to inhabit. Relational psychoanalysis is a powerful movement in the USA and the UK, (Holmes, 2011). There has been a pull away from the comfort of the private consulting room towards an engagement with wider social issues (Altman, 2009). The person of the therapist is now more acknowledged as vitally there, present, and seen by "client" or "patient", as not neutral, but as far as possible impartial, not observing an individual psyche objectively, but interacting with the other. Psychotherapy is now seen as based on intersubjectivity (Holmes, 2011, p. 309), consisting of the exchanges between the intrapsychic processes of subjective fields of consciousness. Group therapy could be the ideal form of treatment in which this process can take place. Without careful leadership, however, the group might not necessarily be that therapeutic milieu.

Bion (1961) elucidated the defensive nature of much group dynamics, arising from the conflict within each of us about our membership of any group. His description of the individual is often quoted: ". . . a group animal at war with his groupishness" (Garland, 2010, p. 104). Thus, a group resorts to defensive postures, designed to repudiate the threat to individual identity posed by the group. Some of these defence mechanisms become irrational and rigidified, as if psychotic processes, inhibiting any work the group may be required to do. Hume (2010) shows that Bion's was not a model for individual treatment in a group setting and that he gives little guidance as to how the therapist might work with a group. Instead, Bion remarked on how common it is that patients are convinced that the group ". . . is no good and cannot cure them" (Hume, 2010 p. 110). Interpretations in this model are addressed only to the group, and reflect on its method of dealing with the failure to fulfil the needs of the individual. Hume (2010) goes on to quote Sutherland as observing that Bion's group ". . . takes away the anchorage of the adult self-identity". However, for people who urgently need to change maladaptive forms of self identity, this disillusionment can be put to good use. Hinshelwood (2008) has suggested that the Foulkesian model and technique, allowing, as it does, more space to the individual, is less stressful to those who might need to reorientate their relationship to what Foulkes called the "matrix" of their social world.

The "foundation matrix" is what Foulkes called the shared mental operations between people. "Dynamic matrix" refers to a more specific level, the "web of communications in the here and now within the group" (Foulkes, 1975, pp. 131–132). This is built up and developed by a process of "free group association" (Foulkes, 1975, pp. 95–96), in which each group member is encouraged to respond to each other's communications as freely as possible. This material consists, in effect, of spontaneous interpretations by the group of each other's contributions. The therapist's role is to guide, contain, and, at times, illuminate, as he or she amplifies certain features and damps down others; confusion and chaos in the group, for example, is useful only up to a certain point, beyond which the therapist needs to be more active. Foulkes draws an analogy with the conductor of an orchestra who co-ordinates the interplay of parts in order to make a coherent whole (Foulkes, 1964, p. 285). (Indeed, he preferred "conductor" to "therapist", though this is usually retained in the clinic setting.)

Interpretations about an individual's internal world are problematic in group therapy; they exclude other group members, and, if prolonged, reduce the others to an audience who must wait their turn. However, when patients are encouraged to relate to each other, there is an immediacy of therapeutic experience for group members on a collective basis. There is a far greater range of possibilities of meaning than was previously known to the individual. It is as though the unconscious emerges in the present reality rather than being signposted by the one "expert": "Is this how I come across to others? Perhaps this is a side of me I don't want to recognise. But in that case . . . who am I really?" Increased self-knowledge can produce new identifications. Instead of denying the identity that others in the group reflect back, the person is led to accept that he may not be quite what he thought he was: for example, not the innocent victim of injustice that he had defensively maintained. Identification is a process that takes place unconsciously. Identity, on the other hand, is an attempt that each individual makes to organise conflicting identifications in order to achieve what might, after all, be no more than an illusion of unity. Questioning this destabilises a person's view of himself. Joining a group and staying with the process has to be acknowledged at the outset as hard work, especially in order to dispel the fantasy of comfort and consolation that some might bring as their goal of treatment.

The Groups Book (Garland, 2010) shows how varying aspects of an individual's internal world are picked up on by different group members, including the therapist. "The internal world becomes visible and alive, active in the relationships lived out in the room" (p. 57). Orientated more to Bion than Foulkes, Garland and her contributors focus on the group's task, and the basic assumptions that may, or may not, unconsciously facilitate a therapeutic process (Garland, 2010, pp. 104–110). By contrast, the Portman model owes more to Foulkes, though it has been adapted, most notably by Welldon (1997, pp. 9–10). This is worthy of comment, since the emphasis on destructive group process is much less in Foulkes's theory than Bion's, even though Portman patients have been referred for predominantly destructive behaviour. It might be that the group therapy culture in the Portman clinic has been determined by a need to ensure, as far as possible, that the group remains a safe place, especially for people who have done dangerous things, despite the group also providing an exploratory, uncovering, and interpretative function.

Developing Bion's theory of the basic assumptions that inhibit the work of the group, Hopper (1997) has proposed a fourth basic assumption, "incohesion", particularly relevant to groups of people affected by trauma, and where thought and work have to be avoided because awareness is associated with too much pain. Hopper goes on to elaborate concepts of "aggregation" and "massification", two forms that operate the incohesion that itself becomes a threat to the survival of the group. In these states, role differentiation is made impossible because of envy and fear of destruction. There might be a "fantasy of perfection" that, for a paedophile group, can have sinister overtones; this is where the therapist has to provide an active form of leadership.

> The group was bemoaning the impossibility of loving sexual relationships and the therapist began to feel oppressed by the repetition of these complaints. He commented that the group was bonding with an implicit idea that sexual exploitation was inevitable. Then a group member responded to someone who had been complaining that he keeps being drawn into anonymous sex: "Until I met you, I thought I was the only person who could lie so successfully to myself. Can you not see that in

going to a sauna, where you know men are going to be looking for sex, you are going to be propositioned?"

How differently this critical stance would have been perceived by the patient had it been put by an individual therapist. Perhaps a key question is that, given the background and personal histories of group members, what prevents them from becoming *en masse* perverse and/or delinquent? The rest of this chapter, and perhaps the whole book, attempts to address this issue. It is unusual for Portman groups to fall into destructive processes, because they are ever-present and always being worked with. The question will be investigated in more detail, but part of the answer arises from the valuable qualities of group therapy generally. Clearly, the power differential between client and professional is radically altered. Group therapy is fundamentally a democratic and egalitarian form of treatment. It meets a need in most people, especially those who have had severe problems in their lives, for recognition, belonging, and emotional support. This can become the basis for change. Group members report a sense of empowerment, being no longer in a passive position in relation to their therapist, but actively involved in their own and others' work. Thus, we speak of group "members", rather than "patients", and they are invited to take part, to a certain extent, in managing their own treatment setting: for example, writing to absentees, and in other ways which will be evident throughout this book. This is not to say there is no conflict or frustration at the conflicts that inevitably arise:

> Exasperated by Roger's arriving again clearly intoxicated at the group session, even though he insisted he had "only a half a pint for God's sake!", the group debated whether they could take a decision demanding that he not come to the session if he has been drinking. He accepted this limit, but found it much harder to give up his other compulsion, paying for sex with "rent boys". The group would not accept his protestations that these male prostitutes were of legal age. Group members were too aware of the damage of sexual abuse, and how it is repeated in prostitution. Confronted continually with this conflict, he decided to leave, much to the chagrin of some, but relief to others. For the therapist, the sense of failure with Roger was mitigated by the sense that the group had at least confirmed their own limits to acceptable behaviour, and "who knows?" someone in the group workshop conjectured, "Roger himself may have got the message."

The peer group, siblings, and the law of the mother

"Horizontal" relationships in a group, based on equality and common purpose, rather than the "vertical" transference evoked in other therapeutic structures, facilitates independence and autonomy (Welldon, 1997, p. 17). This is a process that is particularly useful for people who have come into conflict with the authority of the law. Oedipal conflicts are mitigated by multi-dimensional sibling transferences (Welldon, 2011, pp. 126–128). This is not to deny powerful ambivalence and conflict in the group setting as well. Freud conjectured that at an early stage of cultural evolution, a "horde of brothers" banded together to murder the father, in order to have rights over the mother; they are then held together by guilt and fear of retribution (Freud, 1939a). This he regarded as fundamental to what we would now call group dynamics. Idealisation of a group leader, such as Hitler, promises relief from guilt and shame. Klein, on the other hand, commented that the bond between siblings might provide relief from parental sadism and neglect (Klein, 1927, p. 119). Wellendorf (2011, p. 4) points out the annihilation anxiety aroused by the arrival of a new sibling which, if not dealt with, is repeated in damagingly competitive relationships. Coles (2003) describes the crucial role of siblings in structuring the psyche of individual development. Joyce (2011) has shown the developmental value in managing aggression and rivalry between siblings.

The significance of siblings for the development of personality has been extensively explored by Mitchell (2003). She takes the view that psychoanalysis has focused excessively on vertical relations between parents and children, to the neglect of lateral relations and their influence on individual development, especially on relationships in later life. Sibling experience evokes existential conflicts, the trauma of being annihilated by another, and might also provide the first experience of differentiating self and other. The mother, in Mitchell's view, has a crucial role in mediating this process. The "law of the mother" introduces sharing, a concept of seriality, and mutuality, all of which militate against narcissism and omnipotence, the most blatant manifestation of which is to be seen in the incest perpetrator. Whereas breaking the barrier of incest goes against the "law of the father", albeit at the cost of entry into the symbolic (social) order (Lacan, 2007, p. 67), breaking the "law of the mother" produces primitive fantasies of power over life and death, and the pathway to adult sexual perversion is opened up. (The clinical material about the pregnant therapist in Jessica Yakeley's chapter can be seen as a wonderful instance of re-establishing the law of the mother.)

The single therapist is often the object of a maternal transference, and it has become expected in the therapeutic culture at the Portman, following Welldon's pioneering work, that a sole female therapist may effectively work with groups of men; some may well have been violent, but come to accept the authority acknowledged her by the group (Welldon, 1997 p. 17, 2011, p. 202). Whether the solitary therapist is male or female, their nurturing and consistent role fills a gap and a need in the experience of the patients' lives. We might say that for the delinquent or offender patient, the law of the father has failed, and that sometimes a male therapist seems to evoke more aggression in the patient or group. Neither has the renunciation of a primitive union with mother happened in the development of perverse fantasy life. In group treatment, the sexually perverse patient has an opportunity to renegotiate his relationship to the social world at a profound level. A move into the social world brings the possibility of being no longer excluded from the symbolic order. What also may be supplied by a treatment that derives more from the law of the mother is a restitution of earlier pre-oedipal experience, and repair of early infantile emotional trauma.

> The group is debating whether to write to Patrick, who is now absent for the third week. Martin says he does not feel like writing because Patrick did not seem motivated to change; "Quite frankly I'd prefer it if he didn't return." The group seem nonplussed by this, while the therapist is thinking about Martin recently revealing his grievance at the suicide of his brother, and being made to feel guilty for neglecting his brother's obvious mental illness. The therapist comments that it might be useful for Martin to express some of that to Patrick, since he obviously felt rather let down by him.

How does forensic group therapy work?

Aims

The therapist and a prospective group member formulate the aims of joining a group. These have to be realistic and achievable. Cure is a notion that usually has to be modified. The greater likelihood of gradual change, at the patient's own pace, puts the individual in a more autonomous position. "Finding out the real reason why I compulsively exhibit myself" might be achievable, but will knowing the "real reason" enable the person to manage his life better? Above all, the group provides a forum for experiencing and, therefore, thinking about relationships. So, such a question may be reframed as, "What am I doing to people by my behaviour, and why?" Bion expressed this as a transition from "narcissism to social-ism" (Garland, 2010, pp. 34–36). The first step is for the new group member to engage with an idea that there might be a benefit to be derived from sharing their experiences with people who have "problems somewhat like" their own. The immediate result is to reduce the shame and sense of isolation with which they have been burdened, in many cases, for years. Then the work begins.

The purpose of the group

Doubts are often expressed when group treatment is recommended: "Sharing my innermost thoughts with a bunch of strangers? I've got enough problems of my own, I can't take on other people's!" The group therapist needs to have a concept, based on training and experience, of the value of taking such a leap into the unknown, but might respond with something simple: "You may learn something about yourself through sharing with others." The process is most elegantly put in a classic group analytic paper titled "Taking the non-problem seriously" Garland (1982). The presenting problem that the person brought to the group fades into the background as the foreground is occupied by those aspects of the personality and behaviour that have an impact upon other members of the group. Opening his mind to new possibilities presented by the group, an individual may be released from his repetitive and self-destructive mode of being. This is not always easy to convey to a candidate for group therapy. More readily agreed in the Portman context is the forensic focus. This has to be made explicit, since an emphasis on the presenting problem changes the traditional non-directive stance of the psychoanalytic therapist.

The forensic focus

The aims of psychodynamic group therapy are described usually in terms of self understanding and relatedness to others, (Garland, 2010, pp. 12–13). What forensic treatment adds is twofold: (a) to develop an understanding of the offending or perverse behaviour and its unconscious determinants, and (b) a working through, as far as possible, of the trauma that is presumed to have been defended against and converted into acting out (in so far as the patient is able to do so). Once this work commences, then a shared culture develops in the group. This expectation is confirmed every time a new member joins. The convention is that pre-existing members introduce themselves, saying what brought them to the group, where they are now in their lives and in their therapy. This method of induction stabilises the newcomer and enables them to open up about what brought them here. It avoids the danger of secrecy, one that these patients are particularly prone to, having lived with shameful secrets for so long.

> After hearing the others' introductions, Timothy describes his self-harming masturbation. He says, "I don't need to tell you it all but it does involve trying to strangle myself. It's too shameful to say everything." Martin says, "Well, what I do is pretty self destructive, only in a different way."

Confidentiality

A question much debated among colleagues is the question of reporting on information shared by patients, especially in relation to questions of child protection. Group members, too, will ask about what degree of confidentiality they may expect from the treatment. Clearly, the treatment will require a degree of confidentiality, but privacy, in the context of abuse, easily becomes secrecy, and patient confidentiality can be perverted into collusion. We strive as far as possible to preserve a therapeutic space, because a patient who has committed offences needs to be able to explore his thoughts and impulses before they lead to action. If, however, criminal actions are brought into the treatment, the response might have to recognise that confidentiality cannot be absolute. It is not possible to be impartial about child abuse (Woods, 2003). While we have the prerogative of clinical judgement, we also have the responsibility to support child protection and prevent child abuse. Reporting has been rare in the collective experience of Portman group work, and this largely because the sharing of such problems with colleagues has meant that a therapeutic intervention has usually managed to minimise the risk to any child connected with our patients.

The activity of the group

Interacting with others, sharing experiences, taking on their feedback and impressions produces an increased awareness of self and other, and, gradually, the interposing of thought before action. As the network of communication builds, so it becomes an experience of containment, which is eventually internalised. Confidentiality is usually taken for granted, though occasionally has to be reaffirmed. Since all are in the same boat, so to speak, there is usually an assumption that, for mutual benefit, each can count on the respect of others, though this does not preclude a degree of confrontation and conflict. It is a shock when the boundaries of trust are disrupted, when someone, for example, attempts to gossip outside the group—or worse.

> Michael discloses that Larry had persuaded him to go for a drink and then suggested a sexual encounter. A row ensues, with anger from the group, outrage from Michael, denial and indignation from Larry, who then proffers his loneliness and depression as excuses. It feels touch and go in the session whether the group can survive, or at least that someone has to leave. Finally, Larry accepts the group's response that he was also trying to destroy the group and with it any therapy that he and Michael might receive.

The role of the therapist

The therapist stands for reality and truth, in opposition to the illusions and deceptions of perversion, and represents something healthy in the larger social matrix, that which Foulkes called the group norm (Foulkes, 1948, p. 29). However, in so far as that has to be mediated through the individuality of the therapist, the group's functioning becomes a reflection of the person of the therapist, albeit sometimes unconsciously communicated. Positive therapeutic outcome has, in fact, been linked to the availability of the group therapist as someone with whom the group can identify (Catina & Tschuschke, 1993), but since the therapist is far from omnipotent, there will, at times, be group dynamics that cannot be controlled, perhaps only monitored, and maybe elucidated. This is not to say that that therapist attempts a "neutral" stance, though he or she needs to be impartial in dealing with the group. Evidence suggests that a non-directive approach is unproductive (Andrews, 1990). Experience provides the means to achieve a balance between how much to intervene, to maintain boundaries and aims, and how little, to enable spontaneous expression of the individual's use of the group. Brown and Pedder (1979, p. 134) describe a "modelling function", whereby a group therapist may helpfully demonstrate actively the ways in which a group member interacts and responds to the communication of others. The aim here is to promote engagement, something that would be inhibited by interpretations about attacks on the setting.

Pines (2000) has very usefully provided a "conductor's therapeutic map", which distinguishes three aspects of the therapist's role: *dynamic administration*, which refers to selection and composition of the group and managing the setting, *boundaries*, the facilitation of group communication, and *interpretation*, which may be seen as the provision of new information to the group about the meaning of what is going on, particularly in regard to previously unconscious or transference content. At times, however, the group, especially with a new member, might launch into uncharted territory:

> The therapist had recently introduced a new member, Ron, who disclosed that he had sexually abused his own son, penetrating him anally, and had served a prison sentence for it. He put this in such a way as to imply that he felt it unfair because he had "only done it once", had been drunk at the time, feeling very let down by his wife, and, in any case, he said, "it's no big deal." This was a very different version of events than he had given to the therapist at assessment, where he had expressed appropriate remorse. The group were sceptical about Ron's minimisation of his offence, but Ron was slow to take this on board. The group became despondent, feeling they could get nowhere with this. Phil began a session, saying to Ron, "I dreamt you had me gripped by the balls and were forcing something into my mouth." Ron seemed to relish this image, and wanted to explore it further, but the therapist intervened, saying that he thought the group also perhaps felt assaulted by the introduction of someone who was saying that sex between adult and child was permissible; they might even, he said, feel rather abused by the therapist. This seemed to release the group to say that Ron could only be accepted in the group if he could see the harm done to children by sexual abuse. We then heard about Ron's own experiences and the severe emotional damage that had resulted.

This was an unusual situation, unanticipated by the therapist, and the role of dynamic administrator suddenly had to be adapted to include an interpretative function. Note the need for an "analyst centred" interpretation (Steiner, 1992), since the therapist had to accept the fact of having created the situation. To have interpreted the forbidden paedophilic impulses as belonging to the group would have undermined the therapeutic process (Alvarez, 1992, pp. 161–162).

Usually, the therapist will have formed a view from the preparatory meetings that someone is likely to engage with the group openly and honestly, at least to a degree. It should not be forgotten that for anyone it is a tall order to take the risk of revealing their innermost self to others who are, to begin with at least, total strangers. This is only possible via the therapist, who enables a transition from a one-to-one contact in assessment to the experience of being in a group. The therapist has to manage the relative loss of intimacy for the new member, creating the possibility of a shared therapeutic space. The introduction of poorly prepared patients might undermine the group, and be a repetition for the individual concerned of the injurious and traumatic events originally experienced years before. In preliminary meetings, it might be necessary to dispel the notion of the group as a kind of social club where people make friends and meet up outside sessions. There has to be a capacity at least to think about the meaning of antisocial acts, but the therapist also needs to know that an overriding tendency to action will, from time to time, reassert itself. A balance has to be achieved between knowing the individual well enough from preliminary meetings to support their joining, but not so much as to develop a dependency that would exclude the presence of others in the therapeutic space. A group therapist develops a lightness of touch through which each group member feels that they are recognised and are significant to the therapist, while also allowing space for interaction with the others.

> Joe had told the therapist of his HIV positive status in a preliminary meeting, and how he had come to expect rejection, fear, and revulsion in others. He said that he could reveal this to the group. However, when he did so, there was an absentee, Mark, who, it was said by those present, would be intolerant of some one with AIDS. The therapist was slow to pick this up. Joe remained silent in subsequent sessions when Mark was present, who tended, as he always did, to dominate proceedings. The therapist drew Mark's attention to the fact, (not for the first time) that he could be intimidating, especially to a new person. "But" (and this was addressed to the group generally) "no one is going to be abused here." Mark, for his part, was saddened to think that he had been so feared, and said it was

"only" his anger about what had been done to him, and that he could let go of his prejudices when he met someone face to face and with whom he knew he shared problems.

The therapist's own reactions need to be continually monitored. Listening to traumatic experiences from group members, whether as victim or abuser, is bound to evoke painful affects. Identifying with Joe's fear in the above illustration enabled a sensitive exploration. The issue of HIV/AIDS was, of course, bound up with the traumatic experiences of child sexual abuse. Focusing upon the task, and taking care to provide a containing setting for the patient, are ways for the therapist to hold disturbing feelings in her or himself. Muddles over boundaries might threaten that the original trauma comes flooding back. Processing these feelings is a large part of the work of the therapist, trusting not only to self-knowledge derived from his own therapy, but also to the ongoing support of colleagues via the group therapy workshop. As Bion put it, the group is the container (Bion, 1961) and the therapy depends on what kind of container.

Handling boundary incidents

Following their session, the group began to hang around the steps of the clinic to smoke and chat. The therapist was unsure what to do about this, not wanting to fall into a superego role. He discussed the matter in the group workshop, where colleagues helped him deal with feelings about recent sessions, which were becoming dull, boring, and repetitive, with much lateness and absenteeism. Subsequently, the therapist took the opportunity of saying to the group that they seem to be waiting for their real session to begin at the doorstep, and "could it be there are things you don't want me to hear about?" Mick then said that he was bothered by the fact that on one such doorstep occasion he had been shown pornographic pictures by another group member. This led to some productive discussion about the corrosive effect of the "smoking" group.

Foulkes envisaged the conductor as less concerned with interpretation of meaning than with facilitating communication. The "smoking group" did not need so much to be interpreted as destructive (although, of course, it was), but to be drawn into the field of communication within the session. In Foulkes's view, there is an inherent therapeutic power of a group, which, however, has to be mobilised to overcome symptoms of disorder, which have primarily an antisocial meaning: "[Symptoms are] . . . highly individualistic, group disruptive in essence, and genetically the result of an incompatibility between the individual and the original group, i.e. the family" (Foulkes, 1964, p. 156). To restore this connectedness with others, the conductor intrudes as little as possible, and only in so far as would enable participation, preventing anything that would deter good communication among group members. Interpretations by the conductor are less important in this model, just as the precise nature of transferences is less relevant than the relatedness of group members to each other. Reid puts it a different way when she says, "becoming a group is the therapy". Members might start out as self-centred individuals in discord with others, but move towards "a recognition of the needs, wishes and feelings of others" (Reid, 1999, p. 257).

Less extreme forms of boundary incidents may be understood as arising from members' need to be special, to be recognised and cared for. The history of neglect might have meant that this person has been treated as a part object by parents and carers, without the acknowledgement of feelings of his own or the need for safety. Although the therapist and group might not be able to provide the love that was so lacking, they could, nevertheless, provide a model of firm and caring adherence to boundaries. One is helpfully reminded at these times of the process of adolescence, where acting out under the pressure of need for change is to be expected at that stage of development. Transference, however, will dictate that there will be resistance to dependency or trust.

> Graham brought in a self-help book, which he said was relevant to the problem described by another group member, Jim. When Jim hesitated, the therapist intervened and said that it would be better if, instead of reading from the book, we heard from Graham about what was stirred up in him by Jim describing his problem last week. Graham was evidently disconcerted, but Jim said later he was relieved because he could not stand self-help books but would have felt anxious about rejecting it.

Know your group

Most, if not all, forensic patients come from a background of neglect and abuse, to varying degrees. Group members will, therefore, bring a sense of deprivation deriving from trauma directly into the treatment. The sense of grievance might stand in the way of accepting any benefit from the experience. If criminality and antisocial attitudes of arrogance have been employed by some group members to hide their shame and otherwise crippling insecurity, these defences will break down. Many will have been leading a double life, or at least one of secrecy, which will, of itself, produce an enormous emotional strain, and might, indeed, become the occasion for seeking help. The habit of (self) deception might be repeated in the treatment, sometimes with disastrous consequences. Since there is such a limited capacity for tolerating anxiety, acting out might well occur as an old and not very effective defence.

> Steve informed the group, "It happened again. Some guy in a van—they think they own the road, cut in, made me slam on the brakes, so at the next lights I got alongside him, gave him the V sign, which annoyed him. OK, maybe I shouldn't have done it. He swore at me, I wound down my window and swore back. The lights changed, I drove off, he followed me. I led him a dance until there I was in a cul de sac, no way out. I got out of the car with the big spanner I keep just in case, and stood there. "Come on then," I said. That did it. He could see I meant business and so he fucked off." Leslie said, "You know, Steve, you say you shouldn't have done it but in fact you seem really happy about the whole thing and you keep the spanner there 'just in case?': Steve answered, slightly sheepishly, "OK, but there was no damage this time. No harm. I suppose there might have been. I just remember thinking, 'No one is going to mess with me'." Leslie said, "Well, your mood is certainly a lot lighter than when you were telling us about being bullied by your wife . . ."

The therapist's understanding of perversion and violence

"Perversion is a condition in which a person does not feel free to obtain sexual genital gratification through intimate contact with another person" (Welldon, 2011, p. 31). Instead of what could be regarded as healthy relationships, the person suffering from a perversion has compulsions of a more or less bizarre and asocial kind, but which always involve harm to the self or other. This is a statement not of moral condemnation, but about emotional and psychological health, and is nothing to do with sexual orientation (unless the sexual interest in children be regarded as a sexual orientation, rather than a perversion (see Chapter Six)). What is perhaps more important than social sanction is our understanding of how the perversion might have come about. The "core complex" theory of Glasser (1964), a former director of the Portman Clinic, is a set of ideas much employed by Portman therapists. In brief, this refers to a dynamic of a certain kind of object relationship developed in early childhood and which operates as a powerful determinant of current relationships that can be described as based upon sexual perversion. As a first condition, there is a longing for fusion or merging with the maternal object, a sense of being "at one" with the object, but this gives rise to fears of annihilation of individuality. There is then a flight from the object, but in the absence of a safe place, this means, in effect, a narcissistic withdrawal. There are consequent problems of isolation and fears of abandonment, so that attempts at controlling the object are made. Aggression is used not in order to remove or destroy any realistic threat posed by the object, but to keep it at a safe distance. According to Glasser's theory, sadism and sexualisation are used in varying degrees in order to maintain an illusion of power and to triumph over, and protect against, fears of loss. This pattern is seen time and again in our patients and produces distortions in everyday relationships, which will also be evident in the group.

> Michael complained of his wife's "intolerance". Upon discussion with the group, it becomes clear that he feels that she is supposed to accept his habitual use of prostitutes, instead of having a sexual relationship with him. He said how he likes the ritual of dressing up and pretend beatings that he can give the prostitute. "It's only playacting." Then he could be sexually aroused. He said he could not face his wife if he were to show her that side of his character.

From the time of Freud's (1940e) conceptualisation of fetishism, based on disavowal in the little boy of the female's lack of a penis, to Chasseguet-Smirgel's (1985) concept of the "anal universe", it has been clear that a predominating feature of perversion is the tendency to erase differences and to deny reality. This, too, will manifest itself in the group, as sometimes group members will presume a familiarity with the therapist, or claim a triumphant attitude at having all the sex they want, through pornography.

Gone are the days when homosexuality was regarded as a perversion, or, indeed, as a crime. It is now recognised that deviant sexuality is independent of object choice and that the work of the forensic therapy group is to extricate as far as possible a healthy sexual function from the corruption of narcissism, omnipotence and destructiveness.

> Frank describes how he feared his masturbation was getting more "weird". It was not enough to tie himself up; now he found himself inserting large hard objects into his anus. Group members ask if he is causing himself pain. He says, yes, but it enhances the pleasure of ejaculation. He can feel himself, he said, to be both male and female at the same time. "That is why I've never stayed with a girlfriend, even though I've had sex with them; I think they are having more pleasure than I am. I don't want to do the poking, I want to be poked."

The changing nature of the patient population

It had been thought that voyeurism was not suitably treated in group therapy since the group member would simply watch others and not be able to participate (Welldon, 2011, p. 68). However, the recent explosion of internet pornography, including the compulsion to watch illegal images of child abuse, has meant that each Portman therapy group currently has members bringing this as an ongoing problem. Perhaps this compulsion to pornography, and concomitant masturbation, differs from more traditional forms of voyeurism: it is not yet clear; theoretical research suggests that new forms of psychopathology are being created (Wood, 2007). What is certain is that our groups have adapted and provide considerable help for people to manage their addiction, to understand the underlying causes, and get the support that they need in order to change. Similarly, one group that was reserved for patients who came with contact offences against children has had to adapt to include offences of downloading illegal images of child abuse. This has helped a reconceptualisation of "paedophilia" as but one manifestation of what may be termed "paedo-sexuality" (see Chapter Six).

The inhibited capacity to mentalize and the tendency to act

The awareness of the relationship between internal and external reality is not universal; it is a developmental achievement (Fonagy &

Target, 2000), one that many forensic patients only partially attain at best, and, therefore, need to recapitulate. These authors go on to explain the need for the infant to integrate two mental states: "psychic equivalence" and the pretend mode. Psychic equivalence is shown in the above instances: Michael's frustration with his wife derives from his creation of her as the embodiment of his sexual conflict and sadism. His "playacting" with prostitutes gives him a sense of real power, just as Frank's anal penetration makes him feel that he is actually a woman. It is not enough for him to participate in a woman's pleasure; he has to possess it. In neither case is it possible for these men to appreciate symbolic reality, or to imagine that the thoughts and feelings of others are different from their own. In the ordinary social world, we do not know, or directly experience, the thoughts and feelings of others, but we can infer them, recognise them as connected to an outer reality, and use them to reflect upon our own thoughts and feelings. Opportunities for this process, which have been so lacking in the past, may be found anew in the therapy group.

> Derek (challengingly to the therapist). "Sometimes I think you're disgusted with us. Actually, I think you are most of all disgusted by me. Oh, I know you don't say it, you have to be the therapist, professional and everything, but I can see it in the way you look away sometimes. Especially when I speak." The therapist remained silent, allowing the next question to be asked by Derek himself. "About what, I suppose, you would have to ask." He looked at the others appealingly, perhaps for support. They waited for him to continue. "About masturbating to children's television programmes ... That must be the most despicable thing. Apart from abusing a child, which I would never do. I only have my fantasies. I hate myself, so why shouldn't you? And yet you go on listening to it. When is it going to change, you should ask?"
>
> "As if I could make you change," said the therapist.
>
> "If only you could," he said, sadly.

The question of gender

Due to the preponderance of males in forensic referral, therapy groups often find themselves single-sex, with some exceptions (see Chapters Five and Seven). Similarly, in prison, the vast majority is male. While in some ways unfortunate in not providing a truer social experience, this feature does enable the group to engage in an intense reassessment of masculine identity. It seems, in Western culture, that masculinity is so often equated with power, especially in the area of social deviance and law-breaking. Gilligan (1999) has shown how violence, "our deadliest epidemic" (the subtitle to his book *On Violence*), is often employed by perpetrators as a solution to problems of severe low self-esteem and shame, tied especially to fears about masculinity. Violence is felt to be the solution to feelings of powerlessness. The violent patient gets rid of anxiety about his powerlessness. If a boy experiences the trauma of sexual abuse it is often felt to "feminise" him; masculinity has to be reasserted when there is an intolerance of weakness. Thus, violent males grow up unable to manage feelings of loss and more ready to resort to violence in order to restore a fragile sense of masculinity. Perelberg (1998) suggests that an extreme fluidity in masculine and feminine identifications might lead to an act of violence as an attempt to repudiate a feminine identification in favour of a more potent male identity. Women are feared, and so become the target of male violence. What lies beneath the violence is the perpetrator's fear and vulnerability, though different in each case, which needs to surface in the treatment. For men, the opportunity to explore their own vulnerability, to own projections of hostility and damage, and to question their blame of women, can lead to a new conception of themselves.

Crucial to the development of a masculine identity is the role of the father. Discussing the origins in childhood of the male tendency to violence, Fonagy and Target (1998) point to the paternal function that can facilitate separation from mother. The one-to-one mirroring between mother and child is modified by an early triangulation and a transition away from that intense relationship. Father normally enters the psychological world in the first year, and in the father the child sees a representation of himself as a psychological entity *in relation* to mother, not engulfed by her (Greenson, 1968). If the father has himself been abusive or absent, or both, this will fundamentally distort the growing boy's concept of himself in relation to the feminine. Although absent from the group, women are ever-present in the minds of the men, and may be symbolised by a maternal function that the group comes to represent, as described in the clinical illustration below.

The addiction model

The forensic group therapist needs to know about the compulsion that lies behind much sexually deviant or abusive behaviour and should not be surprised when it recurs. It is, therefore, helpful to know something of the addiction model (Carnes, 2001). This is especially useful because many "sexually addicted" patients avail themselves of the support offered by the twelve-step programme, much of which is complementary to the work of psychotherapy. Sex Addicts Anonymous (SAA) offers an opportunity to understand the triggers to acting out, and strategies for control. The experience at the Portman Clinic has been that, by and large, patients who, for example, have shown a compulsion to internet pornography, are very much helped by a combination of psychotherapy and attendance at twelve-step groups.

> Nigel spoke with difficulty about his visit from the police. "I have to tell the group they found something. I had kept some images [i.e., erotic images of children] not because I was going to do anything or look at anything illegal, it was just to have them there. I even forgot about them. I was astonished when the disc was found." The group was angry about his concealment of his perverse imagery, and the therapist, too, had to think how he had been duped into a collusive belief in Nigel's avowed intention of developing "adult" sexual relationships. "You're like the alcoholic," another group member said, "you have to keep a bottle hidden, just in case . . ." Nigel bowed his head and said, "I know. I can stay away from it, but I can never not need it."

Symbolisation as a key therapeutic ingredient

When boundaries have, to some extent, been internalised by group members, and the possibility of thought rather than action becomes part of the culture of the group, then symbolisation may begin. Segal (1991 pp. 24–37) suggests that symbolisation is the creative way to deal with and process anxieties and desires. The unattainable object may be represented and internalised instead of becoming persecutory by its absence. Terrors of the past may be faced rather than avoided. Traumatic and perverse experiences are regularly presented in group treatment and, necessarily to an extent, being re-experienced, but in manageable doses.

The all-male group had been resentful and hopeless about their various failed sexual relationships. Geoff then said he wanted to talk again about something he had brought up last week. "I said what happened, like I'm supposed to, but no one understood. Well OK, there wasn't enough time." He then recounted the events that led up to his assault on his wife. At first, he presented the story angrily, with circumstances intended to minimise his responsibility, but it became clear that he had been actually unable to cope with various frustrations before the assault. "It was all to do with the bloody sink. I was trying to fix it myself. I couldn't find my tools. I'm terrible with my tools, can't organise them. I couldn't afford to call a plumber, they cost a bloody fortune! Undid the pipe. Nothing there, but still it won't drain. The wife was saying "Can't you unblock it?" I was keeping my temper and she was saying, "Don't get so upset. Leave it, if you can't manage it. We'll call someone in, if you can't do it." "I can do it," I said. So I went downstairs, undid the bloody pipes there, and out comes all this filthy water; a lot of shit flooded me, and this dirty great hairy rat-like thing, unbelievable. It was my wife's hair, and I've told her not to wash her hair in that sink, it hasn't got a proper filter, so I take it upstairs and she starts going on at me for making a mess on the carpet. "It's your fucking mess," I said. She pushes me, and I've told her not to do that . . . so I thumped her."

There is silence in the group.

Jim said, "I think it was all about control. You couldn't control the sink, you couldn't control your wife. You hit her to try and get back control. You're a control freak."

Geoff is angry: "Don't give me that bullshit! So I'm a control freak, how do you think I even survive? I control myself. Mostly. I tell you, the things I could do . . . I could have gone on hitting her. But I stopped myself. It was only the once."

Mark asks whether this has been reported, since, he reminded us, Geoff is, after all, known to the Multi Agency Protection Panel.

Geoff: "No, not this time. But, she says it's the last time. If I do it again, ever, she's had enough. She's off. She will. She's done it before."

Mark: "But she came back?"

Geoff: " I felt so awful when she wasn't there. I didn't go out. I drew the curtains. Stayed in the dark, didn't eat."

Mark: "You put yourself in prison."

Geoff: "Yes, that's where I belong. But if I went back I'd probably try to do myself in again."

Mark: "Haven't you got someone to ring if you get into that state again?"

Geoff: "Maybe I do, but I didn't think of it."

Silence. The therapist comments that Geoff seemed to feel it was only his wife who had the power to report this.

Geoff: "Well, maybe Sarah (his probation officer mentioned before) would listen. She told me I could ring anytime. But maybe I'll be recalled to prison.

Jim: "I would say mate, that's a chance you got to take."

Fred: (who had been silent up until this point) "I wouldn't tell them anything. The old bill? They'll just lock you up any chance they get."

Jim: "I think you owe it to your wife to do all you can to stop yourself doing it again."

Geoff wept and said that he could not live with himself if he hit her again. "The worst thing," he said, "is feeling that I'm no better than my Dad, who used to beat my mum all the time. Until he cleared off." As the group seemed attuned to Geoff's grief, the therapist said that something had perhaps been unblocked here, that the anger and frustration had given way to feelings of sadness at losing, or not having, the kind of relationship that was wanted. (In subsequent sessions we learnt that Geoff did report himself to the probation officer and he and his wife were able to get more support, instead of him being recalled to prison.)

It appears from this sequence of material that the group was eventually able to provide a place where Geoff could think about his violence, and the meaning of it. Initially condemnatory, this led to a more rational consideration as to whether his behaviour needed more management, and to raise the question of whether he could do something to take more responsibility. It could also be asked whether the therapist had a duty to report, and it is a matter of careful clinical judgement as to whether the patient has the capacity to keep bringing the problem and to find his own solution. In the event, the therapist had to give little more than a nudge in order to get Geoff to think about the responsibility to manage his own violence. In a different case, the therapist might be under more pressure to discuss with colleagues what the boundaries should be. As it was, the psychodynamics of the violence were presented as organised around the frustration of the blocked sink. The little boy's frustration at not coping, in the absence of a good father, is enacted on the mother. The triangulation discussed by Welldon also symbolises an oedipal pattern and provides space for thought and the development of an identity separate from the mother, who has been created in a perverse image of fear and sexualised control (Welldon, 1997). Although it was not articulated explicitly, the metaphor of the blocked sink was very relevant to the group at this particular time, blocked as they were in terms of their emotional life and, consequently, in their relationships. As Geoff unblocks his feelings, difficult as they are, the group responds and participates in his experience; indeed, they contribute powerfully to his learning. How different would this have been if he had simply been instructed by a professional to turn himself in? He might have done so, but there would have been little therapeutic learning on his part. Alternatively, the refusal to consider the external implications of his actions would have come dangerously close to collusion. These dilemmas are less acute in the group because there is more space to think.

Conclusion

The final clinical example above shows how a mature group can reach a point where it can work to produce change. In this vignette, the foreground was occupied by one member, but clearly the other voices had their own character, and the session could be retold from an entirely different point of view with equal validity. A group session is like a constantly shifting kaleidoscope of meaning, which at times might feel chaotic, especially to those inexperienced in therapeutic groups, but which stimulates all concerned to ask questions, explore meanings, in order to produce change. The different voices responding to Geoff's situation could be seen as his own inner conflicts, sometimes feeling evasive, (Fred), accusatory (Jim), or helpful (Mark). The individual revisits his trauma, that is, both what he has done and what has been done to him. In so doing, he rewrites his own story, or reinterprets it, and the group, in a larger sense, revisits human destiny. As a microcosm of society, the group provides an opportunity for members to discover a new sense of social responsibility in a nurturing context, rather than in the blaming mode they are used to. However, that depends on probably the most significant development: the opportunity to develop a capacity for thought as opposed to action.

Freud pointed out the process of identification that operates in the formation of a group (Freud, 1921c). As an individual develops a sense of belonging, his aggression is modulated by positive feelings, which tend to foster the development of thinking. In a therapeutic mode, the group develops the capacity to understand and process violent impulses and the painful affects of fear and grievance that might underlie them. Such insights need to take place in a nurturing environment. How is this achieved, given the histories of such deprivation, in such brief sessions? While it would be unrealistic to attempt to provide the kind of love these individuals so lacked in their development, nevertheless there is available a relationship that can symbolise the sort of nurture that was absent. This experience can be seen in terms of a new attachment; some group analysts refer to attachment theory and show how a group can repair damage to previous attachment relationships (Glenn, 1987). Although the group necessarily raises the traumatic past, it also provides a positive experience: the respect each shows the other, as modelled by the therapist, being listened to and listening to others, responding genuinely; all this cumulatively leads to a belief in a non-abusive world, as each individual feels more fully known by others than elsewhere.

References

Altman, N. (2009). *The Analyst in the City: Race Class and Culture Seen through a Psychoanalytic Lens.* New York: Analytic Press.

Alvarez, A. (1992). *Live Company.* London: Routledge.

Andrews, P. (1990). Does correctional treatment work? *Criminology, 28*: 369–404.

Bion, W. R. (1961). *Experiences in Groups.* London: Tavistock.

Blackmore, C., Tantum, D., Parry, G., & Chambers, E. (2012). Report on a systematic review of the efficacy and clinical effectiveness of group analysis. *Group Analysis, 45*(1): 45–69.

Brown, D., & Pedder, J. (1979). *Introduction to Psychotherapy.* London: Tavistock.

Brown, S. (2010). *Treating Sex Offenders: An Introduction to Sex Offender Treatment Programmes.* London: Willan.

Burlingame, G. M., Fishman, A., & Mosier, J. (2003). Differential effectiveness in group therapy: a meta analytic perspective. *Group Dynamics; Theory, Research and Practice, 7*: 3–12.

Carnes, P. (2001). *Out of the Shadows: Understanding Sexual Addiction*. Hazelden: Information & Educational Services.

Catina, A., & Tschuschke, V. (1993). A summary of empirical data from the investigation of two psychoanalytic groups by means of repertory grid technique. *Group Analysis*, 33(3): 433–447.

Chasseguet-Smirgel, J. (1985). *Creativity and Perversion*. London: Free Association Books.

Coles, P. (2003). *The Importance of Sibling Relationships in Psychoanalysis*. London: Karnac.

Dolan, B. M., Warren, F. M., Menzies, D., & Norton, K. (1996). Cost offset following specialist treatment of severe personality disorders. *Psychiatric Bulletin*, 20(7): 413–417.

Fonagy, P., & Target, M. (1998). Towards understanding violence, the use of the body and the role of the father. In: R. Perelberg (Ed.), *The Psychoanalytic Understanding of Violence and Suicide* (pp. 51–72). London: Routledge.

Fonagy, P., & Target, M. (2000). Playing with reality III: the persistence of dual psychic reality in borderline patients. *International Journal of Psychoanalysis*, 81: 853–873.

Foulkes, S. H. (1948). *Introduction to Group Analytic Psychotherapy*. London: Maresfield Reprints, 1984.

Foulkes, S. H. (1964). *Therapeutic Group Analysis*. London: Maresfield Reprints, 1984.

Foulkes, S. H. (1975). *Group Analytic Psychotherapy*. London: Maresfield Reprints, 1986.

Freud, S. (1921c). *Group Psychology and the Analysis of the Ego. S.E.*, 18: 69–143. London: Hogarth.

Freud, S. (1939a). *Moses and Monotheism. S.E.*, 23: 3–137. London: Hogarth.

Freud, S. (1940e). Splitting of the ego in the process of defence. *S. E.*, 23: 275–278. London: Hogarth.

Garland, C. (1982). Taking the non-problem seriously. *Group Analysis*, 15(1): 4–14.

Garland, C. (Ed.) (2010). *The Groups Book*. London: Karnac.

Gilligan, J. 1999). *Violence: Reflections on Our Deadliest Epidemic*. London: Jessica Kingsley.

Glasser, M. (1964). Aggression and sadism in the perversions. In: I. Rosen (Ed.), *Sexual Deviation* (pp. 279–300). Oxford: Oxford University Press.

Glenn, L. (1987). Attachment theory and group analysis. *Group Analysis*, 20: 109–117.

Greenson, R. R. (1968). Dis-identifying from the mother; its special importance for the boy. *International Journal of Psychoanalysis*, 49: 370–374.

Hall, Z., & Mullee, M. (2000). Undertaking psychotherapy research. *Group Analysis*, 33(3): 319–332.

Hinshelwood, R. D. (2008). Group therapy and psychic containing. *International Journal of Group Therapy*, 58: 283–302.

Holmes, J. (2011). Donnel Stern and relational psychoanalysis. *British Journal of Psychotherapy*, 27(3): 305–315.

Hopper, E. (1997). Traumatic experiences in the unconscious life of groups. *Group Analysis*, 30(4): 439–470.

Hume, F. (2010). Bion and group psychotherapy. In: C. Garland (Ed.), *The Groups Book* (pp. 110–128). London: Karnac.

Joyce, A. (2011). Why the Ugly Sisters and Cinderella? In: *Proceedings of the European Federation of Psychoanalytic Psychotherapy, Krakow, October 2011*.

Klein, M. (1927). The sexual activities of children. In: *The Psychoanalysis of Children* (pp. 111–122). London: Vintage, 1997.

Lacan, J. (2007). *Ecrits*. London: Norton.

Leichsenring, F., & Leibing, E. (2003). The effectiveness of psychodynamic therapy and cognitive behavior therapy in the treatment of personality disorders: a meta-analysis. *American Journal of Psychiatry*, 2003: 223–232.

Lorentzen, S. (2000). Assessment of change after long term psychoanalytic group treatment. *Group Analysis*, 33(3): 353–372.

Mitchell, J. (2003). *Siblings*. London: Polity Press.

Morgan, R. D., & Flora, D. B. (2002). Group therapy with incarcerated offenders. *Group Dynamics: Theory, Research and Practice*, 6(3): 203–218.

Perelberg, R. (Ed.) (1998). *The Psychoanalytic Understanding of Violence and Suicide*. London: Routledge.

Pines, M. (2000). *The Evolution of Group Analysis*. London: Jessica Kingsley.

Reid, S. (1999). The group as a healing whole. In: M. Lanyado & A. Horne (Eds.), *The Handbook of Child and Adolescent Psychotherapy* (pp. 247–260). London: Routledge.

Saunders, D. G. (2008). Group interventions for men who batter. *Violence and Victims*, 23: 156–172.

Segal, H. (1991). *Dream Phantasy and Art*. London: Routledge.

Steiner, J. (1992). The equilibrium between the paranoid–schizoid and the depressive positions. In: R. Anderson (Ed.), *Clinical Lectures on Klein and Bion* (pp. 45–56). London: Tavistock.

Taylor, R. (2000). *A Seven Year Reconviction Study of HMP Grendon*. London: Home Office Research Unit.

Welldon, E. (1996). Group analytic psychotherapy in an out-patient setting. In: C. Cordess & M. Cox (Eds.), *Forensic Psychotherapy* (pp. 63–82). London: Jessica Kingsley Publishers.

Welldon, E. (1997). Let the treatment fit the crime. *Group Analysis*, 30(1): 9–26.

Welldon, E. (2011). *Playing with Dynamite*. London: Karnac.

Welldon, E., & Van Velsen, C. (1997). *A Practical Guide to Forensic Psychotherapy*. London: Jessica Kingsley.

Wellendorf, E. (2011). Sibling rivalry: psychoanalytic aspects and institutional implications. *Proceedings of the European Federation of Psychoanalytic Psychotherapy, Krakow, October 2011*.

Wood, H. (2007). Compulsive use of virtual sex and internet pornography. In: D. Morgan & S. Ruszczynski (Eds.), *Lectures on Violence, Perversion and Delinquency: The Portman Papers* (pp. 157–178). London: Karnac.

Woods, J. (2003). *Boys Who Have Abused: Psychoanalytic Psychotherapy With Young Victims/Perpetrators of Sexual Abuse*. London: Jessica Kingsley.

Yalom, I. (1972), *The Theory and Practice of Group Psychotherapy*. New York: Basic Books.

CHAPTER TWO

On the containing structures required by forensic group psychotherapy

Andrew Williams and Anne Zachary

Group psychotherapy can contain the disturbance of some patients in a way that individual psychotherapy sometimes cannot. The presence of other group members brings breadth, depth and often creativity, but also explicit boundaries and active challenging when required. The wealth of resources available in the group setting can provide a capacity to contain even the most fragile and volatile patients. Glasser's concept of the core complex dictates that patients tend to feel either overwhelmed or abandoned by those with whom they are intimately involved (Glasser, 1979, 1992). For some patients, the intensity of the one-to-one setting can be overwhelming. For these patients, treatment in a group can help to dissipate the intensity of the therapeutic encounter so that it is more manageable.

The child's need to test out boundaries within the family forms a normal part of healthy child development. Hence, for patients who can resort to primitive and child-like states of anger and rage, whether expressed through direct violence or through sexualised forms of aggression, it is to be expected that a key aspect of any effective treatment setting is the capacity to contain the individual's "power to disrupt, to destroy, to frighten, to wear down, to waste, to wangle", as Winnicott described it (Winnicott, Shepherd, & Davis, 1984).

It would be difficult for forensic group psychotherapy to take place effectively outside an institutional setting; the holding capacity of a responsive surrounding network is essential. There is a need for an external "third position", representing the reality of the outside world, whether held by a GP, psychiatrist, or probation officer. However, there also needs to be adequate resources available to each group therapist within the clinic itself to enable them to manage the risks and projections that patients inevitably bring to the group. The theme of early failures of containment often seen in the personal histories of forensic patients requires that the group itself will, one hopes, eventually mature and develop a capacity to contain high levels of disturbance by itself. In this way, a capacity for holding is necessary, so that the work of exploring and understanding can take place (Winnicott, 1965). There are certain times, especially in the early stages of a new group, or when a group is going through a difficult period, perhaps with high levels of acting out, in which the onus falls upon the group therapist to provide much of this holding function. The aim of this chapter is to describe the main structures that enable this holding to take place.

The setting

Rey's concept of the "brick mother" is very relevant to patients who tend to act out in perverse, violent, or delinquent ways (Rey, 1994). The Portman Clinic exists in an Edwardian era house that stands separately from its bigger sibling next door, the Tavistock Centre. "Patients often comment on the fact that the clinic feels like a separate and safe place where, despite the staff who work there knowing what the patient has done, they are treated with courtesy and respect." One patient in the early stages of treatment spoke about a story in a comic book, in which there was a school where "mutant" children, born with special powers but rejected by society, were welcomed, cared for, and nurtured.

Much of the sense of security that patients experience when they arrive at the clinic is provided by the receptionist and the administrative staff. We have been fortunate enough to have an experienced receptionist who has worked at the clinic for many years. She knows the patients well and is effective in maintaining a calm manner when patients make pressured demands upon her. Similarly, the administrative staff who work in the office behind the reception are familiar with most of the patients, especially those who have been attending for a long time, sometimes helping them out with reimbursing their bus fare, or passing on messages to their treating clinician. We are also fortunate enough to have an experienced clinic manager who may step in to deal with difficulties as they arise. It is easy to underestimate the importance to the environment of the input of non-clinical staff, and the value of good communication between non-clinical and clinical staff. Indeed, one of the Department of Health's initiatives to reduce the frequency of untoward incidents in forensic services has been the attempt to improve "relational security", which emphasises the importance of effective communication between staff (Department of Health, 2010).

As might be expected, patients who tend to act out often behave in particular ways on the doorstep, in the waiting room, in their interaction with the receptionist, or on the way to the consulting room. Notification by the receptionist that, upon arrival, a particular patient "seems to be having a bad day" can be invaluable in preparing the therapist for what might lie ahead.

Clinical vignette: an unconventional entrance

A patient had been in treatment for eighteen months, presenting with a history of violent outbursts towards his partner. Following a group session, the receptionist telephoned the group therapist to inform her that a patient in her group had entered the clinic via the back door used by clinic staff, coming through the back garden, which is out of bounds for patients. The receptionist told the patient that this entrance was out of bounds. He dismissed her comment with a charming smile, and6promised not to do it again. The receptionist informed the group therapist about this after the session. When the therapist reflected upon the session, she recalled that the patient had spoken in the group about feeling that he had made a "major breakthrough" in his relationship with his partner, and that he did not think that he would be violent again, or perhaps even need to continue with his treatment. This had seemed markedly out of keeping with his usual attitude, that conveyed a genuine sense of his need for treatment. The therapist struggled to think about how to introduce the notion that on the day of the session in question, the patient had committed a "violent act" by entering the clinic through the prohibited entrance, and, to his mind, had got away with it through his dismissal of the receptionist's comment. It was decided, following a discussion with colleagues, that the therapist would mention this in the group, attempting to avoid the split that would otherwise have been enacted between the boundary of the clinic and the boundary of the group setting. The patient felt somewhat aggrieved by the therapist's intervention, but the patient's aggression became more available for discussion within the group itself.

Preparing patients for a group

Estela Welldon, in her pioneering work with groups at the Portman Clinic, has written eloquently about selecting and preparing patients for group treatment (e.g., Welldon, 1997). In view of the fragile nature of many of the patients seen at the Portman Clinic, a culture has developed of seeing patients on an individual basis on more than one occasion before they start in the group, usually two or three times. It can often be helpful to allow a robust attachment to the group therapist to be formed through these individual meetings, especially for those patients who are particularly anxious about joining a group. An attachment to the therapist can enable the patient to remain in treatment when the "going gets tough", as it often does in the early stages. This must be done with caution, however; it is important to balance the positive impact of establishing a good relationship with the therapist with the risk of encouraging an overly strong attachment to the therapist, as this can make the transition to sharing the therapist with the rest of the group difficult. In addition, the patient can be helped by the individual sessions to talk about his "problematic behaviour" from the outset. Supportive encouragement by the group therapist can be invaluable in enabling the patient to start working on his difficulties from the first group session.

During the preparatory meetings, the group therapist will discuss the "rules" of the group with the patient. It is stated that confidentiality is of the utmost importance, and that first names only are used, and that matters discussed in the group should not be discussed elsewhere. Patients are often relieved upon hearing this emphasised. Second, patients are advised that they are discouraged from meeting outside the group setting: this request is explained in terms of the fact that any communication outside the group will make the therapy less effective. It is important to attempt to identify ambivalence about joining a group with each patient and discuss this—especially to acknowledge that most patients find joining a group to be daunting.

Establishing a setting that feels confidential and safe is crucial in any form of group psychotherapy, but especially in working with forensic patients. An important feature that distinguishes patients who tend to enact their pathology upon others is that they have committed acts that cannot be reversed. Patients might have hit, kicked, or sexually assaulted someone, and there is no turning back the clock. It is often only in the later stages of treatment that patients are able to truly start to think about feelings of guilt and shame about what they have done. It feels crucial that the group remains a safe enough place in which to do this.

Patients in forensic groups often struggle to settle into the group during the early stages of treatment. There is often a high level of anxiety and an increase in the urge to act out. It is a rule of thumb that the group therapist, in her individual meetings with the patient, will emphasise that the patient might feel worse before they start to feel better. Some clinicians specifically tell the patient that they might experience strong feelings of alienation or disorientation in the group, and a wish to leave. Sometimes, the ways in which patients might initially feel within the group can be anticipated from what is learnt about the patient during the assessment and the individual sessions with the group therapist. It is important that any anticipated difficulties are put to the patient, so that they feel less overwhelmed when they encounter these within the group setting. It is sometimes useful to tell patients that they will derive benefit from the group as long as they continue to attend, and that feeling a wish to leave means that something therapeutic is already being stirred up by the treatment.

Is it not uncommon for patients to make a request for individual psychotherapy in the early stages of group treatment. One way of understanding this is that forensic patients display a high prevalence of histories of deprivation, and, therefore, find sharing the group therapist with six or seven other patients extremely difficult. It is not uncommon to hear patients who have been referred to a group say that they feel that they have been "short-changed", or that group therapy is only being offered because the clinic wants to save money. This can represent the patient's re-experiencing of a depriving parental figure that is unable to provide the child with what he needs.

Clinical vignette: Alan

Alan presented to the clinic as he was worried about the fact that he found himself compulsively downloading illegal images of children online. During the assessment, he presented as keen to start treatment, and engaged well with the assessor, feeling that he was listened to and understood. When offered treatment, however, he announced that as he was often required by his employer to travel, he would be away too much to be able to commit to weekly group treatment. Although the assessor interpreted his inability to commit to treatment as a difficulty in coming to terms with the seriousness of his problems, the patient politely but firmly insisted that he would like to go away and try to change his working arrangements so that he could start treatment. The assessor agreed to offer him intermittent review appointments every six weeks in the meantime. Six months later, it became increasingly clear that the patient had started to use the intermittent appointments as an opportunity for "confession", in which he would discuss his use of child pornography but continue to resist committing to treatment. This enabled him to be able to continue to rely upon his use of illegal pornography as a way of managing difficult affects, but relieving his guilt by confessing, providing the illusion that he was getting help with this. After a few "confessional" sessions, the assessor eventually put to the patient that he would no longer be able to see him on this basis, but that he could return to the clinic should he change his mind about treatment, explaining that it was important for him to take responsibility for prioritising his treatment. Although initially angry and hurt, the patient reluctantly agreed to join a group, with the agreement that his work commitments might mean that he would be unable to attend consistently. Although he did attend erratically for the first few months, after much support, encouragement, and tactful challenging by the group, Alan was able to eventually tell his employer that he was now attending group therapy and would not be able to travel abroad as often as before. He soon became a consistent and committed group member.

The group workshop

The group workshop holds several important functions. All clinicians who run groups meet for an hour each week, the meeting being chaired and brief minutes taken. This makes it possible to refer back to earlier discussions about patients, since useful insights through group discussions can sometimes be forgotten. In a practical sense, the workshop provides a setting for the discussion of new referrals, for discussion of any difficult clinical issues, and is a forum in which clinicians can share their experiences and learn from each other. On another level, the group workshop serves as a containing structure which, removed from the "coalface" of the group setting, provides a space for detoxifying and thinking about complex projective processes. The workshop can prove to be a rich resource and learning experience for clinicians who are new to running such groups. It also functions as a work group in itself, sometimes mirroring the processes taking place within the patient groups, and serving as a useful source of information about the unconscious processes that emerge.

As long as a clinical problem can wait until the next group workshop (this is usually the case, even with the more concerning problems), drawing on the collective experience of other clinicians can enable a thoughtful but active response.

New referrals for group therapy are discussed at the group workshop. Welldon has written about the indications for group therapy: please see appendix A for a summary of this (Welldon, 1996). Clinicians concluding their assessment who feel that group therapy might be indicated can either send a written referral or attend the group workshop in order to discuss the patient. This can be an extremely helpful process, as not only will a patient's suitability for group psychotherapy be discussed, but also the allocation of the patient to a group that is likely to suit their needs best. For example, a fragile patient displaying a significant level of denial about his problems might do better in a mature group which would be able to sensitively but assertively challenge their denial, whereas a patient who is more prepared to confront their own and others' difficulties might do better in a less mature group and be suitable for a newer group. The discussion of new referrals at the workshop also helps to maintain a collaborative dialogue with clinical staff who are not involved in running groups.

It could be said that the containment offered by the group workshop and, in turn, the clinic around it affords a sense of concentric containers, much like a Russian doll. A structure exists within which the group setting, group workshop, the case managers (see below), and the outside network all interact to provide an experience of a "good-enough" setting in which patients can start to open up and discuss their fears, thoughts, and vulnerabilities (Winnicott, 1953).

From the perspective of the group, it could be said that the therapist, supported by these concentric structures, embodies the containment provided by the surrounding structures.

The case manager

Each patient in treatment has an allocated case manager. This tends to be the clinician who assessed them, although this might not always be possible. Patients are often very relieved to be told by their assessor that they will remain available in the background should difficulties arise during the course of treatment, and it is surprising how rarely this offer is misused. In our experience, it is very useful that the patient has a person in his mind that he could potentially turn to if treatment becomes overwhelming. Some patients forget that they were ever told that they had a case manager—the absent or unreliable parent, perhaps. For those patients who were in an enmeshed relationship with an intrusive or violent parent, the availability of a third person to turn to can sometimes rescue a treatment that might otherwise break down when the intensity of the work increases. Patients who are experiencing difficulties during their time in the group can be helped to continue to attend the group by offering them an appointment with their case manager. Patients who struggle to make sense of what has been difficult to manage in the group can be helped to clarify what has been difficult in their own mind and, ideally, to convey this to the group. Although some might argue that this facility clashes with a more "purist" group therapy approach, we have found this to be extremely helpful. The appointment with the case manager could be seen as equivalent to the disturbed pupil who needs extra support at times of crisis in order to avoid school exclusion or refusal. The successful negotiation, with the support of the case manager, of a situation in the group that appeared insurmountable to the patient can be a powerful therapeutic development.

Clinical vignette: George

George was in group treatment at the clinic following a conviction for indecent exposure. During his assessment, he presented as an isolated man, who had few friends and had lost contact with most of his family, apart from one sister. There was an early history of emotional neglect within a large and somewhat chaotic family. Upon starting group therapy, although he was encouraged to talk about his offending in the group, he rarely did so, preferring to focus instead upon his depression and the possible causes of this. About eighteen months into treatment, his sister, to whom he was close, died. The group pointed out that he seemed relatively emotionless and distant as he spoke about this, although he had mentioned on several previous occasions that she meant a lot to him. His response to a comment of another group member that he might be protecting himself against more painful feelings about her death was dramatic—he stormed out of the group and wrote a letter the following week to say that he would not be returning. Following a discussion at the group workshop, it was decided that his case manager, the clinician who had originally assessed him, would offer him an appointment to discuss what had happened.

In this meeting, he described his outrage that another patient was "daring to tell me how I should be feeling—he was obviously trying to push his stuff on to me". He also spoke about how the group seemed to be encouraging him to get back in touch with his family, whereas he remained adamant that he had given up on them as a potential source of support. The case manager pointed out that he seemed to be replicating his relationship with his family within the group. A link was also made between his tendency towards living in an isolated state and how this had predisposed him to his offence. George agreed to try to go back to the group in order to talk about his feelings more. He managed to return to the group and continue to work on his difficulties in relating to others, how starting to share his feelings made him feel terribly "exposed", evoking feelings of vulnerability and insecurity in him.

The attendance sheet

Each group member signs an attendance sheet at the beginning of each session. Patients are invited to write their first name on the sheet (without surnames to protect confidentiality) and to tick the box for every week they attend the group. The group therapist fills in any missed weeks with "DNA" (did not attend), "CBP" (cancelled by patient), or "CBC" (cancelled by clinician). Although, on first appearance, the attendance sheet might appear to be reminiscent of schooldays, for patients who are predisposed to denying or splitting off their own and others' enactments, it is extremely helpful for group members to be able to have a concrete record of who has been, or not been, to the group. Patients are actively encouraged by the group therapist to reflect upon the meaning of lateness, absences, and cancellations. Indeed, in some cases, the group may write to patients who have not attended in order to encourage patients to attend the group. This is often in itself a helpful process for the group, since the members can feel empowered by the fact that they can let another group patient know that their absence is affecting the group. For patients who, as children, might have felt powerless in relation to inconsistent or absent care-givers, it can be extremely powerful to come together as a group to respond in an active way to an absent fellow patient. The degree to which patients are able to sensitively but assertively offer an interpretation to a fellow patient with encouragement for them to return to the group is often impressive.

Patients who do return after a period of absence have often commented that they were surprised to learn that the group had been actively trying to understand why they had not been attending. This could be seen as a reparative form of "re-parenting", as the alpha-function provided by the group enables an attempts to decipher the patient's communication through his absence (Bion, 1956). Patients are actively encouraged to write to absent group members. This can be a very powerful way of letting absent patients know that they are in the group's mind, and is usually effective in enabling a patient to return to the group.

Clinical vignette: absence as a communication

> Stephen was a sixty-two-year-old man who had a long history of engaging in masochistic relationships, getting involved with abusive and sometimes violent partners. This behaviour stopped shortly after he began group treatment. Now in his sixth year of treatment, he had become a thoughtful and insightful group member, offering well-placed and sensitive comments to other group members. However, there were also prolonged periods of absence from the group, and, upon his return (often prompted by a letter from the group encouraging him to return), he described how he had entered into a depressed state in his flat, only going out at night to buy food but otherwise depriving himself of human

contact. The group felt very concerned about him during periods of absence, knowing that he was probably in the middle of another depressive episode, but feeling unable to do anything to help him.

Following another period of absence, the group was encouraged to actively explore the meaning of Stephen's absence. One of the other group members recalled how Stephen had spoken previously about how neglected he had felt by his family; he was one of several siblings, and had felt himself to have been inferior to the others. He had self-harmed on numerous occasions as a child, banging his head against the wall or, less consciously, by being accident-prone. It was possible to see how Stephen's periods of absence from the group were a repetition of this early dynamic: by masochistically depriving himself of proper care in a depressed state (replicating his emotionally deprived childhood), the group members were forced to watch him suffer and felt helpless in the process. Dynamically, this reflected a projection of Stephen's feelings of helplessness and distress into others.

Communication with outside agencies

As a general rule, therapists are reluctant to provide reports on patients: rather, this role is referred on to the patient's general practitioner or mental health worker, where possible, in order to avoid a contamination of the therapy. However, there are exceptional occasions during which it might be necessary to provide a supportive letter or report; in these cases, it is helpful to encourage the group to offer an opinion regarding such requests, as this often results in a new insight or view about the patient involved being expressed. This culture of transparency is important, as it conveys a message of the group environment being one in which an exploration of all aspects of a patient's life is encouraged. This helps to avoid a "behind the scenes" exchange involving the therapist, the patient's case manager, or other clinical staff.

Psychiatric intervention as "paternal container"

The relationship between traditional psychiatry and psychotherapy is complex, not least because of the ways in which, from the patient's perspective, one approach can sometimes seemingly contradict the other. For example, it can be confusing for patients who are given a psychiatric diagnosis and a clearly outlined management plan by their psychiatrist to encounter in the course of a psychotherapy assessment that there is a movement away from categorical diagnosis towards a more exploratory approach.

Despite these differences, it has been our experience that using a more traditionally "psychiatric" approach, whether involving medication, a risk assessment, or clarification of a diagnosis, can provide an important function for forensic patients who are in treatment. This is partly due to the fact that it is not uncommon for patients in treatment to "decompensate" as they give up their acting out, a behaviour which they have previously relied upon to provide a sense of internal equilibrium. States of clinical depression, high levels of psychotic anxiety, and sometimes frankly psychotic episodes are all psychiatric entities which patients might experience during the course of treatment. During these times of high anxiety for the patient, the intensity of the relationship to the "group mother" can be helpfully managed by a collaborative intervention by the "psychiatric father".

Referring a patient to a psychiatrist colleague, whether within or outside the clinic, can help in several ways. Within the clinic, depending on previous allocation, this might or might not also happen to be the case manager. In providing a space in which the patient can be assessed away from the group, there is opportunity for psychiatric assessment, including diagnosis and risk assessment, with referral to colleagues working in general psychiatry when needed, whether to a crisis team for brief intervention or to the local community mental health team for longer-term external holding. As well as helping the patient, it can be extremely containing for the group to know that a psychiatrically unwell group member receives extra input when required; the group is often provided with an anonymised version of the referring letter (usually written by the case manager) when possible. The process of referring the patient on to a psychiatric colleague, with the patient improving as a result, communicates to the group that psychiatric illness can be managed, the source of the deterioration in mental state understood, and that psychotherapeutic work can continue.

Clinical vignette: Mark

Mark, a forty-two-year-old mechanic, was attending the group due to his compulsion to visit prostitutes, sometimes as often as six times a day. He presented to the clinic for help because his use of prostitutes was not providing him with the same sense of relief from symptoms of anxiety and depression as it had previously. Within six months of attending the group, he stopped visiting prostitutes and was starting to address underlying issues which he had avoided dealing with for most of his life. These were early issues of sexual abuse by his stepfather and his difficulties in relating to women as a result. Perhaps not surprisingly, during the course of these issues emerging, he started to feel worse, was more depressed, and finding it difficult to function in his everyday life. About a year into treatment, he expressed concerns that a neighbour was planning to attack him, and was avoiding going into work as he felt that his colleagues were plotting against him. Within the group, he accused another group member of mocking him, and also reported thinking that the group therapist might be meeting with this group member outside the group in order to discuss him. The group therapist, concerned about the patient's mental state, arranged for a psychiatrist colleague from within the clinic to see him outside the group. The psychiatrist's letter, inviting the patient for an appointment, was copied to the group as follows:

Dear Mark,

I understand from your group therapist Mr W that you have been experiencing some troubling thoughts which have concerned you and the group. I wondered whether it would be helpful for us to meet in order to discuss these and to think about whether anything can be done to help. I can offer you an appointment to discuss things on Oct 23rd at 3pm. I do hope that you can attend then.

Yours sincerely,

Dr Smith

In the meeting, the patient outlined his concerns as described above, and the psychiatrist felt that these symptoms suggested a psychotic episode, requiring a referral to the patient's local sector psychiatrist. A referral was made and the patient was started on antipsychotic medication. The patient was able to continue attending the group through this period and felt supported by the rest of the group. As the medication took effect over the next few weeks and the symptoms subsided, the group were able to help Mark to see that his ideas about the neighbour wanting to attack him might have been a projection of his own violent thoughts towards his abuser. His experiencing the other group member as mocking him in conjunction with the group therapist was interpreted as an externalised experience of the collusion between his stepfather and his mother (the therapist), whom he felt had turned a blind eye to, and therefore colluded in, the abuse.

In this example, it is possible to see how the recruitment of an external agency, in this case a local psychiatrist, brought a containing function that enabled therapeutic work to continue despite the patient's fragile mental state. This could be seen as the psychiatrist holding a function representing external reality for a patient whose mental state meant that he had become psychotically preoccupied with a persecuting object (the group/the neighbour/parents).

Of course, it is important for such occurrences within the life of a group to be properly worked through, as they can be disturbing to the other group members. The therapist must remain alert to material that relates to this. In groups in which several, if not all, patients use acting out to protect them from psychotic anxieties, the disturbing impact of a patient developing frank psychotic symptoms within the course of treatment should not be underestimated.

Responding to violence within groups

Physical violence is extremely rare within the group setting, and shocking if it occurs. It could be said that one of the group tasks is to maintain an environment in which thinking and understanding can occur, acting as a form of dialysis for toxic disturbances which might otherwise result in violence. It is the group therapist's responsibility to respond actively to escalations within the group session that suggest imminent physical violence, stopping the session or asking a patient to leave if necessary. The following vignette describes how the impact of a violent incident might require a response from several components of the clinic's overall structure in order to allow the event to be properly processed.

Clinical vignette: a violent incident

Colin was intensely involved in a "pairing" with Brendan, a long-standing and dominant group member. Colin was a new group member, and, as a result, they had not had an opportunity to learn much about each other's background histories. There were several episodes of sado-masochistic exchanges between them, usually with Colin accusing Brendan of bullying him, but provoking him into doing so in the process. Brendan would respond in his usual ebullient manner, loud and opinionated. The excitement between the two patients had been escalating and the pair seemed reluctant to hear the therapist's interpretations about the destructiveness of their interactions for the group as a whole.

The following week an incident occurred and a window was smashed. The pairing between Brendan and Colin had been intense. Colin was, as he described, "standing up" to Brendan (literally, from his sitting position), but with an obvious sadomasochistic pleasure that became salacious in quality. At the height of the exchange between them, Brendan spat at Colin, and then rose out of his chair and approached Colin, gesturing a punch but not touching him. He then turned and picked up a plant pot and hurled it through a window. The group all stood up, the patients moving to protect the female therapist. The therapist asked both Brendan and Colin more than once to "move away", but in the context of the high level of arousal in the room, neither of them seemed to hear her. Eventually, another patient, in his mild-mannered professional way, persuaded Brendan to leave the room by escorting him to the door. A telephone call to the receptionist, whose voice was calm and carefree, established that Brendan had left the clinic quietly.

The group sat down for the remaining fifteen minutes. Colin said that he found the therapist to be controlling, and complained that she had not asked him whether he was all right. The patients were supportive of him. Slowly, the group settled itself and it was agreed with the therapist that she would discuss what had happened with her colleagues in order to consider the appropriate way to proceed.

Brendan rang later that day to apologise and to offer to pay for the damage. This was most important in terms of assessment of risk and in planning a response to what had happened. The group therapist's initial feeling was that Brendan should be suspended. However, in the group workshop the next day, the other workshop members and the clinic director, who attended the workshop in view of the seriousness of the incident, felt inclined to think that the clinic should accept his offer and wait to see if he returned the next week, which he did.

The next group was very difficult: both Brendan and Colin attended. Brendan did apologise but said that he had felt provoked, which was partly true. The group split in two and took sides, everyone spoke at once, and the therapist felt that they were looking for a male authority figure to step in and take control (it had been explored before, and was being worked through, that the previous therapist for this group had been a man, to whom the patients had often referred favourably following his departure). Colin suddenly got up and left the group early, complaining that he had almost been a victim of violence and that the issue was now being brushed under the carpet. Another patient followed Colin, trying to persuade him to return.

When Colin did not reappear at the group the following week, the group, including Brendan, wrote him a very caring letter urging him to return and to accept that such strong feelings towards the therapist and group members are often to do with earlier difficulties in one's family background. The group had not consciously formulated things, Colin being such a new member of the group, but this was clearly a difficult repetition of Colin's experience that his parents, particularly his mother, had preferentially poured their resources into a younger sibling who had physical health problems. Colin wrote back to the group with gratitude, but saying he would not return. Following an appointment with his case manager, Colin did eventually return to the group and was able to work through what had been a traumatic experience for him.

The group workshop spent much time exploring what had happened. Colin's family background influencing his difficulty in managing what had happened within the group seemed relatively clear, but what had fuelled Brendan's eventual breakdown into violence? The violence was viewed as an attack on the therapist/mother's body, perhaps as an attack on the therapist for not protecting him from Colin's goading superciliousness and better start in life. There had not been sufficient time for them to get to know each other and realise that both had had mothers who abandoned them emotionally in childhood, but perhaps there was an unconscious recognition of that in the immediate competitiveness that was set up between them.

There was a strong view in the group workshop that Brendan should have been expected to pay for the damage. This would enable an opportunity for him to make a very real contribution, but also to enable the act to stay both within his own and the group's mind to facilitate the work of "repairing" what had happened psychologically through developing some understanding of what had taken place. The significance of the breaking of the window, as a part of the fabric of the clinic walls, came to be understood as an attack upon the holding function of the therapist and group.

The sadomasochistic opportunity provided by the payment of the instalments meant that they were much delayed in starting. One week, Brendan said that he had forgotten to bring the first instalment; the next week he did not attend. But once he settled into a routine of paying, he became very conscientious about the instalments, appearing to appreciate the specific contact with the receptionist that it required. There were further delays according to his access to funds, so that it looked as if he was monitoring his future place in the clinic, that it could be endless because of the debt still to be paid. However, an end to the payments did come into view, by which time Brendan had become much calmer and more solid in his interactions in the group.

In this example, one can see how, in the context of a serious enactment within the group setting, multiple components of the group's supporting network (the therapist, the receptionist, the clinic director, and the group workshop) were required in order to contain and eventually develop an understanding of what had taken place. Only then could a reparative process occur.

The importance of good communication between staff

An ethos of openness and availability between clinicians can be said to be crucial to the clinic's functioning. It is this spirit of being able to discuss difficult cases or situations at the drop of a hat that contributes to the clinician's capacity to remain sensitive and responsive to the patients' needs.

Some of the alarming risks that patients might present during the course of treatment requires the therapist to remain alert to these, and not to "turn a blind eye" to abuse, neglect, or cruelty, just as many care-givers before might have done. This requires that the therapist feels sufficiently contained so that he or she is able to be in touch with, and express, any worries about group members as treatment progresses.

It is also important that the clinic can maintain a balance between holding a robust position in relation to patients' requests and being flexible to patients' needs. It is not unusual to receive requests from patients to change group, for the possibility of individual psychotherapy to be reviewed, or to stop their treatment. In these cases, it is important that the therapist can engage with the request in a considered and thoughtful way, involving the group in the process, but also keeping in mind that a request to change the frame of treatment might be a response to the emergence of something difficult, but therapeutically valuable, within the course of treatment.

Conclusion

This chapter has outlined the main structures required to offer sufficient containment so that the work of forensic group psychotherapy can take place. These include the way in which the administrative staff interact with the patients and the physical building of the clinic. It also includes the way in which patients are prepared for group therapy, the allocation of case managers, and the ways in which the group itself is run. The availability of external support, when necessary, is also crucial. It is only when the group and the group therapist feel sufficiently contained that the work of enabling patients to understand their destructive and aggressive tendencies can occur. Winnicott's concept of holding and Bion's concept of containment are crucial to an appreciation of the importance of these structures. Good, clear, and regular communication between all involved professionals is key to enabling the network to perform its containing function effectively.

References

Bion, W. R. (1956). Development in schizophrenic thought/A theory of thinking. *International Journal of Psychoanalysis, 37* [reprinted in *Second Thoughts*. London: William Heinemann Medical Books Ltd, 1967].

Department of Health (2010). *See Think Act, Your Guide to Relational Security* (available online at: http://www.rcpsych.ac.uk/pdf/Relational%20Security%20Handbook.pdf).

Glasser, M. (1979). From the analysis of a transvestite. *International Journal of Psychoanalysis*, 6: 163–173.

Glasser, M. (1992). Problems in the psychoanalysis of certain narcissistic disorders. *International Journal of Psychoanalysis*, 73: 493–503.

Rey, H. (1994). *Universals of Psychoanalysis in the Treatment of Psychotic and Borderline States*. London: Free Association Books.

Welldon, E. (1996). Group-analytic psychotherapy in an out-patient setting. In: C. Cordess & M. Cox (Eds.), *Forensic Psychotherapy, Crime Psychodynamics and the Offender Patient* (pp. 63–83). London: Jessica Kingsley.

Welldon, E. (1997). Let the treatment fit the crime: forensic group psychotherapy. *Group Analysis, 30*(1): 9–26.

Winnicott, C., Shepherd, R., & Davis, M. (Eds.) (1984). *Deprivation and Delinquency.* London: Tavistock.

Winnicott, D. W. (1953). Transitional objects and transitional phenomena—a study of the first not-me possession. *International Journal of Psychoanalysis, 34:* 89–97.

Winnicott, D. W. (1965). *Maturational Processes and the Facilitating Environment: Studies in the Theory of the Emotional Development.* London: Hogarth Press.

CHAPTER THREE

Acting out, the repetition compulsion, and forensic group therapy

Andrew Williams

Working psychotherapeutically with patients who express their disturbance predominantly through action requires a careful consideration of the meaning behind behaviour. Understanding the significance of a particular form of sexualised or violent behaviour can provide a sense of relief to patients, offering meaning to a pattern of behaviour which might have previously been experienced by the individual as senseless, repetitive, and compulsive. For many patients starting in group treatment, starting to make links between their history, their current situation, and their particular form of acting out conveys a sense that behaviour can be understood, and, thus, some control gained: knowledge is, indeed, power.

Anna Freud, in her 1968 paper "Acting out", differentiated between the acting out which occurs in neurotic patients and that which occurs in patients who tend to act out in their daily lives before coming into treatment (e.g., those suffering with perversions, psychosis, or addiction). She stated that for patients suffering with neurotic symptoms, the analytic setting provides a forum in which, through the use of free association and the analytic technique, the id pushes with increasing force against the ego. Acting out in this case represents an expression through action of a repressed memory, impulse, or wish, the therapeutic task being to develop an understanding of the repressed material as the acting out occurs within the transference relationship. In patients who act out before coming into treatment, however, the task is different. These patients tend to behave in more impulsive ways, whether in treatment or not, and action has long been used as a way of avoiding thinking. Thus, the aim is to enable the patient to move their form of acting out into the transference relationship so that it can be properly understood (Freud, A., 1968). For the perverse or violent patient, it is the movement of acting out into the forum of the group setting that presents an opportunity for understanding and lasting change.

Many patients present for treatment at the Portman Clinic because their particular form of acting out no longer provides the same sense of relief that it did previously—the perversion or violent act has "broken down". In this way, the behaviour no longer serves as a solution to the underlying conflicts from which it might have previously provided relief. This could be underlying trauma, depression, a feeling of emptiness, psychotic anxieties, or all of these. Indeed, it is not uncommon for patients to present for the second time for treatment years after they initially presented for help, having disengaged from the assessment or early into treatment the first time around. This might be because, on first presentation, consideration of the notion of giving up a perverse solution provoked too much anxiety.

Freud, in his 1914 paper, "Remembering, repeating and working through", introduced the concept that repetitive behaviour might represent the patient's inability to remember some earlier trauma: to quote Freud's oft-repeated but invaluable description of acting out:

> We may say that the patient does not *remember* anything of what he has forgotten and repressed but *acts* it out. He reproduces it not as a memory but as an action. He *repeats* it without, of course, knowing that he is repeating it. (Freud, 1914g, p. 150)

Although he initially regarded acting-out as a hindrance to the progress of the analysis, he later formed the opinion that when this occurred within the relationship with the analyst, and could be understood, a curative process could occur. He went on to state, "As long as the patient is in the treatment he cannot escape from this compulsion to repeat; and in the end we understand that it is his way of remembering", later on stating,

We soon perceive that the transference itself is only a piece of repetition, and that the repetition is a transference of the forgotten past not only on to the doctor, but also onto all the other aspects of the current situation. We must be prepared to find, therefore, that the patient abandons himself to the compulsion to repeat, which now replaces the impulsion to remember, not only in his personal attitude to the doctor but also in every other activity and relationship which may occupy his life at the time. (Freud, 1914g. p. 151)

Freud later noted that resistance to change was particularly unyielding in persons who seemed to persist in seeking outcomes that led to unhappiness and suffering. In these cases, he noticed that these patients tended to be unable to learn from experience. From these observations, fuelled by his pessimism about treating these patients, he went on years later to describe the death instinct:

I drew the conclusion that besides the instinct to preserve living substance and join it into even larger units, there must exist another, contrary instinct seeking to dissolve those units and to bring them back to their primaeval, inorganic state. (Freud, 1930a, p. 118)

The role of the death instinct in relation to the repetition compulsion has been previously conceptualised as representing a hatred and intolerance of all those things that stand for life and creativity (Feldman, 2000). Although the purpose of such an instinct is difficult to understand, the reality of its manifestations is impossible to avoid. When viewed as an "anti-life" instinct, the relationship with envy becomes clearer. Perverse and violent patients sometimes display behaviours that could be seen as destroying or attacking anything perceived as therapeutic progress. In some patients, there is a pull towards not changing, or remaining in, a lifestyle which restricts the patient's sense of being alive. There are some patients in whom it seems that the tendency to stay the same, so as not to develop creative interests or relationships, is very powerful. An example of this, sometimes observed in forensic psychotherapy, is the patient who, in response to having made some progress in his personal life, finding a girlfriend or starting a new job, soon immerses himself in a weekend full of sexual acting out but does not know why.

The concept of the repetition compulsion is of particular relevance to patients presenting with perversion and violence. Several authors have recognised that in the treatment of perversion, it is the analysis of the perversion as it unfolds in the transference–countertransference relationship which is important, as it is understanding the way in which the individual distorts, controls, or manipulates relationships which is the crucial task enabling therapeutic change (Malcolm, 1970; Meltzer, 1973; Ogden, 1996). Group therapy can be said to embrace this principle, as patients develop transferences not only to the therapist, but also to each other, to the group as a whole, and to the institution in which the group takes place. One of the benefits of group psychotherapy, as opposed to individual psychotherapy, is that the complex range of interactions occurring within each group session allow for a wealth of information to emerge from which to explore each patient's psychopathology. The group could be said to be a sort of laboratory in which the patients can start to explore their everyday interactions, learning, questioning, and challenging the way in which they relate to themselves and others. With the help of the group therapist, it is important to attempt to promote a culture of constant enquiry about the material that each patient brings to the session.

Clinical vignette: Jonathan

Jonathan, a twenty-year-old man, had been in weekly group treatment for about a year. He was attending the group because he had engaged his younger sister in sexualised behaviour when he was seventeen. This had been kept secret for the months during which it had taken place, only coming to light much later when his sister disclosed this to his parents. Following the involvement of social services and the police, he continued to live at home with his sister and parents. His girlfriend was now pregnant and social services were concerned about the risk to his future child. He remained a quiet and passive group member, which was understood by some group members as his being "shy" or possibly depressed. About a year into treatment, the clinic manager reported that he had approached her following a group session and requested a list of the times he had attended the clinic. When the clinic manager said that she would need to discuss this with his group therapist, Jonathan became irate, demanding that it was his right to be allowed to have a record of attendance. When this was brought back into the group by the therapist during the following session, a discussion ensued about Jonathan's motivation for attending the group. Jonathan explained that he wanted to strengthen the case to have access to his unborn child. Some group members thought that he might be attending "to look good" for social services rather than wanting to learn about himself. The group were then able to point out the parallel between the way in which Jonathan had kept his request out of the group setting and demanded something from the clinic manager and the way in which he had perpetrated the abuse by isolating his sister and demanding something sexual from her. It emerged that this sexual acting out was in the context of feeling neglected by his parents; it could be said that his silence in the group represented a replication of the family situation in which he felt neglected and acted in a hostile way in return. This formulation was indeed difficult for Jonathan to consider, but he was later able to acknowledge the secretive way in which he had gone about his request.

Melanie Klein developed Freud's ideas about the relationship of the death instinct to envy. She suggested that the good aspects of the breast represent maternal goodness, patience, generosity, creativity, and that a good relation to it is vital if the infant is to establish a good internal object to provide a foundation for future development. Envy threatens this goodness and becomes a major obstacle to development of healthy character and relationships (Klein, 1957).

Developing theory in relation to envy, Bion described that it is the link between objects that that is difficult to tolerate, since, for patients who prominently display the repetition compulsion, receiving something good evokes feelings of humiliation. In order to avoid these feelings, the individual instead repeatedly turns away to possess the goodness through identification rather than dependency, so that he is in a position to give and not receive. In this way, the individual "becomes" the source of goodness in a self-feeding way, rather than maintaining a dependent relationship with a good object (Bion, 1959). This may be achieved through a manic defence against dependency and the depressive position, which attacks creative links and prevents change (Joseph, 1959).

Clinical vignette: a shameful act

Two years into treatment, Jonathan anxiously revealed to the group that as a teenager he had drunkenly got into his sister's bed and touched her inappropriately while she was sleeping. He was extremely ashamed of this, and had worried since then that he had harmed her psychologically in some way. He had been adopted, while his sister was a biological child of his adoptive parents, and he felt that her arrival when he was aged five caused a total displacement of his parents' attention. In exploring the possible reasons for what he did to her, one group member talked about his envy of an older sibling and the preferential treatment he felt that she had received: "Sometimes I wanted to beat her up just so she wouldn't feel so special." A further discussion ensued in which it was suggested that Jonathan's actions towards his sister might have represented his prominent envy of her status as the biological child of their parents, and his wish to take something away from her through touching her inappropriately. During the following session, Jonathan spoke about feeling quite taken aback that his behaviour could be thought of in terms of his own feelings of envy, rather than judged solely as an attack upon his sister.

In "Formulations on the two principles of mental functioning" (1911b), Freud emphasised the way in which thinking provides an experimental space in which an action can be imagined without having to carry it out. He later conceived of thinking as a way of playing with possibilities: "Thinking is an experimental action carried out with small amounts of energy, in the same way as a general shifts small figures about on a map before setting his large bodies of troops in motion" (Freud, 1933a, p. 89). For many patients who act out, the shift from "action" to "thinking about action" can be said to be a key therapeutic aim, something that might not be achieved until several years into treatment. For many patients who have relied upon their actions as a means of managing disturbed states of mind, the experience of sitting in a group on a weekly basis in order to think about how they behave, and how their behaviour affects others, can be a new experience.

Clinical vignette: Adrian

Adrian was in his fourth year of group treatment. He was in a specialist group for patients who had committed contact offences against children. He had received convictions for downloading illegal images of children as well as serving a prison sentence for inappropriately touching an eleven-year-old girl. One of the aims he wished to address in therapy was to attempt to build up his life again after losing his job as a gas fitter when he was given a custodial sentence. During the first three years of treatment, he had spoken on numerous occasions about his wish to befriend young girls, "nothing sexual, I just like their company". He would also talk in the group about his wish to be in an adult heterosexual relationship, but kept struggling to meet women as he had relatively little contact with others socially. During one group session, he recounted how he had been shopping in the supermarket and spoken to a girl in one of the aisles while her mother was nearby. It was a pleasant chat, all above board, and Adrian felt that there was no risk of anything untoward happening. It was only when the group enquired further about this that he eventually disclosed that he had gone home afterwards and masturbated while thinking about her. Adrian's denial that there was anything to be concerned about in this encounter was challenged actively by the group, and a discussion followed about whether turning a situation into sexual fantasy constitutes something worth worrying about. There were mixed views, but later in the same session, another patient was able to talk about the fact that he had often felt guilty about "sexualising" the experience of being on the beach in the summer when there were children present. A discussion followed about whether it is more sensible to avoid these types of situations altogether.

In the above example, it is possible to see how, through a process of connecting with each others' experiences, the group was able to consider the significance of *fantasising* about doing something illegal as against actually acting it out, and the internal significance of this. In this way, a culture gradually establishes itself within the group against which the individual patients can start to recalibrate their own sense of right and wrong. This is especially important for patients who have acted out paedophilically, as early abusive experiences that have been internalised can mean that the usual intergenerational boundaries have been violated in some way. A sense of moral code arising from such group discussions can, one hopes, be internalised by the individual, leading to his developing a better capacity to evaluate the moral aspects of his behaviours.

Winnicott (1971) emphasised how psychotherapy occurs in the area of overlap between the therapist and patient's areas of play, an important task facing the therapist in helping the patient move from a position of not being able to play into a state of begin able to do so. Parsons (1999), developing this notion, emphasised the way in which the therapeutic domain serves as a "paradoxical reality, in which things may be real and not real at the same time". It is this paradoxical setting which makes play between therapist and patient possible, a safe space where ideas, conflicts, and a freedom to explore new ways of thinking can occur (Parsons, 1999). This freedom to explore the meaning of fantasies and actions is a crucial aspect of the group's function. Although some of the acts perpetrated by forensic patients are sometimes difficult to put into words, and evoke feelings of revulsion in those who hear about them, a movement towards considering what motivated such actions encourages a sense of enquiry. The "real–not real" environment of the group, in which words and not actions are the currency, means that group members eventually develop a sense that actively exploring their own and others' motivations can help them to develop a sense of mastery over the impulse to act.

In her paper "On acting out" (1990), Chasseguet-Smirgel commented upon her finding that, in the case of patients who display a propensity to act out prior to entering analytic treatment, there is a "persistent lack of psychic elaboration throughout the treatment" and acting out should be tolerated over a significant period of time. This has certainly been our experience at the Portman Clinic, where patients can continue to act out in various ways as treatment progresses. The quality of the acting out can change; some patients who initially present with perversion might display more evidence of aggression further into treatment as the aggression previously contained within sexuality becomes more available in a "purer" form. Similarly, violent patients who were previously thought not to display sexually deviant behaviours might describe these later in treatment.

The magical quality of omnipotent fantasies common observed in delinquent patients was emphasised by Adam Limentani, a psychoanalyst who worked at the Portman Clinic for many years. Referring to the notion that patients who frequently act out tend to believe in the magic of action, he proposed that omnipotent fantasies are a central part of the psychopathology of the delinquent:

> Undoubtedly the most serious technical problems are encountered in those cases where the belief in omnipotence at the service of denying impotence is fed by the feeling of being in control of the environment and being capable of provoking pre-set reactions in people. Acting out for these patients is the oxygen of their psychic life. (Limentani, 1966, p. 280)

For patients who have relied upon their actions for many years as a means of maintaining a psychic equilibrium, the notion of starting to think about giving up these behaviours can be very frightening, experienced almost as a matter of life and death.

Klein developed Freud's ideas about acting out in her view that the patient's acting out represents the way the patient originally turned away from the primary object. Developing this idea further, Rosenfeld expressed his view that the extent of the infant's aggression is a crucial determinant for acting out in later life. He linked this very clearly to the early experience of the infant: that excessive hostility during the first months of life (whether through innate temperament or evoked through the interaction with the mother, or both) means that there is a rigid split maintained between the good and bad primary object. In less hostile babies, there is more integration of the good and bad object and, thus, guilt and depression can be experienced, which centre on the fear of losing the good object. This increases his capacity to feel love and to introject a good object more securely, which again strengthens the ego and makes it possible for him to bear his frustrations with entirely losing his love, that is, the depressive position. He went on to describe the implications of this for later life: that when the healthier patient is full of hostility towards the analyst for one reason or another, and, therefore, acts out by turning to the outside world to find good objects, the patient retains some good relationship with the analyst and, consequently, some co-operation and insight in the analysis. Under such circumstances, it is possible for the patient to work through the negative transference with the analyst, thus avoiding potentially catastrophic acting out (Rosenfeld, 1965).

Clinical vignette: Derek

Derek was a thirty-two-year-old man who was referred to the clinic because his use of Internet pornography was out of control. He could spend hours at a time looking at pornography or engaging in webcam sexual encounters with both men and women online. He worked full-time as an office clerk for a legal firm but would still find time in his busy schedule to engage in his compulsive Internet behaviours. He decided to seek help because his wife had caught him masturbating at the home computer one evening while engaging in a live online chat with a woman.

He told his wife about his problematic use of the Internet; she was initially shocked, but remained supportive, given his promise that he would seek help for his problem.

During the assessment, he revealed that he had two children, a son who was seven and a daughter who was entering adolescence. He told the assessing clinician that his mother suffered with depression as far back as he could recall, and that his father was often absent from the family home, having affairs with other women, he discovered as an adolescent. He had one older brother, whom he thought had a closer relationship to his mother than he did, something he felt very envious of for most of his childhood. As an adolescent, he had struggled with talking to girls, finding himself extremely anxious in their company. He met his wife at the age of nineteen and they married a year later.

He described how, on some occasions, he could spend large amounts of money on accessing pornographic material and speaking with women online. He seemed eager to access treatment, although he had little sense of what psychotherapy involved. The assessor was able to make some tentative links between his Internet-related activities and his underlying anxieties about being a good husband and father. He conveyed a sense of desperation—that he needed to go online in order to hold himself together in some way, yet realised that this had to stop, something which worried him greatly.

When he joined the group, the therapist noted that he had a sense of pressure and urgency about him. He looked very stressed throughout the first session, and talked openly about his distress about his "addiction", that he needed to do something about his problem urgently before it destroyed his marriage and family. The group, a reasonably well-established cohort, took his anxiety in their stride and started to explore his background with him. Although initially open to this, halfway through the session, he exploded and said that this was useless; why should he be thinking about his childhood when his problems were troubling him now? This was all just wasting time and he needed to stop what he was doing straight away. The group, by now familiar with demands and complaints from newer group members, held a steady position and reassured the patient calmly that although it might seem frustrating now, thinking around his problem would probably help him in the long term. There are no "quick fixes", they assured him.

During the next session, Derek returned to the group in a complaining state of mind. He told the group therapist (not the group members) that this treatment probably would not help him and that his "problem behaviour" had deteriorated in the last week. He had increased his use of the Internet within the family home, shutting himself away in the computer room for several hours on the pretence of working on figures for his job. He also spoke about how he had been thinking of ending his life, revealing that he had taken an overdose a few years ago during a period of depression.

The group were becoming anxious about his suicidal tendencies, but also irritated by him. One group member pointed out that Derek seemed to be demanding an instant cure. Another suggested that he seemed to be trying to make the group feel responsible for him, whereas he should take responsibility for both limiting his use of the Internet and keeping himself safe. Derek responded in a shocked way, saying that he had presented for help at the clinic and did not expect to be told to get on with it all by himself.

After a few more sessions, the group formed two opposing sides: some members felt sorry for him and encouraged him to explore the problems he might be experiencing in his day-to-day life. Other group members felt less tolerant towards him, complaining that he was dominating the group and not allowing anyone else time to speak. One group member challenged what they felt to be his aggression towards his family, pointing out that if he did take an overdose, it would be his wife or children who would find him comatose or dead. Another group member pointed out that he was doing something quite aggressive towards his children by sitting at his computer for hours on end instead of spending time with them or his family.

The group therapist tried to gather these views, all of which were true in their own way. He said, "I think that Derek is showing the group what it feels like to be where he is. He is desperately asking for help, but when this is offered in the form of an invitation to explore things, he says, 'What you have to offer won't help, I'll kill myself'." After a prolonged silence, Derek said that he was worried that his wife was going to leave him. One shrewd group member suggested that perhaps Derek was worried that the group would reject him. He was taken aback at this comment, and went on to say that he had been thinking of leaving the group as he had been researching a Sex Addicts Anonymous (SAA) group which met locally. He had an idea that this would help him deal with his problems more quickly.

The group put to him that he was looking for a "quick fix"—a bit like the idea that the "fix" which he regularly took of Internet sex in order to provide instant relief, albeit temporary, from his problems. The reality would be that, if successful in his attempt to kill himself, he would be leaving behind two children and a wife who need him.

Derek started to talk more about his problems in the two subsequent sessions. He spoke about his anxieties about his capacity to be a good husband and father, how disgusted he felt with himself for doing what he did, and how when left with too much time to think about things, such as his relationship difficulties with his wife, he would feel much worse. He thought that he used the Internet as a way of escaping all of this. The group started to explore with him why he felt the way he did about things. However, after a particularly good session, in which it felt as if he had made some progress, he then wrote a letter to the group the following week to say that he no longer felt that he was getting benefit from the group and had decided to leave. The group wrote to him to attempt to persuade him to return, but with no response. The group therapist wrote to both the patient and his referring psychiatrist to encourage him to return to the group, but he did not come back.

In the above example, it is possible to see how Derek's early experience becomes replicated within the group dynamic. His early experience of an emotionally unavailable mother and a father who was often absent from the family home becomes manifest within his relationship to the group. Although he makes a good contact with the assessing clinician, starting to be able to make some links between his sexual acting out and his past, his capacity to continue with this work quickly subsides once he is in the group setting. His engagement in sexual acting out increases, probably linked to an increase in anxiety accompanied by starting to engage with his problems. Derek complains to the group that he is not being helped by them—that they should "do more" to help him. In this way, he is complaining not only to the group, but also to a depressed and unavailable mother who could not respond to his needs. Therefore, he turns away from the group, perhaps in identification with his father, who looks outside the relationship for something better. Thus, his chances of remaining in a therapeutic relationship with the group are sabotaged.

The split evoked with the group revealed something of Derek's internal world: a split in which he attempted to be sympathetic with himself (in coming for help, also embodied in his wife's support of him), but also felt hateful and rejecting towards himself in relation to his difficulties. There was little sense of a couple which might have worked together to contain him, whether this coupling was between

Derek and the patient, the therapist and the group, or the split aspects of the group coupling together to form a whole. Contained within his sexual acting out was a repetition of an early experience of feeling abandoned, in this case projected into his wife and children. It was only when the group pointed out the neglect that Derek perpetrated towards his own family that he started to realise the pattern that was being repeated. In this case, Derek was unable to tolerate the frustration of having to wait for the therapy to take effect; his relationship to his early objects probably did not allow for sufficient integration of good and bad parts of the group to allow him to tolerate the challenge of remaining in contact with a group that he experienced as both nourishing and frustrating.

Conclusion

In the context of forensic group psychotherapy, the concepts of acting out, repetition compulsion, and the movement from action to thought are all key ways of conceptualising a model for therapeutic change. Further, the concepts of the death instinct and its relationship to envy help us to understand and tolerate the inevitable attacks upon progress, and the frequent conflicting pull between life and death that occurs when treating patients suffering from perversions. "Relapses" during the course of treatment can be dispiriting for the treating clinician; indeed, this might include the patient's absence from treatment for periods of time. However, seeing these as a necessary part of the treatment process can help both patient and clinician tolerate the frustrations of forensic psychotherapy. By providing a consistent presence within the group, the treatment becomes a place in which the patient's internal conflicts and emotions can emerge, allowing scope for understanding, tolerance, and eventually therapeutic progress.

References

Bion, W. R. (1959). Attacks on linking. *International Journal of Psychoanalysis*, 40: 308–315.
Chasseguet-Smirgel, J. (1990). On acting out. *International Journal of Psychoanalysis*, 71: 77–86.

Feldman, M. (2000). Some views on the manifestation of the death instinct in clinical work. *International Journal of Psychoanalysis, 81*: 53–65.
Freud, A. (1968). Acting out. *International Journal of Psychoanalysis, 49*: 165–170.
Freud, S. (1911b). Formulations on the two principles of mental functioning. *S.E., 12*: 218–226. London: Hogarth.
Freud, S. (1914g). Remembering, repeating and working-through. *S.E., 12*: 147–156.
Freud, S. (1930a). *Civilisation and Its Discontents. S.E., 21*: 64–146. London: Hogarth.
Freud, S. (1933a). *New Introductory Lectures on Psychoanalysis. S.E., 22*: 81–111. London: Hogarth.
Joseph, B. (1959). An aspect of the repetition compulsion. *International Journal of Psychoanalysis, 40*: 213–222.
Klein, M. (1957). Envy and gratitude. In: *The Writings of Melanie Klein, Vol. 3: Envy and Gratitude and Other Works* (pp. 176–235). London: Hogarth Press, 1975 [reprinted London: Karnac, 1993].
Limentani, A. (1966). A re-evaluation of acting out in relation to working through. *International Journal of Psychoanalysis, 47*: 274–282.
Malcolm, R. (1970). The mirror: a perverse sexual fantasy in a woman seen as a defence against a psychotic breakdown. In: E. Spillius (Ed.), *Melanie Klein Today, Vol. 2: Mainly Practice* (pp. 115–137). New York: Routledge, 1988.
Meltzer, D. (1973). *Sexual States of Mind*. Strathtay, Perthshire: Clunie Press.
Ogden, T. (1996). The perverse subject of analysis. *Journal of the American Psychoanalytic Association, 44*: 1121–1146.
Parsons, M. (1999). The logic of play in psychoanalysis. *International Journal of Psychoanalysis, 80*: 871–884.
Rosenfeld, H. (1965). An investigation into the need of neurotic and psychotic patients to act out during analysis. In: *Psychotic States* (pp. 200–216). London: Hogarth Press.
Winnicott, D. W. (1971). *Playing and Reality*. London: Tavistock.

PART II
THEMES AND APPLICATIONS

CHAPTER FOUR

My first year as a forensic group therapist

Aikaterini Papaspirou

This is an account of my first year conducting a treatment group for men referred for violent and sometimes sexually violent behaviour. From the very beginning, they have continued to surprise me.

Axis one: history lines

Before the beginning

A few months into my training in forensic psychotherapy at the Portman Clinic and while still finding my feet, I was invited to take over a group from a senior staff member upon her retirement. Despite my initial anxiety, I was tempted by the idea of a group that had been going on for a while and I was open to the possibility of learning how to be a group therapist by sharing the experience with colleagues at the Group Workshop. My supervisor suggested that he would help me develop my own style of conducting a group. I had extensive discussions with the departing therapist, and I spent some time looking at the patients' files. I eagerly waited for my first session.

The baptism of fire

It felt strange to be a newcomer in an already formed group, maybe even more so if one is supposed to be the therapist. I decided to use my intuition along with some theoretical concepts to ground myself. In the first session, I concentrated on listening for themes, keeping an eye for shifts in the affective atmosphere, and being mindful of the transference of the group as a whole on me.

At the start of the session, the members of the group introduced themselves; looking back, I can now see that in doing so they also unravelled some patterns of relating to each other that are still noticeable. For a while I felt excluded, almost wiped out, until a theme about deaths of relatives emerged, only to be quickly followed by discussions about one of the members needing to move to a different home. I commented there seemed to be a theme of loss, but that this was difficult for the group to bear and that there was a tendency to concentrate on moving on. This comment led the group to acknowledge my presence.

There followed material about getting stuck in depression and living in the past. I linked this to their feelings of loss for their previous therapist. This turned the group's attention to my person. They seemed to be both curious about me and also wary about how I would be able to cope with them; I noted their anxiety about the boundaries I would be able to keep and about whether they would be able to trust me. Implied also was the question of whether I would be able to trust them.

When our time was up, I had a sense that a couple of members almost ran to the door. I was left feeling that they were interesting and challenging, but that we had to deal with grief and also with learning as a group how to move on. It seemed that I was already linked to the Portman: there was an implication that if the clinic had chosen to appoint me as their new therapist, that must have meant that I could not have been a completely random choice and, therefore, untrustworthy. The Portman and I were some sort of a couple for them. Their attitude conjured in my mind the idea of the institution as an internal object upon which I might also be able to rely. In times to come, this would prove invaluable, in both abstract and concrete terms.

The honeymoon period

In the following session, only one of the members turned up. I felt rather disappointed and concerned about whether the group would be able to come together with me as their new therapist. However, the session after this was better attended, and the group gave me a taster of how they were able to work together. They began giving details about the main issues in their lives, past and present, and I felt I was slowly getting to know them. Their respective narratives already hinted at what I would later come to recognise as each member's key themes, which would repeat themselves in a number of variations.

The group members who attended each session varied to the extent that I felt I was seeing a different group every week. Nevertheless, the ones who were present seemed to be invested in keeping the group afloat. On one occasion, they wrote a thoughtful letter to a fellow member who had not attended for a while, inviting him back. They acknowledged that, as much as it might be difficult for him to take other members' difficulties into consideration, he might benefit from their support.

It was evident that the group was often able to keep absent and previous members, as well as its previous therapist, in mind. Members expressed their feelings of grievance about my having replaced the latter and having changed the time of the group. They also relayed their appreciation of some of my predecessor's interpretations, comparing me, occasionally unfavourably, to her while expressing some reluctant acceptance of me.

As I slowly settled more comfortably in the therapist's seat, I began to notice more of my reactions to their material. There were occasions when I felt rather affected, almost as if I was one of them, and yet I was aware of being different to them, being the one mainly responsible for processing what they were sharing with the group and providing them with a different perspective.

I was able to comment on how they seemed to be feeling as a group about myself. In the material, I felt I was being represented as an oppressive father figure, a neglectful mother, or the female figure with whom they would engage in an inevitable power struggle. Interestingly, there were increasing references to the current political situation. Those would usually come at the end of the session and would leave me curious about their significance.

Protests

Slowly the political references moved to more central parts of the sessions. There was a theme about protests and the reaction of the police and the state to them. This sometimes felt like a distraction from the work of the group, but it often seemed to be highlighting a testing of the boundaries and an attempt to explore the nature of my authority. I interpreted their anxiety that I would either be rather strict, like the police, or else I would allow too much freedom and then things would get out of control.

In a particular session, I felt I was being pushed into a corner, as if I was a protester faced with a potential eruption of violence on the street and limited choice as to how I could respond: the options given to me were that one could either retaliate and become "justifiably" violent, or run. I was surprised by the intensity of this experience as much as by my response: I was able to maintain some freedom of thinking and invite the group to consider how one could provoke violence as well as choose not to, and refrain from engaging in unwitting battles as a result of taking into consideration the possible consequences.

There were other times when I found it encouraging that the discussion centred on how important it was for communities to come together and work for the benefit of their members. I felt this conveyed an acknowledgement of the group as a potentially collaborative space that would counter its members' feelings of disempowerment and persecution.

Departures and turbulence

The next phase was marked by the coming and going of certain members. Some went for good; some appeared briefly only to leave after a short period of time; some struggled with either turning up on time or with remaining for the whole of the session.

This was a difficult period for me and the group. Certain external circumstances contributed to some of the members' capacity to contain their anxiety and aggression being overwhelmed. Still, there was a sense that we were pushed to our limits and that my ability to contain the group from session to session was faltering. Thankfully, there were no violent incidents, but the emotional blows experienced by the remaining members when others had walked away in fury were almost palpable. They felt powerless, desperate, and worried that the damage could not be repaired. They even posed the question on one occasion as to whether they should return the following week for their session. They decided they would. And they did.

What helped me to keep my ability to function as a therapist and my hope for the survival of the group was my link with the institution. Some conflicts within the group necessitated management intervention on my part, and I was helped both by the Group Workshop and my supervisor to think about the meaning of the actions of the patients as communications and about how I could make the most of the institution as a wider container. There were occasions when some communications took the form of verbal and written complaints that required the involvement of clinical and non-clinical managerial staff with whom I worked closely. I felt well supported and trusted, and that helped me rely on my clinical judgement as much as on my relation to the Portman Clinic as a good enough internal object that would sustain me emotionally.

Sometimes, group members needed to use the therapeutic space as a space for resolution of practical issues that were experienced as matters of life and death. When I strove to preserve some space for thinking rather than action, I was met with hostility, contempt, and violent rejection. I was experienced as someone who was unable to understand them and who was not just unhelpful, but even obstructive. At times, both I and the clinic were experienced as neglectful parents who allowed abuse and harm. This reflected their experience as children as well as how some viewed themselves as parents.

This phase came to an end with a session in which, despite the pressure, I maintained clear and firm time boundaries even though I was concerned about the repercussions this might have. In the session the week after, the group was able to reflect on their responsibility to come along on time and actually work, in order to benefit from this needed and valued experience. There was also a sense that the group was present for them week after week and that this was something they could keep in mind.

Consolidation

What followed was a period during which attendance was more consistent and the group members engaged with more conviction and liveliness with each other. They were more open and more willing to talk about their difficulties and seek each other's point of view. This felt like an attempt at reparation of the damage done recently. The theme of the neglect they had suffered as children and its consequences on their lives was predominant, but there was also an expression of a wish for new members to join the group with the hope that they would provide different perspectives.

Deliveries

The arrival of two new members to the group, though, was actually met with reticence, resentment, and suspicion, as well as with some reserved curiosity. There followed a period of inevitable turbulence. The old members reacted mainly by putting pressure on the newcomers to catch up, to the extent that there were intense exchanges in the process of exploring their history that I experienced as interrogations. There was an increase in competitiveness and conflict between the group members. At times, I felt I had to be more active to ensure the space was allowed for each of them to complete their sentences before the next question would be asked. I was left with the impression that they felt the resources available to them were not enough.

At the final session of the first year, the group remembered and talked about members who had left, as well as their previous therapist, with scepticism, fondness, and some thoughtfulness. I noticed that they were more acknowledging of the importance of the group for them. I felt that the existence of a history thread running through the group, keeping it together, was a manifestation of their faith that the group could survive despite their struggles and their attacks: the group could recover and be used as a means for their own development.

Axis two: going round in circles

Recurrent themes

As much as I have a sense that the group has moved on somewhat in the year I have been conducting, I have noticed there are some themes that are repeated, often as if they had never been explored before.

One of the group's characteristics is the members' tendency to resort to sadomasochistic ways of relating. Relationships usually were experienced as battles for control and domination. This has had transference implications and has caused me a lot of strain in terms of maintaining a neutral stance and a frame of mind that would allow me to refrain from either retaliating or colluding with them. As much as they would protest against the prospect of strict boundaries, their anxiety would become palpable when they experienced me as potentially offering them too much freedom to use their own minds. It has not always been easy for me to find a balance between being invited (if not provoked) to act as either a mindless police force or a corrupt government. Things become further complicated when the wish for me to be an all-forgiving, all-encompassing mother church becomes evident.

Moreover, there were instances when I felt that, by virtue of my gender, I was put in the position of the excluded, and even occasionally helpless, female observer who was superficially respected but was expected to silently witness their attitude of sexual objectification of women. When I brought to their attention the broader relational context of sexual encounters and how they used exciting conversations about sexual matters as a means of distracting themselves from psychic pain, they often reacted by attempting to appease me in fear of being punished by me. Still, occasionally, they were able to acknowledge and explore the function of sexualisation as a way of defending against feelings of mistrust, despair, regret, and threatened loss.

What I find striking is the difficulty these men experience in making use of a space where there can be some trust, where mistakes do not bring the end of the world, and where conflict can exist in creative tension with collaboration, a space in which they could be safe enough to repair the damage they have inflicted upon others and themselves. The group members have damaged with their actions not only their direct victims, but also the possibility of having a more ordinary life as fathers, partners, relatives, and friends. Their roles have been compromised, and there is anger as much as guilt about that.

Feelings of guilt are generally less accessible for this group of patients; usually their exploration causes them to feel overwhelmed and brings about a desire for a manic flight into a state of mind less connected with the reality of the group. Alternatively, they resort to more paranoid solutions: they look for someone to blame, be it in the group or outside it, or they become invested in comparing the seriousness of different kinds of abuse. Still, some hope remains, and they become able to express their regrets and own up to their feelings of depression and loss. They then feel able to make choices guided by an increased ability to acknowledge the fantasies that distort their perception of the external reality.

The presence of members who have not been convicted because of their offending behaviour also gives an ambiguous feel to the group at times: what is the truth of the matter as against the proof that the law requires? More recently, the emphasis has been on the tension between legality and morality as factors preventing reoffending. At times of more mature functioning, the group is able to consider feelings of empathy, and to develop a capacity to put oneself into another person's shoes. This, in turn, leads to an ability to make different choices when faced with the compulsion to repeat certain dysfunctional patterns of acting or relating.

Another poignant theme in the group is the contradiction of having been a victim of neglect and abuse while having then become a perpetrator. Very often, the preferred position is that of the powerless victim who can attract sympathy and attribute responsibility to others. Then again, at times of integration, the group grasps emotionally the paradox of the co-existence of the victim and the perpetrator within them and the sadomasochistic dynamic that is perpetuated intrapsychically and acted out interpersonally.

My presence in the group as a female therapist who has a mind of her own, who is essentially neither a victim nor a perpetrator of abuse and neglect, and who can think with them about issues of identity, male sexuality, and relationships in general, seems to have opened up a possibility for the group members in the long run to experience women as whole persons as much as men. Thus, they have perhaps gained some confidence in their capacity to develop more creative relationships with females that can be sustained and repaired. When this is manifested in the group, it often corresponds to a feeling within me of having the freedom to relate to them and to be related to as a receptive female adult with a capacity to be facilitating of growth rather than the more frequent experience of being forced into the position of the terrifying punishing mother or the passive–aggressive partner.

Axes one and two: a spiral of a process

What I have learned so far

This has felt like a long and complex journey. Having been a newcomer to this group, I went through what felt like an initiation rite that included learning the history of the group as a whole as well as that of its members. These histories were both narrated and enacted at different times.

My previous experience in individual psychodynamic psychotherapy led me to put more emphasis on interpreting the transference of the group as a whole on me. It took me a while before I found the freedom to address individual members at times, or to make interventions such as inviting the group to look at the process and comment on how the shifts might indicate defensive reactions to material too painful or simply unbearable for them to contemplate.

The paradox of being part of the group and yet also a somewhat detached observer is fascinating. It has not always been easy to allow myself to be affected while also maintaining the necessary psychic distance to process their material and introduce helpful links for them. Robert Caper, in his book *A Mind of One's Own* (1999), speaks of the need for the analyst to be receptive to the patient's projections, but also not to identify with them: this allows for the projections to be recognised as such and for reality testing to take place. I felt this was a crucial capacity to develop as a group therapist.

I have been impressed with some of the members' ability to offer sensitive and accurate interpretations that I would not have thought about. In that sense, I feel that the group is contributing to my development as a therapist.

With time, I have felt more confident in becoming less active in my interventions and leaving space for the group to do the work. There have also been occasions when I felt I almost had to put intense physical effort into helping the group to move from a more obstructive way of functioning to a freer and more constructive one.

Overall, when the group works well, it feels like a spinning wheel: if it slows down, it only takes a gentle nudge to get it moving again. At other times, it feels like a cog wheel: a lot of force and energy is needed to get things going when stuck.

My perception of the group's experience of me has been that as much as I am often turned in their minds into an object of hate, contempt, disbelief, and mistrust, as well as of admiration and, I suspect, so far unspoken excited feelings, I remain alive and concretely present week after week apart from breaks. There is an awareness that I continue to reliably provide, along with the Portman Clinic, a space for exploration of their difficulties, their fears, their hopes, their psychic pain, their destructiveness, and their potential creativity. Despite the trials and the tribulations, they seem to appreciate this and to acknowledge that they need to continue processing what has been brought to the group between sessions, as well as to practise their thinking capacities in each session. On the whole, the group has so far been able to sustain a sense of liveliness—not because they do not lose it at times, but because they manage to recover it.

Acknowledgements

Supervision has been crucial in sustaining me, helping me contain my anxiety but also giving me an opportunity to see the group as a whole, its members and my role as a therapist from a different perspective, and to ground my learning experience. It has also helped me maintain an open mind, especially when the material has challenged my sense of what is acceptable and what is understandable.

The Group Workshop, a weekly workshop for clinicians who conduct groups at the Portman Clinic, has been a source of immense support; it has been a space where I could develop my therapeutic skills both by presenting clinical material and by listening to other colleagues' work and reflecting on their experiences of group therapy.

Last, but not least, the Portman Clinic as a lively group of clinicians and non-clinicians working together to provide a safe setting for psychotherapy with perverse and violent patients becomes a meta-container, making feasible the existence of open-ended group therapy. In this way, it fosters the possibility of a creative intercourse between therapist and group.

Reference

Caper, R. (1999). *A Mind of One's Own: A Kleinian View of Self and Object*, Volume 32 of New Library of Psychoanalysis. London: Routledge.

CHAPTER FIVE

Therapist as "perverse female": the implications of therapist gender for working with perverse and violent patients

Jessica Yakeley

Introduction

Group therapy is often said to be modelled on a paradigm of family dynamics, the group situation replicating the familial–social microcosm of the component patients/members (Welldon, 2011) where the therapist represents the parental figure, and the patients relate to each other as siblings. For a group composed solely of male patients with a female therapist, the latter might quickly be experienced as a powerful maternal transference figure, composed from the group's collective unconscious fantasies of mothering, which in turn derive from each patient's individual experiences of his own mother, real and wished-for. However, group therapy does not only recreate the early family situation, it is also a living experience in the here-and-now in which troubled adults seeking help from their symptoms come together and interact with each other in complex ways, revealing patterns of relating based not only on familial experience, but influenced also by specific cultural and societal values and mores. These will include stereotypes and constructs of sexuality and gender which will have shaped each group member's attitudes and beliefs regarding sexual roles and relating, and will inevitably affect the male group's experience of their female therapist.

In this chapter, I explore the experience of both patients and therapists in the psychoanalytic therapy groups run at the Portman Clinic, focusing on how groups composed of male patients who are already struggling with a disturbance of sexuality and/or gender relate to the female therapist. Although there is a rich literature exploring issues related to the gender of the therapist, there is little, if any, reference to gender differences between patients and therapists for patients referred specifically for difficulties with problematic sexual and violent behaviours, as are the patients referred to the Portman Clinic. First, I highlight our experience of some of the ways in which such male patients in a group relate individually and collectively to their female therapist in general, and then describe what happens when the therapist becomes pregnant, a unique situation in which the sexuality and maternal function of the real person of the therapist becomes overt, which might severely challenge the group's therapeutic boundaries and the resilience of patients whose grasp of sexual and generational differences is already tenuous.

Effects of therapist gender: review of the literature

There is a substantial literature exploring issues related to the gender of the therapist: preference of patients for therapist of one gender or the other, patients' experiences of the therapist linked to their perceived sex roles, and the effect of the therapist's sex on outcome of therapy (for example, the common belief that same sex pairing between therapist and patient lead to better therapeutic outcome). Most research studies were conducted in the 1970s and 1980s, reflecting the peak in interest in gender and feminist issues at this time, and most have examined gender issues in the patient–therapist dyad of individual psychotherapy or counselling, rather than in the group setting.

Although there is little evidence that the sex of the therapist predicts outcome (Bowman, Scogin, Floyd, & McKendree-Smith, 2001), it is clear from the literature that both patients and therapists may be strongly susceptible to stereotyped ideas regarding sex roles and gender differences that will affect treatment decisions and experiences. In studies examining patient–therapist preference or matching in individual psychotherapy or counselling, while it is often reported that patients, especially women, would prefer to have a therapist of the same sex (Pikus & Heavey, 1996), it has also been reported that patients in general prefer male therapists (Goldberg, 1979; McKinnon, 1990), or therapists who have a masculine style. These patient preferences appear to be linked to their perceptions of opposing therapeutic styles of authority as opposed to nurturance, associated by patients with male and female therapists, respectively. Therapists who exhibit more emotional responses are experienced as more nurturing, while those who provide more interpretative statements are seen as authority figures. Male therapists are more likely to be perceived as authority figures regardless of therapeutic style, while female therapists who adopt a stance of minimal disclosure and non-responsiveness are seen as least nurturing, even when compared to male therapists who adopt the same style. Male therapists tend to establish a positive, idealised transference which, if not analysed, will hinder the emergence of more negative transference feelings, whereas female therapists have less difficulty in facilitating a negative transference, but might inhibit its verbalisation because of the patient's perception of her apparent fragility. In one study of patient preference for sex-role orientations, "the feminine male therapist" received the lowest ratings, which the authors interpreted as reflecting a societal prejudice in which the male dread of being feminine was a universal component of masculinity (McKinnon, 1990).

Mills (1964) was one of the first researchers to investigate the effects of the gender of the therapist in the group setting. He found that when the group leader and patient are of the opposite sex, this intensifies the desire for exclusive union and the inhibition of the expression of hostility towards the leader. Other studies have examined how therapeutic style and sex of the therapist influences the behaviour and feelings of the group members. Thus, Perlman (1978) found differences in how hostility was expressed by group members to the group therapist depending on their gender. Patients tended to be more overtly hostile towards male therapists, while their aggression towards a female therapist was expressed in more covert ways, often by displacement or ignoring the female leader altogether. Group members were also more prone to make comments to the female therapist that implied a need to protect her, or that she was vulnerable or inadequate in comparison to the male therapist. Other researchers have found that female group leaders who adopt a stance of non-responsiveness are perceived as contemptuous, distant, and less friendly compared to male therapists with similar styles who are experienced as more friendly (Wright & Gould, 1977). These findings suggesting that female therapists are perceived more negatively than men in parallel authority roles have been understood as reflecting the patients' cultural expectations of women being more nurturing and emotionally responsive than men. When this is not encountered in the female therapist whose stance is more withholding, the unmet expectation leads to an aggressive response by the group member, which cannot be overtly directed towards the woman therapist due to her perceived fragility, but instead is directed towards the self or other group members.

Conlan (1991) examines in more detail the unconscious dynamics of both mixed and single sex female analytic groups and the transference that emerges in relation to the female therapist or conductor. Interestingly, she does not comment on the all male group with a female therapist, perhaps because this constellation is unusual in group analytic practice. She emphasises that the more overt expressions of hostility and aggression projected on to the group's leader defend against underlying feelings of infantile dependency and helplessness that are reactivated in a group setting and are linked to unconscious anxieties and fantasies of an all powerful, castrating, phallic mother, a pre-oedipal fantasised constructed image of the woman who commands malevolent power and resonates with the image of the omnipotent mother in us all. The unconscious fantasy of a malignant, controlling, and persecutory maternal object located by the group in the female conductor creates much primitive anxiety in the group, which defends itself by splitting and projection, attempting to rob the female therapist of her autonomy and authority, and to attack her competence and creativity. The force of these projections might be so powerful as to force her into a depressive stance which could literally render her powerless if the group's projections resonate with her own internal unconscious fantasies of woman and mother. The therapist's own unresolved fusion between herself and her internalised mother will contribute to countertransference responses of denial or collusion, and the danger that she will respond to the group's attacks either by retaliation or by overcompensating in being overly compliant or solicitous.

More recent studies have looked at the effects of therapist gender in groups treating specific conditions or experiences, such as eating disorders or adult survivors of childhood sexual abuse, but none, to our knowledge, has examined gender issues in group therapy specifically for violent or perverse patients. This raises the question as to how the particular psychopathology of individuals who resort to aggressive or problematic sexual behaviour may influence their experience of a female therapist in the group setting. Do their reactions and responses reflect the findings from the literature in general, or do their pervasive difficulties with intimacy and very primitive anxieties in relation to the maternal object distort their perceptions of the therapist in a particular perverse direction?

Gender differences in perversion and violence

The majority of the psychotherapy groups run at the Portman Clinic contain only male patients. Although certain key clinicians working at the Clinic over the years have specialised in the study and treatment of female perversion (notably, Estela Welldon, Dorothy Lloyd-Owen, and Carine Minne), the majority of individuals who are referred for treatment for problematic sexual and/or violent behaviour are men. This situation, however, does not simply reflect the higher rate of violence and perversion in men than in women, but is also due to female violence and perversion being less often recognised or diagnosed as pathological. Most of the obvious violence perpetrated in our society is by men, whether this occurs in the home in the case of domestic violence, in the community in fights, muggings, robberies, and murder, or in the large-scale group violence of warfare, terrorism, and genocide. Although a minority of women can indeed be very violent towards others, for example, members of female gangs, the majority of female violent behaviour is more private, experienced as shameful, and, therefore, not acknowledged and kept hidden. Clinicians have long noted that women tend to direct their aggression internally by harming themselves, such as by cutting or overdosing, rather than hurting others. What is less often recognised, however, is that other psychopathologies more common in women, such as anorexia nervosa and bulimia, can be understood as aggression that has been internalised to attack the female body. Welldon (1988, 2011) has been prominent in highlighting the subtle and perverse manifestations of female aggression and violence, which might be directed not only against the woman's own body, but towards that of her child, who is experienced not as a separate being, but as a narcissistic extension of herself. Welldon highlights here an important gender difference in the location of the "object" or target of the perverse or violent activity. She notes that, although both sexes use their reproductive functions and organs in perversion, for men, abnormal sexual behaviour is overtly focused on the male genitalia, since many use their penises to carry out perverse activities such as fetishism, exhibitionism, or paedophilia, all of which are more common in men, whereas for women, perverse activity and relating involve their whole body, and, importantly, will include their mothering functions.

Despite the increasingly reported occurrence of mothers who sexually abuse their children, mothers who fabricate or induce illness in their offspring, and the criminal act of infanticide (which, by its definition, must be perpetrated by the mother of the murdered infant), society is still not ready to accept that some mothers have perverse and even murderous, albeit often unconscious, motives towards their children, and Welldon received much public criticism when she first dared to challenge, over two decades ago, the unspoken but cherished belief that maternal love was universal and innate. What this means for our society, which continues to firmly locate harmful sexual and aggressive behaviour in the realm of the male and tends minimise, ignore, or miss altogether such behaviour in women, is that these women and their victims (most often themselves, their partners, and children) are denied appropriate treatment and understanding, and unhelpful gender stereotypes are perpetuated. What this means for the smaller object of our study, the all male Portman group led by the female therapist, is that while the manifest task of the group might appear to be exploring the underlying causes and psychodynamics of the disturbed activities of the male group members which are their "ticket of entry" into the treatment group, a more hidden and unconscious agenda will be the recreation of a perverse and violent woman seen in the person of the female therapist. Exposing and understanding the unconscious transference fantasies that underlie the male group's construction of their woman therapist, based on the collective experience of each member's own experience of perverse and sometimes violent mothers and other female family members, family and sub-cultural attitudes, and the split-off internalised feminine aspects of themselves, will be an important long-term task for the group.

Core complex and pre-oedipal anxieties

Many psychoanalytic writers have located the origins of violence and perverse behaviour in a pathological early relationship between mother and infant that prevents the child developing a sense of separate identity. Many of the patients who seek treatment for aggressive or abnormal sexualised behaviours have experienced childhood traumas, abuse, or rejection, from parents who showed excessive aggression or neglect. Others might not have experienced overt trauma, but had parents or care-givers who were emotionally absent or failed to recognise their child as a separate individual in his own right, confusing his own mental states, wishes, desires, and feelings with their own. The pathological effects of the overprotective mother, who overgratifies the infant and confuses her narcissistic needs with his, may be as detrimental as the absent or abusive mother. This leads to fears in the child of being overwhelmed or consumed by the maternal object, which can only be averted by an aggressive response. However, the child whose mother or parents appear to have malevolent intent towards him is placed in an impossible dilemma. Because he is dependent on her love and care, any aggression that he feels cannot be directed at the mother, as this would destroy the person on whom he is dependent, but must be directed against himself or others. Glasser (1996) illuminates this fundamental conflict in his concept of the "core complex", a particular constellation of interrelated feelings, ideas, and attitudes that he proposed were fundamental in the genesis of violence and perversion. He believed that all of us oscillate between wishes to be emotionally close to significant others and fears of becoming dependent, anxieties which are rooted in the early relationship to the mother. If this relationship is pathological, this might predispose to primitive and pervasive anxieties persisting into adulthood, which will interfere with the person's capacity to form intimate relationships with others. Intimacy is now experienced as merging with the other person, so that the person's identity is completely subsumed and obliterated. To defend against such annihilatory anxieties, the person retreats to a "safe" distance. However, he is soon overwhelmed with feelings of loneliness and isolation, and the desire to be close to the maternal object again propels him to seek contact once more, so that the core complex has the qualities of a vicious circle.

Aggression is a central component of the core complex. The annihilatory fear of a loss of separate existence provokes an intense aggressive reaction on the part of the ego. In order to preserve the self, the object—usually meaning the mother at this very early developmental stage—has to be destroyed. This, of course, would mean the loss of all the goodness of the mother, the security, love, and warmth embodied in her milk, that she offers. The infant has only two options: to retreat into a narcissistic state or to resort to self-preservative aggression against the obliterating mother. Glasser proposes that the perverse person finds a unique solution to the vicious circle of the core complex. This is the sexualisation of aggression into sadism. Here, the direct aggression that the person feels towards the other person (originally the mother) is disguised by converting it into sexual excitement, gratification, and sadistic control. The (m)other is now preserved and no longer threatened by total destruction, as the intention to destroy is converted into a wish to hurt, dominate, torture, and control, but ultimately to preserve, the object. Although perverse behaviours such as fetishism, exhibitionism, and sadomasochistic practices might appear to be sexually motivated, on closer examination they are revealed to be practices that are used, albeit unconsciously, by the perverse individual to aggressively control the other person and defend against anxieties of becoming too emotionally close and having his psychic existence obliterated.

Violent and perverse behaviours can, therefore, be understood as symptoms of disorders of attachment and narcissistic development in which true separation from the maternal object has not been achieved. The perverse or violent behaviour can be understood as a desperate attempt to create space between self and other. The internal world of many violent and perverse individuals is a terrifying place in which pre-oedipal object relations and primitive defence mechanisms such as splitting, projection, and projective identification predominate and predispose to destructive aggression and violent enactment. The internalised maternal imago is based on a fantasy—rooted in the reality of the person's early experiences of a pathologically intrusive and symbiotic maternal relationship—of a mother who is omnipotent, malevolent, and engulfing. Psychoanalytic writers such as Perelberg propose that the violent person holds an unconscious fantasy of a very violent primal scene dominated by the pre-oedipal phallic mother, who is engulfing and also violent. The violent act can be seen as an unconscious attack on the mother's body, the mother experienced in fantasy as not only being in possession of the child's body, but also the child's intellectual and affective experiences. The function of violence is, therefore, survival in the face of a maternal object that is experienced as obliterating, with no conception of a paternal object present.

The contemporary psychoanalytic understanding of perversion also highlights the importance of early experiences and pre-oedipal relations in the development of perverse behaviours and states of mind. This represents a shift from Freud's (1905d) original theory of component instincts of infantile sexuality that had escaped repression to a conceptualisation in which perverse behaviours and phantasies have a defensive function against not only castration anxieties, but also against much more primitive pre-oedipal anxieties and aggression towards the maternal object. Cooper (1991) believes that most, if not all, perversions defend against a core trauma of the experience of terrifying passivity in relation to the pre-oedipal mother who is perceived as malignant and omnipotent.

Therapist as "perverse female"

One of the ways that perverse and violent men defend against this persecutory and castrating internalised maternal object to achieve a semblance of normal interpersonal functioning is by utilising primitive psychic mechanisms such as splitting, projection, grandiosity, and projective identification. Thus, their views of women are commonly split between, on the one hand, an idealised version of a (wished-for) mother who is the source of altruistic love for her children, is selfless and pure (and implicitly asexual), but ultimately ineffectual in the face of the superiority of male physical and intellectual prowess, and, on the other hand, a denigrated version of a woman castigated as whore, impure, dangerously seductive, and evil. Such perceptions inevitably enter the group therapy arena and can be detected in the transference relationship with the female therapist. Thus, commonly, the male group members will become engaged in a debate about a typically male pursuit such as sport, or in an intellectual discussion, often of a philosophical nature, which excludes the female therapist, who is viewed as intellectually inferior. As Perlman (1978) noted, the group's hostility towards the female therapist is covertly expressed by ignoring her interpretations and denial of her leadership. Fears of dependence are consciously refuted, but enacted in group members' erratic attendance or concurrent participation in other therapy groups (commonly Sex Addicts Anonymous's twelve-step group therapy). Alternatively, the female therapist is accepted as an honorary member of the male club, often by using her professional qualifications as an entry ticket. In a more split-off fashion, group members might refer to her as "the doctor", exploiting her authority role to avoid acknowledging that she is a woman at all. One male patient, referred for group therapy with history of domestic violence, had recently broken off contact with his daughter as he felt she was behaving like a prostitute in having sex before marriage, but treated the medically qualified female therapist, whom he referred to as "Doc", with the utmost respect and veneration.

Such positive attitudes towards the female therapist are more prominent when a group first starts or new members join, but, as the group develops, these idealised defences start to break down and more negative transference experiences and reactions emerge. An image of woman as sexually promiscuous, omnipotent, and castrating becomes more evident. This is, of course, rarely overtly verbalised towards the female therapist, but might emerge in the material of the group's discussions to be explored by the group.

> Toby, a longstanding member of an all male psychotherapy group, who had originally been referred following convictions for deception and fraud, related to the female therapist and the other professionals involved in his care with an attitude of apparent gratitude and deference. Although he rarely missed a session, he was often reticent in the group, saying that he preferred others to speak as he did not like people to find out about his criminal history that he was deeply ashamed of. His demeanour hinted of a voyeuristic quality, as if he were obtaining gratification from hearing the stories of others while giving very little away himself. In his history, his mother had refused to look after him and paid private foster carers to raise him. At puberty, he was returned to his mother's care, and experienced her as sexually seductive. He had a three-year-old son whom he kept at a distance, struggling with conflicting feelings of wishing to be a good father yet feeling terrified of the responsibility.

One day, he told the group how much he hated the mother of his son, who had entrapped him in a sexual relationship and tricked him into having a child, with whom he was now burdened. The group pointed out how Toby rejected all responsibility for his own part in the sexual liaison that resulted in the birth of his child, viewing himself to be the innocent victim of a dominant and predatory sexual woman who was only out for herself, as he had experienced his own mother. The therapist added that Toby perhaps also experienced her in the same way, submitting himself to her leadership of a group which he attended very dutifully, but which he also secretly resented. However, as he could not openly express his resentment, he instead expressed this by more deceptive and covert means by not fully participating in sessions, as if he were "stealing" others stories, without revealing his own. His experience of women as deceitful and duplicitous was enacted in his own fraudulent activities of taking things from others that he felt he deserved himself—the love of his mother that she withheld. The following week, Toby told the group that he had thought about what the group had said, realised that he was still dependent on his mother, and had decided to stop accepting the money that his mother continued to give him and live on his own means.

Bion (1961) described primitive reactions that he called "basic assumptions" that can occur in groups when unrealistic demands or threats to its security occur. These are unconscious defensive manoeuvres of the group that are mobilised to defend against primitive anxieties of dependence, aggression, and sexuality. Such anxieties are, of course, present in all of us, but may be overwhelming in violent and perverse patients who are operating at a pre-oedipal level. Experiences of separation, such as the therapist's holidays, might leave the group feeling neglected and abandoned, as they were by their original care-givers, mobilising powerful group defences which might cause dangerous acting out both outside of and within the group. Welldon (1996) described two specific ways in which the group can defend itself from such infantile oral and separation anxieties. The first is where a violent threat is used as defence. Here, an angry patient both terrorises and excites the group by the use of aggressive and abusive language, and, although there might be no overt violence in the group, such behaviour represents a repetition of actual violent acting out within the group. The second is where erotisation of the group is used as a defence. This is when the group starts acting in an excited way by unconsciously promoting one of its members to talk about sexually perverse material in a provocative and repetitive manner. Although this might appear as if the patient is opening up to the group by trusting them, it becomes apparent that he has cast the group as an audience to his perversion in the seduction and excitement of the other group members through his exhibitionist behaviour. The female therapist is placed in the no-win position of being experienced by the group as a prohibitive authority figure who forbids any sexual pleasure if she intervenes, but if she does not, being experienced as voyeuristically colluding or being seduced and corrupted by group forces beyond her control.

> This group session occurred in a therapy group that had been running for only a few months, and was the last session before a break during which the group would not meet for two weeks. John, a man with a borderline personality disorder and a history of getting into fights with other men, as well as seeing prostitutes behind his wife's back, started the group session by relating a dream in which he had been having sex with his sister-in-law. He related the dream in graphic detail, using explicit language, and appeared visibly excited, giggling and making lewd gestures. He said that his wife refused to have sex with him since having their daughter two years ago, so he was thinking of seducing her sister. He added that she was an attractive professional woman, a high-flying psychologist. Another patient, Simon, asked John why he wanted to do this, and said that he still had fantasies of wanting to have sex with his mother, and used to dress in his mother's underwear in secret as an adolescent, but accepted that this was not normal. Other members of the group looked uncomfortable but animated. Tony said that his mother used to undress in front of him and sleep in his bed as a child, which made him feel very confused. Matt asked if John was angry with his wife. John denied this, but said he was going to have sex with her sister anyway.

> The therapist pointed out that the group appeared to be in an excited state, and linked this to the group's excitement and anxiety at having a female therapist. She suggested that John's dream contained the anxieties of the group regarding women, mothers, and wives who were being seen as either dangerous sexual predators, or hostile and neglectful women who rejected them, as perhaps they might feel she was doing by going away for two weeks. The group denied this, saying that of course she was entitled to take holiday, but the mood in the group became more sombre and a discussion ensued about whether women could be trusted. For the first time, John told the group that the cousin who had abused him had later committed suicide, and he wondered whether she had been sexually abused herself.

Here, we can see how the group's manifest sexual excitement and erotised transference towards the therapist is a sexualised defence against underlying anxieties of abandonment, despair, and suicide, triggered by the therapist's forthcoming absence from the group. The group's rage at the abandoning mother/therapist and her omnipotent control—the group cannot meet without her—is enacted in the sexual fantasy that they can replace her with another woman whom they will control and seduce (the psychologist sister-in-law). Women are depicted as interchangeable, untrustworthy, and either sexually promiscuous or frigid, abandoning their partners to look after their children (the wife who refuses sex after the child is born) or abandoning their children to have sex with other men. This generational confusion is a central feature of perversion and reflects a toxic version of a family in which generational boundaries are blurred and incest taboos are broken. Within the familial microcosm of the group, the female therapist becomes a sexually perverse maternal object, born of the group's experience of a malignant version of dependence in which the mother/therapist not only overwhelms the child/patient, but corrupts him as well.

Toxic parental coupling

Where there are co-therapists, one of each sex, in a group of violent and perverse male patients, powerful unconscious group defensive processes could operate to split the therapeutic couple, projecting all the positive qualities into the female therapist, and locating all the badness and negativity in the male therapist. Thus, the female therapist is described as nurturing, kind, supportive, and truly understanding of the patients' difficulties, whereas the male therapist is experienced as withholding, critical, domineering, and unhelpful. The projection of negative attributes into the male therapist serves the function of maintaining the female therapist as an idealised maternal figurehead, who will protect the group from the authoritarian and abusive father. Such a version of the parental couple accords with the patients' early childhood experiences, in which the child choosing to hate the abusing father and side with mother protects him from consciously acknowledging even more painful and conflictual feelings towards a mother who neglects him or turns a blind eye to abuse. The experience of relationships for these men is based on an internalised template of sadomasochistic dynamics in which there is little notion of intimacy and mutual respect between two equal, but different, individuals in an emotional partnership. Instead, their paradigm of interpersonal relationships is governed by rules of power and control, in which one partner is always dominant and the other submissive or abused. Such a template is based on an extreme version of the primal scene, where parental coupling is associated with violent and sadomasochistic sexual behaviour.

The psychic level of the group's functioning here is pre-oedipal in nature, enacting an unconscious wish for a mother who will be the sole possession of the group members and where any role for the father is negated. Awareness of the sexuality of the female therapist, who is valued solely for her maternal functions, is disavowed and projected into the male therapist, or other group members. In our experience at the Portman Clinic, the group's unconscious envy and hatred of any notion of an oedipal couple will be enacted in their intolerance of co-therapeutic functioning and their attempt to split the two therapists apart. For this reason, there has been a long-standing tradition at the Clinic of running groups with a single therapist. Estela Welldon, who worked at the clinic for over thirty years, describes how these patients recreate the primal scene in a very concrete way in their fantasy of the relationship that exists between the co-therapists, whose skills at containing the group's primitive anxieties, intense envy, and destructive impulses might not withstand the patients' own skills in breaking up the "parental bonding" (Welldon, 2011). Such splitting contains a more malignant quality than that described in the general group psychotherapy literature in the different ways in which patients experience co-therapists: the male therapist as more interpretative, the female as more nurturing (Strauss, 1975). This also highlights a possible limitation of one of the central tenets of group analytic theory—Foulkes's (1964) concept of the group matrix, which he believed contained inherent female and maternal properties. Conlan (1991) describes how Foulkes ascribed the role of mother to the group and the role of authoritarian father to the conductor, but that he was reluctant to use the group to explore more primitive preverbal material derived from more negative aspects of the mother. However, the powerful pre-oedipal anxieties that are present in groups containing patients who are struggling with their destructive impulses and sexual identity, anxieties that are further potentiated by having a female group leader, cannot be ignored.

A more tolerated model of a parental couple for such groups at the Portman draws on the wider institutional setting, in which the Portman Clinic itself holds maternal and containing functions for the patients. The administrative staff and receptionist who greet the patients, and the physical building itself—"the brick mother"—are experienced by the patients as a concretisation of their wish for care and protection. Paternal function is not only projected into the group therapist (regardless of his or her gender), but into the external agencies that are also involved with these patients, in particular, the representatives of the criminal justice system, such as the courts or probation service. Careful liaison with such agencies, paying particular attention to matters of confidentiality and disclosure, can be experienced, by some patients at least, as an attempt to integrate both maternal and paternal functions to form a parental couple working together in the patient's best interests, an experience which was not offered by their primary care-givers.

The pregnant group therapist

A therapist's pregnancy is a unique event in the therapeutic setting. The changes in the therapist's body that become a visual reality might be experienced by patients as a bold statement about the therapist's gender and sexuality that she is forcing upon them. Pregnancy is an unavoidable intrusion into the therapeutic space that can act as a powerful transference stimulus, reactivating infantile anxieties and conflicts, and intensifying regressive tendencies in the patient. If handled sensitively by the therapist, her pregnancy and its aftermath could offer a therapeutic window in which unconscious fantasies may be explored and valuable psychic work can be achieved.

There exists a rich literature that addresses the effects of the therapist's, or analyst's, pregnancy, although again, mostly in the setting of individual therapy. In general, it is agreed that pregnancy mobilises and intensifies the transference, which represents a positive opportunity to facilitate the treatment, or can result in heightened resistance and disruption of the work (Bassen, 1988; Etchegoyen, 1993; Friedman, 1993; McGarty, 1988; McWilliams, 1980). It is also consistently noted that common themes about identity, sexuality, abandonment, sibling rivalry, trust, and withheld secrets emerge in treatment when the therapist is pregnant: these occur in response to the real situation of the pregnant therapist, but reflect unconscious dynamically determined aspects of the transference.

In contrast to the literature on the pregnant therapist treating patients in individual therapy, the literature addressing the experience of the pregnant group therapist is scarce. Breen (1977) compared themes and differences evoked by her pregnancies between the patients she saw for individual therapy, and the patients she was treating when she became pregnant as a co-therapist in a group. She noted that the patients in individual therapy tended to react more directly than the group patients to the intrusion of her pregnancy into the therapeutic relationship. Themes regarding sharing of the therapist with her baby or partner, however, appeared less evident in the group patients. Breen suggests that this is because sharing is already a central underlying issue in any group whose members have to compete with each other for the attention of the therapist/mother. In contrast to the individual patients, the group reacted to her pregnancy as a sexual threat, and group themes regarding sexuality became immediately more evident; this encompassed their own sexuality, their parents' sexuality, and that of the pregnant therapist. Breen also noted that the patients were very effective in splitting the two female co-therapists into a good asexual mother (her co-therapist) and a bad promiscuous one (herself), to the point that she and her co-therapist found themselves disagreeing strongly after group sessions. This echoes our experience at the Portman of our patients' destructive hatred and envy of any notion of an oedipal couple, as described above.

Breen also described differences between the male and female patients' reactions to her pregnancy. The men retreated into "homosexual groupings" and were silent on the subject of her pregnancy, in contrast to the women, who became preoccupied with their own wishes for babies. These gender differences have been amply described in the general literature on the pregnant therapist (see, for example, Fenster, Phillips, & Rapoport, 1986; Lax, 1969), in that male patients tend to react with some degree of denial, isolation of affect, and suppression of thoughts and feelings, and reluctance to entertain transference issues pertaining to the pregnancy, whereas female patients more often react with identification, competition, and envy.

These differences might reflect gender differences in the early developmental movement away from a maternal female identification. Greenson (1968) and Stoller (1974) postulated that the male infant must break away from the primal symbiosis with mother to achieve a sense of himself as male, and, in contrast to the female infant, must "disidentify" with mother and identify instead with father. The male patient's need to remain unaware of the pregnancy might protect him against early wishes and experiences of being at one with mother, which, in the case of perverse and violent patients, might activate core complex anxieties of annihilation and abandonment which will be strenuously defended against. The therapist's pregnancy might also arouse in the male patient homosexual longings and infantile wishes to have babies himself (an identification with a pregnant mother), awareness of which would cause feelings of narcissistic mortification and injury (Lax, 1969).

The few papers since Breen that compare the impact of the pregnant therapist in the group setting with that of the individual psychotherapist concur with Breen's findings (Raphael-Leff, 1980; Thunnissen, 1997; Trampuz, 1997) that the individual setting highlights the early mother–baby experience, whereas the group setting replicates later child–family experiences (Whyte, 2004). However, this does not mean that patients in group therapy are necessarily functioning at a more mature psychic level than those in individual therapy. Breen notes that the more disturbed patients in any group tend to set the tone by a regressive pull towards the group functioning at a more primitive level, a view espoused by Bion (1955), who believed that the group experience mobilised the most primitive anxieties of a psychotic intensity. A subsequent trilogy of papers examining patients' responses to the pregnant group analyst in a group analytic setting (Anderson, 1994; Gavin, 1994; Rogers, 1994) emphasise that pre-oedipal, rather than oedipal, themes of orality, dependency, idealisation, and terror of a pre-oedipal mother therapist were prominent in the material of sessions.

Pregnancy at the Portman

The experience of female group therapists who have become pregnant while running groups at the Portman Clinic have encountered similar issues to those discussed in the literature. As noted by Breen and other authors above in discussing the impact of the pregnant therapist on group therapy dynamics, our experience at the Portman is also that the pre-oedipal issues that already dominate our patients' psychic and interpersonal functioning are brought to the fore by the challenge of the therapist's pregnancy. I would suggest, however, that pregnancy offers a particular threat for these men, whose developmental experiences have been so disturbed by early adversity and whose relationships to the female sex have so often been shaped by their experience of perverse mothering. The therapist's pregnancy, exhibited by the concrete physicality of her enlarging sexual body, might be experienced by these patients as recreating very early experiences of a narcissistic, preoccupied mother, or one who has prematurely exposed the child to sexual experiences, mobilising core complex anxieties and challenging the precarious sexualised modes of relating that these individuals have constructed to protect themselves against absolute dependence and psychic annihilation. These intense anxieties and counterphobic reactions are illustrated in the following account of one therapist's experience of becoming pregnant while running a slow-open group of seven men, each referred to the Portman for help with violent and/or sexually problematic behaviours. The group had been running for less than a year.

The group's gestation

When she was five months into her pregnancy, Dr L told the group that she was pregnant. The group members initially appeared shocked, there was a silence, and then one said that they had no idea (despite the therapist showing). Another member asked whether the group would end. Dr L explained that another therapist would be covering for her during her maternity leave. The conversation quickly moved on to something else. Dr L interpreted their difficulty in thinking about the meaning of her announcement. One homosexual group member, Andy, said that he felt angry and upset; he had not told the group before, but he actually felt sexually attracted to the therapist and could not bear the idea of her leaving. He spoke of fears of breakdown and being violent towards his neighbours in the past. The other group members looked very uncomfortable and said that it was completely fair that the therapist should have a life. There was a discussion about attachment and how you cannot get dependent on therapists. Another member, Darren, whose partner had just had a baby, said that having children was a normal part of life, and why should the therapist be any different? He spoke of watching the film *Snow White* with his two-year-old daughter, and how she wanted to kill the new baby.

At the following session, attendance at the group was poor. Andy reported getting angry with an old lady in Tesco after leaving the group the previous week. Themes of being rejected by parents in favour of younger siblings were evident: Bill spoke of his foot fetish starting after the birth of his youngest brother, to whom he felt his parents paid more attention, Darren spoke of dressing in his sister's clothes as a teenager, as he felt his father preferred his sister. Dr L interpreted their feelings of being pushed out by her baby and how they feared they might be forced to turn to their problematic behaviours again to cope. Andy said he was afraid that he might do something awful, and was feeling suicidal. The group wondered whether Dr L could prescribe him medication.

In following sessions, there was curiosity as to whether the next therapist would be a man or a woman. Andy expressed anger at the possibility that the new therapist might need to change the day of the group, and demanded that the therapist tell them her due date—why was she being so secretive? After all, it was "only a baby". He wondered why they needed anyone new at all—they could just continue to meet in Dr L's absence until she was back. When Dr L declined to answer, he confronted her about not telling the group before that she was pregnant, since she must have known for months. Others appeared shocked that he was asking such a personal question, but another member ventured to "joke" that they all had originally been asked by Dr L to commit to attending the group for at least two years, whereas this rule did not seem to apply to Dr L. There was again very poor attendance the following week, and one person sent a message that he had something "personal" to attend to. Those present expressed fears that the group was going to fall apart. Themes of rejection were again woven into their conversation. Richard spoke of being denied the opportunity by his superiors of organising a conference at work for which he felt he had the most expertise. Bill said his girlfriend was beginning to tire of the sexual foreplay involving her unwashed feet that he insisted on, and he was afraid that she might leave him.

The final sessions before the therapist's maternity leave were poorly attended and dominated by Andy reporting that he was becoming psychiatrically unwell. In the last session, he announced that his drinking was out of control, he had withdrawal symptoms, and his psychiatrist and community psychiatric nurse were away. Richard, who had been referred to the group for help with his compulsive use of prostitutes and sex chat lines, announced that his long-standing girlfriend, who had threatened to leave him, was pregnant. The therapist was left feeling as if she were abandoning the group to madness and desolation.

The fostering period

A male colleague, Dr S, took over as therapist for the group for the next nine months. During this time, only three of the original members survived, the other four dropping out of treatment. These remaining three patients worked well together, forming a special bond that at times seemed impenetrable and made it difficult for the two new members that Dr S introduced to the group to feel included. The was little spontaneous discussion of Dr L or the change of therapist, except for their resentment that Dr L's conception had occurred shortly after that of the group, which had not had time to become fully established, and their fears (mostly voiced by Andy) that Dr L would leave them with someone who would not have skills to look after them. No curiosity regarding Dr L and her baby was expressed, despite Dr S telling the group that the baby had been born and all was well.

There was also concern about the fallout of patients and wanting the group to be replenished immediately. Andy told the group about his sexual attraction to Dr L, and that he had the strange idea that he should have been the father of her baby, despite being homosexual. Whenever Dr S had leave from the group, Andy would voice fears that Dr S was going on a date and getting married and not coming back.

Shortly after Dr L had gone on maternity leave, Richard told the group he had persuaded his girlfriend to have an abortion. Nine months later, he ended the ten-year relationship with this girlfriend and started a new relationship at the same time as Dr L returned from maternity leave to become therapist once more for the group.

Reclaiming the group

The first few months of Dr L's return to the group were very turbulent. The group now consisted of five members, two having been introduced by Dr S while Dr L was away. Andy appeared non-communicative and refused even to look at Dr L. Richard expressed anxiety about how the group would be with a woman in it again—could they really be understood by women? He said they had been able to be more frank with Dr S, especially about sexual matters. Attendance at the group was again poor and the group felt very fragmented. One of the new patients, Martin, did not attend the group for several weeks, sending telephone messages saying that he felt too disturbed, and when he finally did attend he appeared to be in a manic, hyper-sexualised state, saying that he had been asked to star in a porn movie. Acting out increased with the other patients. Andy reported picking up men in bars and seducing them, but was left feeling emotionally void. Richard spoke of breaking his mobile phone in anger after his teenage daughter refused to stop dressing in a manner that he thought was sexually provocative. Within the group the tone was excited, even manic: Richard spoke of his excitement at embarking on a new relationship with his girlfriend, and Darren talked about his continuing sexual fantasies towards his mother and urges to dress in her clothes that he had had since puberty, how attractive he found other women in the office, and how the only reason he did not leave his wife was because of his children. Although the group expressed concern about the small numbers and poor attendance by Andy and Martin, they appeared resentful of Dr L introducing two new members after a few months. Richard stormed out of the first session that these two new members attended, stating that Dr L had been giving them all her attention and he did not feel heard.

Discussion

We can see here how the patients almost uniformly reacted to the therapists' pregnancy by ostensibly ignoring her condition, even when it had become visibly obvious. This has been the experience of other therapists who have become pregnant while running groups at the Portman Clinic. Alternatively, one patient, usually of more borderline pathology (in this case, Andy) will be unconsciously elected to be the group's spokesman to verbalise the group's resentment at the therapist's lack of commitment. For the others, any interpretation of their anger towards the therapist is strongly denied, and instead the group ridicules the notion of attachment to a therapist. The group's anger, dependency needs, and separation anxieties, however, are enacted in the patients' erratic attendance or in some dropping out of group treatment altogether, or reversed in the omnipotent fantasy that the group can survive without the therapist. This wish has some basis in reality as group members still have each other, a very different situation from the patient in individual therapy. The group's unconscious fantasies of murderous rage and sibling rivalry, however, find their way into the material of the session in Darren's account of his daughter wishing to kill the new baby, and with their wish for an idealised asexual mother figure, embodied in the fairytale character of Snow White.

The group's feelings of rejection and abandonment become more evident in their discussions of being neglected in favour of a sibling or being left out of their parents' minds altogether (Richard's exclusion from the conference). Andy's demand that Dr L should tell the group her due date, and, therefore, implicitly the date of the baby's conception, may be understood as feeling excluded from the parental bedroom. The therapist's power and control over the group in her choosing to become pregnant when she wishes without consulting the patients are felt in their complaint that she has not made the same commitment to the group that she expects them to make.

The primitive nature of the group's anxieties becomes increasingly apparent as the therapist's maternity leave draws closer. Andy's deteriorating mental state and acting out behaviour confirm the fears of fragmentation and breakdown of the entire group. The group's symbolic and representational capacity break down and the group regress to functioning at a concrete level, demanding teleological solutions from the therapist. Words are now ineffective and only medication might help. Andy's declaration that his psychiatric support network is also unavailable voices the group's feelings of total abandonment by their therapist. The group's individual and collective defences unravel, exposing core complex anxieties of a psychotic intensity. Richard's dramatic announcement in the final session that his girlfriend was pregnant can be understood as a manic defence and acting out in a desperate attempt to avert the breakdown of the group and denial of the loss of their therapist.

The reactions of the patients underscore the function of their defences in the construction of their sexual identity, the fragility of which is exposed by the threat of abandonment by an omnipotent maternal object. Thus, Andy's homosexual orientation was severely challenged by his attachment to Dr L, revealing defensive aspects to his homosexuality. His sexual attraction towards her can be seen as defending against his rage at her leaving him, and his wish to be the father of the baby an expression of his unconscious oedipal desires. Richard's impregnation of his girlfriend is the acting out of an identification with a potent male, an attempt to regain his masculinity and assert his authority and paternal function in the face of matriarchal dominance. However, the thinness of these defensive identifications is evident in Andy's breakdown and in Richard's later admission that his girlfriend had an abortion, the latter action fulfilling the group's unconscious wishes for the abortion of the therapist's baby so that the group itself would not need to be aborted. Although oedipal themes are present in the material, the group is, for the most part, functioning at a pre-oedipal level, where the patients' attachment to the mother therapist has been rudely interrupted by her prioritising her own baby, a fact of life that cannot be tolerated. Reality must be disavowed.

The group's responses to the changes of therapists also highlight their incapacity to tolerate ambivalence, uncertainty, and loss. An unconscious fantasy of fusion with a maternal object that provides an endless supply of milk and unconditional love is enacted in Richard's replacement of the pregnant therapist with a pregnant partner, and in the group's demand for the immediate replenishment of other group members. The old therapist is barely mentioned, and the group are immediately satisfied with the new one, an idealised father figure, although their contempt for him is veiled in their concerns that his skills might be inferior (to mother's milk). Similarly, when Dr L returns and Dr S leaves, Richard terminates the relationship with his girlfriend and starts a new relationship with another. One might argue that providing another therapist for the group so quickly colluded with their wish to forget the first to avoid experiencing much more painful and frightening feelings of rage, humiliation, and abandonment. However, these feelings become more accessible when Dr L returns, again enacted in their poor attendance and disturbed behaviour within the sessions. The sexual excitement is palpable and the group sessions are at risk of becoming cinematographic pornography in which the therapist is cast in the leading role. The patients' anxiety and aggression, however, is barely kept in check and threatens to erupt at any minute. Is the therapist who has returned the same as the one who has left, or is she a cross-dressing imitation of a woman/mother who feigns empathy and understanding—a perverse caricature of a therapist?

Although the group's acting out again may be understood as a destructive, envious attack on the therapist whom they wish to punish for making them suffer, it might also represent a more healthy protest towards the mother who has survived and comes back. This underscores the importance of the therapeutic work that may occur after the pregnant therapist returns following her maternity leave. Reassured by the survival of the therapist, it might be only at this point that the patients dare acknowledge their anger, hostility, and fantasies of damaging her. Furthermore, the transference issues regarding the earliest mother–infant relationship that might arise during the post-partum period may be as pertinent as those that arise during the therapist's pregnancy. Thus, Richard's leaving the session in a tantrum after the therapist introduces new patients is akin to the ordinary traumas of the toddler who jealously protests over the withdrawal of his mother's attention from him in favour of his newborn sibling.

Over time, the group became more settled as the emotional turmoil and instability generated by trauma of Dr L's pregnancy and leave of absence subsided. Like all therapy groups at the Portman Clinic, this was a long-term, slow-open group in which patients left (in a planned manner or more abruptly) to be replaced by new members. The latter, who had not directly experienced Dr L's pregnancy, brought their own preoccupations to the group, and the memory of Dr L's pregnancy and its impact appeared to fade. However, this event in the early history of the group appears to have left an indelible trace in the group's collective memory or unconscious, and still today, several years on, somebody will ask the therapist, as if in jest and usually around breaks, whether she might be having another baby, or occasional curiosity is voiced as to how old her child must be now. A more benign maternal figure has also begun to feature more prominently in the mind of the group, emerging from the patients' transferential experience of a therapist who has been able to return to the group and survive their attacks without retaliation. A sense of the group's beginning to mourn loss and reach a more depressive position was recently articulated by Richard, who found himself yearning for his deceased mother, from whom he had been estranged prior to her death due to his anger at her neglect of him as a child, but whom he now wanted to help him in becoming closer to his own children.

Conclusion

The gender of the therapist might not definitively determine the outcome of therapy but will certainly shape our patients' therapeutic journeys in meaningful and unexpected directions. For the violent or sexually perverse male patient whose disturbed behaviour carries an unconscious communication about his early traumatic history, his experience of the female therapist will inevitably be distorted by his early experiences of his own mother that formed his internal object world, a bleak, persecutory landscape ruled by pre-oedipal modes of thinking and dominated by a terrifying pre-oedipal mother. When such patients come together in a group, the primitive nature of their individual psychic mechanisms and internal objects consolidate to form a collective internal world dominated by a maternal imago that is not only omnipotent and castrating, but is also deceptive and perverse. In such a group, the female therapist will be unconsciously cast in the part of the all-powerful pre-oedipal mother, a character that not only dominates and destroys, but also deceives and corrupts all those she controls.

The therapist who becomes pregnant intensifies this transference and will be unconsciously experienced as an actualisation of the patients' worst fears: she literally becomes the omnipotent mother who abandons them, exposing their core complex anxieties and mobilising primitive psychic mechanisms to protect them from their terror, aggression, and primitive envy. What is particularly provocative for such men is being confronted with the creativity of the therapist: her creativity in being able to conceive and produce a live baby, a creativity that involves intimacy with another person. Perversion could be thought of as a denial of creativity, an attack on reality, and a pathological solution that negates sexual and generational differences. Chasseguet-Smirgel (1984) describes the world of the pervert as an "anal-sadistic universe" in which penis, faeces, and child are all equal and interchangeable, a world of perverse "pseudocreativity" rather than real creativity, where the pervert has complete control over the objects of his phantasies and intimacy with a real person, who might have their own wishes and demands, is bypassed. The pregnant therapist's ability to withstand the patients' envious attacks on the life she embodies will pose the biggest challenge to her therapeutic capability and to the survival of the group.

Finally, the value of the support of professional colleagues and the containment of the institutional setting should not be underestimated in making it possible for therapeutic work to continue when a therapist is pregnant or needs to take a prolonged period of leave for other reasons, such as illness or sabbatical. Our experience at the Portman has been that, if handled sensitively, groups can be enriched through experiencing a change of therapist—sometimes temporary, sometimes permanent—in these situations. The substitute therapist will need to work hard to keep the replaced therapist alive in the group's mind without undermining his or her own role. When the therapists are of different genders, as in the case with Dr L and Dr S, unexpected themes regarding gender roles and fantasies might emerge as food for group thought. These experiences will, in turn, form part of the evolving history of a group that is continually evolving, a group that can survive the symbolic births and deaths of its individual members, both patients and therapists, and provide an essential sense of continuity and containment that underpins the group's therapeutic endeavour.

References

Anderson, L. (1994). The experience of being a pregnant group therapist. *Group Analysis, 27*: 75–85.

Bassen, C. R. (1988). The impact of the analyst's pregnancy on the course of analysis. *Psychoanalytic Inquiry, 8*: 280–298.

Bion, W. R. (1955). Group dynamics: a re-view. In: M. Klein (Ed.), *New Directions in Psychoanalysis* (pp. 440–477). London: Tavistock.

Bion, W. R. (1961). *Experiences in Groups*. New York: Basic Books.

Bowman, D., Scogin, F., Floyd, M., & McKendree-Smith, N. (2001). Psychotherapy length of stay and outcome: a meta-analysis of the effect of therapist sex. *Psychotherapy: Theory, Research, Practice, Training, 38*: 142–148.

Breen, D. (1977). Some differences between group and individual therapy in connection with the therapist's pregnancy. *International Journal of Group Psychotherapy, 27*: 499–506.

Chasseguet-Smirgel, J. (1984). *Creativity and Perversion*. New York: W. W. Norton.

Conlan, I. (1991). The effect of gender on the role of the female group conductor. *Group Analysis, 24*: 187–200.

Cooper, A. M. (1991). The unconscious core of perversion. In: G. I. Fogel & W. A. Myers (Eds.), *Perversions and near-Perversions in Clinical Practice: New Psychoanalytic Perspectives* (pp. 17–35). New Haven, CT: Yale University Press.

Etchegoyen, A. (1993). The analyst's pregnancy and its consequences on her work. *International Journal of Psychoanalysis, 74*: 141–149.

Fenster, S., Phillips, S., & Rapoport, E. (1986). *The Therapist's Pregnancy: Intrusion in the Analytic Space*. Hillsdale, NJ: Analytic Press.

Foulkes, S. H. (1964). *Therapeutic Group Analysis*. London: George Allen and Unwin.

Freud, S. (1905d). *Three Essays on the Theory of Sexuality*. S.E., 7: 125–245. London: Hogarth.

Friedman, M. E. (1993). When the analyst becomes pregnant—twice. *Psychoanalytic Inquiry, 13*: 226–239.

Gavin, B. (1994). Transference and countertransference in the group's response to the therapist's pregnancy. *Group Analysis, 27*: 63–74.

Glasser, M. (1996). Aggression and sadism in the perversions. In: I. Rosen (Ed.), *Sexual Deviation* (3rd edn) (pp. 279–299). Oxford: Oxford University Press.

Goldberg, J. (1979). Aggression and the female therapist. *Modern Psychoanalysis, 4*: 209–223.

Greenson, R. (1968). Dis-identifying from mother: its special importance for the boy. *International Journal of Psychoanalysis, 49*: 370–374.

Lax, R. F. (1969). Some considerations about transference and countertransference manifestations evoked by the analyst's pregnancy. *International Journal of Psychoanalysis, 50*: 363–372.

McGarty, M. (1988). The analyst's pregnancy. *Contemporary Psychoanalysis, 24*: 684–692.

McKinnon, D. (1990). Client-preferred therapist sex role orientations. *Journal of Counseling Psychology, 37*: 10–15.

McWilliams, N. (1980). Pregnancy in the analyst. *American Journal of Psychoanalysis, 40*: 367–369.

Mills, T. M. (1964). Authority and group emotion. In: W. G. Bennis (Ed.), *Interpersonal Dynamics*.

Perlman, L. (1978). Unpublished doctoral dissertation. City University of New York.

Pikus, C. F., & Heavey, C. L. (1996). Client preferences for therapist gender. *Journal of College Student Psychotherapy, 10*: 35–43.

Raphael-Leff, J. (1980). *Psychological Aspects of Pregnancy, Birthing and Bonding*. New York: Human Sciences Press.

Rogers, C. (1994). The group and the group analyst's pregnancies. *Group Analysis, 27*: 51–61.
Stoller, R. J. (1974). Hostility and mystery in perversion. *International Journal of Psychoanalysis, 55*: 425–434.
Strauss, J. (1975). Two face the group: a study of the relationship between cotherapists. In: G. R. Wolberg & M. L. Aronson (Eds.), *Group Therapy 1977: An Overview* (pp. 201–210). New York: Stratton Intercontinental.
Thunnissen, M. (1997). Pregnancy in a psychotherapist. *Tijdschrift voor Psychotherapie, 23*: 122–132.
Trampuz, D. (1997). Why are women allowed to be group analysts? Reactions to a conductor's pregnancy. *Group Analysis, 30*: 245–257.
Welldon, E. (1988). *Mother, Madonna, Whore: The Idealization and Denigration of Motherhood*. New York: Other Press.
Welldon, E. (1996). Group-analytic psychotherapy in an out-patient setting. In: C. Cordess & M. Cox (Eds.), *Forensic Psychotherapy: Crime, Psychodynamics and the Offender Patient*. London: Jessica Kingsley.
Welldon, E. (2011). *Playing with Dynamite*. London: Karnac.
Whyte, N. (2004). The impact of the therapist's pregnancy on the treatment of the borderline patient: review of the literature. *Psychoanalytic Psychotherapy, 18*: 15–26.
Wright, F., & Gould, L. J. (1977). Recent research and sex-linked aspects of group behaviour. In: G. R. Wolberg & M. L. Aronson (Eds.), *Group Therapy 1977: An Overview* (pp. 209–217). New York: Stratton Intercontinental Medical Book Corporation.

CHAPTER SIX

Paedophilia, child abuse, and group analysis

John Woods

The term "paedophilia" refers to a state of mind, a sexual interest in children, "which may or may not be translated into action" (Wood, 2012). Current social preoccupations have meant that concern about child protection has obscured questions about the meaning of this sexual orientation towards children. Public condemnation and disgust at child sexual abuse militates against any desire or need to understand this psychosexual phenomenon. Consequently, interventions have taken the form of prevention against reoffending; treatment for those who have sexually offended against children has tended to be highly structured, and with an explicit value base, that is, declared statements about responsibility for offences, and analysis of power relationships (Brown & Caddick, 1993, pp. 218–230). The preference for manualised treatment programmes reflects the overarching need for treatment to control behaviour, and not only of the offender-patient, but also of the therapist.

A psychodynamic framework for both theory and treatment, however, is well placed to provide information and knowledge about the psychopathology involved as well as providing some valuable therapeutic possibilities. This is not to say that a blind eye can be turned against the dangerousness of further enactments by the patient. An open-ended and relatively non-directive approach need not mean collusion with, or denial of, offending behaviour. Attempts at understanding a sexual orientation to children need to be made, not in a permissive manner, but ultimately to serve the cause of preventing further offences. Work with child sex offenders has been conducted for many years at the Portman clinic, and has led to many developments in theoretical understanding of paedophilia (Glasser, 1964; Welldon, 2011). However, an increase in the number of referrals has led to the creation of a programme of group treatment specifically for people presenting with that problem. This has contributed to our theory building about paedophilia and has provided treatment for more than forty individuals. The discussion in this chapter is limited to work with males; as Wood (2012) notes, the number of female offenders is relatively low, and males predominate in the clinical population at the Portman. The psychological profile of female offenders is quite distinct from that of males (see Welldon, 1988).

While, unfortunately, no randomised control study has been undertaken, nevertheless the effectiveness of the group treatment has led to its continuation for more than twenty years. During that time, only three patients are known to have reoffended.

First, some observations on the nature of paedophilia, followed by some clinical reflections from the group work.

Paedophilia as a developmental arrest

A good deal of knowledge has emerged from this ongoing clinical work, both individual and group, at the Portman (Wood, 2012; Wood & Hale, 2008). Some typical features of the paedophile have been found, including formative experiences from early childhood, latency and adolescence, and adulthood. This information has led to the elaboration of the psychodynamic preconditions for paedophilia and the paedophilic act. Briefly described here, some of these ideas can be found more fully presented in Wood (2012).

Typically, the paedophile's mother is seen by him as narcissistic and inconsistent. Often described by the paedophile is an ambivalent, emotional, and sometimes physical over-involvement with his mother, which might take the form of sensual overstimulation or overfeeding to the point of nausea. The child learns that to maintain contact with the mother, he must accommodate to the experience of revulsion, and even learn to love it if he is to survive. Mutual excitement between mother and child is confused with proper caring and it is the child's body that is the medium for this interchange rather than the mind. This child has experienced little space to develop a sense of privacy or separateness from mother. The father is seen as weak and unable to stand up to the mother. His response is often to absent himself. His diminished sense of self is the damaged masculinity that the child internalises. Siblings will have afforded little or no respite from the inadequate parenting. Rather, they will have been experienced as part of the abusive family system. Group therapy is well placed to mitigate the damage from this developmental lack.

The intrusion into the child's psyche is magnified if there is overt sexual abuse. While far from universal, there is a much higher incidence of abuse in the childhood of those who sexually abuse children than in the normal population (Wood, 2012). Such sexual abuse takes place in the context of emotional deprivation, and offers a dubious solace. Crossing a "body boundary" as well as the generational boundary has a powerful emotional impact. Despite the sense of powerlessness in the acts of abuse, the child is also introduced to the secrets of adult sexuality, which, despite being themselves confusing and traumatic, might also give a sense of secret knowledge and, therefore, the promise of power over the adult world. This contradictory state of being carries on into adolescence, where the typically normal anxieties about development are magnified, and fragile defences cover massive insecurity and feelings of inadequacy.

Although there is no single pathway to paedophilia, there are childhood experiences which might combine in this perverse "solution" to the problems of development. Even in families not obviously materially or socially deprived, there might be emotional abuse, as seen, for example, in the "boarding school syndrome" (Schaverien, 2011). A personal history of childhood sexual abuse is not sufficient in itself to lead inevitably to later paedophilic enactment. The "cycle of abuse" is not immutable, and many of those who experience childhood sexual abuse do not subsequently go on to abuse (Bentovim & Williams, 1992, p. 102). The child abuser uses his sexuality to turn away from human contact, using the child in a power relationship that denies reality rather than engages with it. A social form of treatment that highlights the quality and nature of human contact, that is, group therapy, is precisely what is most needed.

These unhappy childhood histories, often including early sexual abuse and/or abandonment, isolation, bullying, an adolescence with crippling feelings of inferiority, and an adulthood with poor social adjustment, result in a state where adult relationships seem impossible. All this is retold in the therapy group, which becomes a containing experience for the entire person, not just the problem that he presents to society. A hunger for human contact, so long denied to someone labelled "sex offender", provides a good prognosis for treatment.

The paedophilic state of mind

At some level, the paedophile "knows" that adults and children are fundamentally different, yet, in another part of his mind, believes, or insists on believing, that the child can be a sexual partner to him, and that child and adult are somehow equivalent. This can be seen not only as a failure of development, but also as a product of certain psychological predispositions.

Glasser (1964) proposed that for the paedophile, an actual child carries the projection of the idealised child, on whom the individual lavishes idealised "parental"-type love. Thus, he imagines that he is admiring and adoring that child in the way he should have been admired and adored by a parental figure. This "adoration" includes the fulfilment of oedipal and pre-oedipal wishes of the child within the paedophile. At some level, there is an identification with this imagined child which overrides awareness of crucial differences. The child victim might represent the longed-for relationship with the incestuous parental figure; in fantasy, the perpetrator might imagine that he is gratifying this sensuous state, projected into the child, or that he is sadistically punishing the child for such wishes. In other cases, the child might come to represent a pure and unsullied pre-pubertal "infantile" sexuality that the paedophile envies and wishes to spoil.

The "core complex" theory of Glasser (1979) is particularly relevant to the paedophile state of mind. The longing for fusion with the object carries with it the threat of engulfment, and so provokes a desire to withdraw, which, in turn, arouses terrors of abandonment and isolation. The perverse solution to this conflict is to sexualise the aggression felt towards the object, in order to preserve a sadomasochistic relationship based on control and the infliction of pain. Thus, sexualisation can be used as a kind of anti-depressant. Narcissistic relating, and the negation of the needs of the other, are characteristic. The sexualised child is a part object, representing the mother who can be neutralised in the power dynamics of adult–child interaction. The threatening mother figure can be controlled in fantasy. These dynamics become evident not only in the life stories of the paedophile, but also in the treatment relationship, either with the therapist or group.

The issue of whether thoughts and fantasies are translated into action with a child is pivotal. For this to occur, it is as though symbolism has broken down, to a point where, psychoanalytically, the process could be called "psychotic". One incest perpetrator is reported to have said, "I was totally insane that night" (McCarthy, 1998, p. 116). The child is no longer recognised to be a symbol of the idealised, pure, innocent, unsullied child self, or the deprived, needy, pre-oedipal child, longing for intimacy. This deficit in thinking is linked to failures of the original maternal containment described by Segal (1957), who proposed a type of "concrete symbolisation", that is, a direct equation between the symbol and that which it represents. The individual is not capable of thinking about his need to spoil or attack the purity or innocence, or to reconnect with his child self. At the moment when enactment occurs, the child *is* the envy-provoking purity or beauty that must be attacked.

Keogh (2012) usefully distinguishes between "psychopathic" offenders (i.e. "rapists"), whose usually violent behaviour is to be distinguished from the child molester who acts out of a (cognitively distorted) need for affection. These two types are contrasted markedly in the underlying attachment patterns, the one highly avoidant and the other extremely dependent. These types may be usefully distinguished in terms of assessment, and their contrast may be very useful in the work of a therapy group where differences and their exploration provide meaning. Even the less callous-seeming "child seducer" might conceal within himself a more psychopathic core.

The "child abuser" group: clinical reflections

The idea of a treatment group reserved for those who have committed offences against children has been through various stages of redefinition since its inception at the Portman by Dr Robert Hale. It was originally conceived as a measure to deal with the problem of rejection, since it was found that other forensic therapy groups could not integrate those who had committed sexual offences against children. Hearing from people who had actually committed child abuse clearly was anathema to other group members who had their own, but different, problems of sexual perversion and/or violence. Segregation of any type of patient goes against the grain for various reasons; nevertheless, such a measure seemed at least to enable some work to be done.

A "group for paedophiles" was not a very adequate or comprehensive definition; incest perpetrators, for example, do not necessarily belong in the same category because of differences in their psychopathology as well as behavioural patterns (Welldon, 2011, pp. 119–121). There is then the enormous range between the "romantic" paedophile, who "loves" the beautiful child, has a sexual arousal which is more or less denied, and might or might not have actually abused, as opposed to what may be called the "sadistic" or "predatory" type, who gains overt gratification from hurting the child. The two may not be completely distinct, with one side being less conscious, or hidden, by the other. Also, in recent years, there has emerged a whole new category of offenders who download, or otherwise engage in, illegal images of child sexual abuse via the Internet. It is a vexed question as to how much the sexual arousal and masturbation usually associated with this viewing means that these offenders are to be regarded as paedophilic, and are actively engaging in the abuse of children, as the law decrees (Wood, 2012).

A "mono-symptomatic" or homogenous group is often thought unproductive because too much common ground could lessen conflict, producing collusion rather than questioning (Garland, 2011, p. 49). However, there is evidence for the effectiveness and benefits of specialised group therapy for survivors of sexual abuse (Hall & King, 1997). With careful handling, it can be seen that certain patient populations can overcome their sense of isolation from the social world and benefit from interacting with others who have similar difficulties. Differences along the continuum of the "romantic" as opposed to the "predatory" child abuser, or between the incest perpetrator and the paedophile, becomes the material for each group member to see himself in new ways, in order to gain self-knowledge. Difficult questions are debated in relation to the comparison between Internet and contact offenders. There are, of course, dangers of bonding in a perverse fashion; if the remembering of past abuse, either as victim or perpetrator, becomes a repetition of trauma and its sexualisation, then it is re-experienced, rather than processed. This is a danger that is hard to avoid because the group has to have some replaying of experiences, or else it spends its time in evasion (Hale, personal communication). The ideal would be to achieve a balance between the need for adequate common ground (perverse as it may be) and sufficient difference between members in order to promote the internal conflict necessary for work to be done. Active intervention by the therapist is often required. The following clinical illustration (as will all others in this discussion) is not a precise transcript from a session; as well as names being changed, the interactions presented are typical of the group rather than specific.

> Martin complains about young girls in their summer clothes, "with skirts half way up their bum".
>
> *Fred*: "My God, Martin do you have to talk like that, it just makes me want to explode. This is what I'm struggling with every day. I can't think about anything else. It's driving me mad."
>
> *George*: "Yeah. Listen Martin, I object to your graphic language. You're trying to wind us up, aren't you? You get some pleasure out of that!"
>
> *Martin*: "You're only wound up because you cannot face up to who you really are, what you really are. You want to pretend you don't have sexual thoughts about young children."
>
> *George*: "So you give no credit to anyone who is trying not to think about children."
>
> A silent stand off.
>
> The therapist says that the group clearly has to struggle with both sides, accepting the thoughts and managing them. The silence seems to become more thoughtful and the therapist adds, "Would it be good if the sexual fantasy can be admitted, rather than denied, and yet also kept in its place?"
>
> After a short pause, James says, "Well, what stops me fantasising is the thought of the harm I did my kids, so that now I'm not allowed to even see them."

This intervention by the therapist was initially an attempt to contain the interpersonal conflict, because, on previous occasions, quarrels between Martin and the rest had seemed repetitive and unproductive, each projecting guilt and blame on to the other. At times the therapist speaks for social control, as it were, when he reminds the group of the responsibility each has to manage himself. However, James then takes the opportunity to give voice to his painful reality, thereby moving the group on to a level of self-awareness. This is received by the group, which is now more open to acceptance and loss rather than splitting and projection.

Countertransference issues

A therapist in supervision talked about a dizzy spell he experienced in the session that he was reporting, and went on to say that he was finding himself holding his breath in the group. Thinking over his experience of this group, he realised that he could not bear to breathe in the bodily smells of the group members. These were linked to the child's disgust at sexual contact with adults.

Just as a non-abuser patient group has difficulty accepting someone who has abused children, so the therapist might find it hard to maintain a therapeutic stance. As De Masi notes, "However hard the analyst may try, the paedophile's world appears ... incomprehensible, disheartening and distant" (De Masi, 2007, p. 147). In group therapy, we have the benefit of the group members' understanding of each other, but when we enter the perverse world of child abuse, it is never going to be pleasant and there is little relief. As the therapist comes to know more of the world of child sexual abuse, he might experience visceral reactions, as above. McCarthy (1988) suggests this is inevitable in such work, and that the therapist will come to feel as the child might do, burdened by the sexual aggression and pain of the abuser. In forensic psychotherapy, we seek to understand and work with the victim in the perpetrator (Welldon & Van Velsen, 1997, pp. 1–9), but the perpetrator always seeks dominance. Any therapist, especially if they have worked with children, will be aware of the harm done by child abuse, and know that many, if not most, abusers walk free. The emotional strain on those who work with the victims of child abuse has been documented (Erooga & Masson, 1999; West,

1997), but with perpetrators there is a particular twist. The therapist will experience at the very least disapproval, sometimes disgust, and perhaps condemnation of the abuser, who cannot be entirely separated from his actions.

It is easier, perhaps, to know what stance not to take; certainly the "false positive", that is, "you are really a good person", will not get very far. The child abuser knows he is not a very good person and that is what he needs help with. Equally mistaken is the "superego" position, in which everything the patient says is interpreted as deception. The therapist must stand for truth and reality, not lies and illusions, though he cannot be entirely disinterested, since it is not possible to be neutral about child abuse. Just as De Masi describes, it is necessary for the therapist to align himself with healthy aspects of the patient's (or here, the group's) functioning. There is a heightened dependency in a group of this kind that combines with perverse elements. Perhaps there is something that could be called a "paedophile transference", that is, a dependency based on the immature sexual object choice and is characterised by a sexualised and secretive power relationship (Hale, personal communication). It might seem that patient has created a special and more intimate relationship with the therapist. Over time, this can be seen to emerge as an undercurrent, despite ostensibly useful work being done. The group, together with the therapist, might come to be seen as representing the neglectful and corrupt parental system, but, as this is symbolised rather than repeated, so it may be worked with. The therapist has to be able to withstand the dread that not only is there no cure, but that there may be nothing other than further victimisation. Tolerating this despairing perception, the therapist develops a capacity to help the group change.

The purpose of the group and its task

"I shut myself into a box marked 'pervert', and was safe."

We do not aim to cure anyone of his sexual interest in children. Clinical experience shows that, as with other sexual orientations, paedophilia is unlikely to change. However, the collective work of the group is to create something positive from this disappointment, and so to salvage some remnants from the wreckage of their lives. Even more than with other forensic groups, there is pressure to keep the external world in mind, not only with regard to the prevention of child abuse, but also to protect the abuser from his possible actions. The therapist need to be clear about these things from the outset, and provide a "clear moral compass" (Wood, 2012), but also not to moralise, a difficult balance to achieve. There are dangers in an approach that does not encompass a sense of moral values; not only might it convey an implicit message that the abuse of children is acceptable, but it also can be seen to collude in the neglect of the patient's needs. A shared assumption becomes established in the group culture: a fundamental premise, that children should not be abused. In this respect, the treatment could be said to provide a healthy protective superego. This results from the "offence focus" (Bentovim, 1992, pp. 65–90), as explored in Chapter One. However, a therapeutic group offers more to an individual than control of his actions. This is a form of treatment that can address what was done to him, his persisting distress and self-destructiveness, and his capacity for thought. The therapist leads the group towards a capacity for thinking, reflection on the meaning of behaviour, and, ultimately, symbol formation. This becomes possible through the therapist's grasp of an analytic theory, not only of sexual perversion (see Chapter One), but also one which includes ideas about the perversion of truth, the denial of reality, including trauma, and the denial of differences, especially of gender, generation, and identity.

Selection

A "sex offender" is already in a besieged position *vis-à-vis* the rest of society: "I am no longer a member of the human race. Walking in the street I know that if people knew what I am they would kill me."

He is naturally going to be defensive, employing all levels of denial, minimisation, and self-justification. Any hope of personal change will be faint. Rarely will there be much optimism about treatment; rather, there will be desperation, a need for something to mitigate the hopelessness. How to assess whether he will benefit from group therapy? Unfortunately, there is little certainty, and perhaps only clinical experience provides an informed opinion, based mainly on intuition, as to whether a prospective group member can lower those defences. Such a judgement will be based on "reading the signs", that is, what might not be being said, or the emotional rapport, the countertransference. Clinical supervision, ideally by a group of peers who can reduce the subjectivity of this process by pooling their knowledge, is a necessary resource for anyone undertaking this work. A potential group member needs to have at least the inkling of a capacity for relating to others, and be able to show it. He has, in other words, to see himself as possibly once again becoming a member of the human race, and, as so often, one learns through mistakes.

> In his assessment interviews, Roger admitted he had done wrong and deserved to be convicted for having sex with under-age boys. He said he wanted to find out what it was within him that caused him to do this. As a child he had not been sexually abused, but had been brutally beaten by his father. He said that he would "do anything to sort this problem out". However, once in the group, the minimisation of his offences came to the fore, and even more problematic was his continuing sexual behaviour. He would regale the group with excited stories of picking up "rent boys" who might have been younger than they said, but he didn't care, it wasn't his responsibility. The group were offended by this because it went right against the culture of the group, the shared experience of trauma, awareness of sexual abuse against them, their convictions (in both senses), and their struggle against their own paedophilic impulses. When confronted by the group, he protested that they were bullying him, just as his father had, he said, but in following sessions he would provoke again by telling salacious stories of his encounters with young teenage boys. The group responded that he was bullying them with these triumphant stories. Despite the therapist's efforts, this impasse was only resolved through Roger dropping out of treatment.

Secrecy and concealment is a constant danger with this patient population, and the therapist should expect revelations at any point, but particularly at the transition from assessment to ongoing treatment. At one level, the experience with Roger could be seen as a mistake of selection, and it had to be faced that the group was aggrieved that he had been wrongly placed. Perhaps there were signs of his cynicism about the sexual exploitation of children that could have been better noted before he joined the group. His over-compliance might have been seen as a warning sign. However, it is also possible that he could only reveal his psychopathology by creating a scenario in which he could be bullied by the group and be the bully in order to re-enact his triumph over his trauma. He became the scapegoat, as so often before in his life.

Internet offenders

In response to the enormous increase in referrals of people in trouble with illegal images of child abuse, through unrestricted access via the Internet, we have begun to integrate these with the contact offenders, even though they might not have actually had physical contact with a child. It has been suggested that the use of illegal images of child sexual abuse might not be so much about a primary paedophilic impulse in the perpetrator but more about a need to transgress social norms, enact a sadomasochistic relationship to a sexual object, and unconsciously bring about an equivalent to annihilation by society and the law. These "sex offenders from a sense of guilt" (Wood, 2013) are already desperately ashamed and persecuted by their compulsive use of pornography, but might, nevertheless, have a clear boundary against themselves harming a child. As one said, convincingly, "I might have looked at this stuff, but never, ever would I touch a child!" It does indeed seem unlikely that in recent years the sheer numbers of men convicted for illegal imagery reflect a similarly huge number of otherwise hidden child sex offenders. Certainly, in terms of referrals to the clinic, other forms of sexual perversion, or harmful sexual behaviour, have come to be far outstripped by Internet offences. It might be that at the core of all sexual perversion there is the abuse of a child, especially if, as Stoller puts it, perverse sexuality is designed to master early childhood trauma (Stoller, 1976, p. 9).

The conflation of abuser and victim as a response to trauma

Defences against trauma have long been recognised as key to understanding the process by which a victim becomes a victimiser (Bentovim, 1988). One of the reasons why offenders against children are ejected from other groups is that they evoke traumatic responses from other patients with other types of problems. Punitive responses to the child abuser repeat the abuser's own trauma. In his offending behaviour he is often masochistically repeating the attacks on his own victim self, but this is unconsciously defended against by a need for mastery and the drive to take a dominant role in relation to the family or child victim. This can be linked to the gender roles dominant in our culture; the male is expected to preserve some semblance of power over others to shore himself up against the attacks he has felt, and continues to feel, against himself. The "victim" self is driven into the unconscious, as the "abuser" role gains dominance, but the victim remains within, and resurfaces as the abuser brings punishment upon himself, and so masochistically experiences himself once again as victim.

> The group had been preoccupied with physical ailments, some clearly serious, but the therapist began to feel bored and claustrophobic. As the repetition of symptoms and complaints continued, the therapist had a sense that the group was deriving some satisfaction from this.
>
> The therapist said, "Well, at least this group has something that everyone has in common, being ill, and there's comfort in that, certainly no differences have to be thought about." Immediately a group member said, "Well, we are the living dead!" There was some rueful laughter and a relief of tension. The therapist said, "If that's true, then maybe no one could be accused of abusing a child again."
>
> After a few moments, Martin addressed Adrian: "Well? Did you decide to tell your new friend about your past?" There was sudden quickening of interest as the group was reminded of an intense conflict the previous week. In his efforts to create an "adult relationship", Adrian had met someone through a dating agency. He had brought the problem of whether he tells her about his offences. "If I tell her she'll drop me. If I don't and she finds out, it'll be even worse. I can't bear to tell her, but I can't bear to go on being alone."
>
> Some group members were again angry that he was concealing the truth in his new relationship; "How can she make a decision if she doesn't know who you are?" But the group became stuck. There was a feeling of helplessness and little sympathy in the room.
>
> The therapist said that there was perhaps also a painful awareness in them all, and that as each has said at different times, they, too, were leading a solitary and intensely lonely existence. The mood changed, and there was more sharing of experiences of loss.

This illustration shows how defences such as the preoccupation with physical illness could be challenged and then gives way to the sexual problem, represented by Adrian's dilemma of having to conceal, or admit his past to a woman. The emotional "illness" of the group is then projected into Adrian. The group becomes stuck and so the therapist at this point needs to broaden the focus with an interpretation to the group, who became less preoccupied with Adrian's "decision", and more in touch with their own experiences. The debate about honesty with the woman in the external world became a question about honesty with each other. The following week the problem disappeared, as often happens, as Adrian reported that the woman concerned made it clear she did not want an intimate relationship. He was able to use the group to process this painful disappointment, and not let it lead to further grievance against the world.

A view about the functioning of groups affected by trauma has been advanced by Hopper (1997). Developing Bion's theory of basic assumptions that might inhibit the functioning of the work group, Hopper has shown how a group may fall into a state of "incohesion" in which thought and work have to be avoided because awareness is associated with too much pain. Hopper goes on to elaborate concepts of aggregation and massification as being two forms of defensive functioning that can be used to ward off the incohesion that becomes a threat to survival. In states of aggregation, according to Hopper, the group fails to benefit from interaction and "... differences become a source of invidious comparison" (Hopper, 1997, p. 455). "The living dead", as this particular group expressed it, can at least feel safe. The therapist then has to highlight conflict.

Emotional and psychological trauma can cause actual brain dysfunction and damage, as has been well established (Glaser, 2000; Van der Kolk, 1987). The traumatised child may be rendered speechless and strives to erase unbearable feelings. Once employed as a protective device, this cutting off also forfeits the creative possibility of a coherent narrative. Instead of bearing the emotional or psychological experience, the remnants of trauma might be projected on to the treatment. The abused child identifies himself as a victim. Attacks on the other and on the thinking capacity of the other can be understood as attempts to escape from the intolerable thought of oneself in someone else's mind (Fonagy & Target, 1998). This perspective also shows how the incapacity to conceive of an object at a mental or psychological level causes him to seek identifications via the body. "The bodily self becomes a refuge from intolerable feelings of fear and pain at being abused" (Fonagy, 1999, p. 11). In the sequence described above, a symbolic representation of living death was permitted by the group, which paradoxically enabled a member to think about issues of his responsibility.

How trauma is processed in the group

There follows an extended sequence of material, a composite of various critical points that have occurred in groups (in order to protect patient confidentiality) designed to illustrate the sort of situation in which the therapeutic needs of an individual test group limits almost to destruction.

> In his first few weeks attending the group, Patrick tells how he grew up "in care", where he had been sexually abused and brutalised. He connects this with his offences of photographing pubertal boys in erotic poses. He is preoccupied with his father, who left when Patrick was very young, and caused, as he saw it, the breakdown of the family. This resonates with several other members of the group, but the therapist perceives that there is something unrelated about his version of this sadly familiar story. He seems to bear his burden of injury done to him with more than stoicism; rather, he takes pride in having suffered so much. He listens respectfully to the others, but then picks up the thread of his own story with little or no connection to the others.

This is an instance of what Garland has called the "non-problem" that we need to take seriously, (Garland, 1982). This is to say that the group experience reveals the underlying feature of personality that may be hidden by, though significantly connected to, the sexual perversion. The therapist wondered if this new member needed to learn about communication in a very basic way. Therefore, some practical interventions were made about the need to share in a group, to listen, and interact with others.

> Patrick describes how desperately he tried to lead a normal life, creating a family, but because of offences now has lost everything. George gets angry with Patrick, and confronts his apparent enjoyment in suffering. As he is criticised, Patrick appears to wallow in his feelings of worthlessness and the rest of the group begin to show contempt rather than sympathy.

Here we see the group playing out mutual projections, and enacting a powerful victim–abuser dynamic. After discussion with colleagues, the therapist interprets the scapegoating as a shield behind which other group members may hide their own guilt and shame.

The group turns its attention elsewhere, but, not to be ignored, Patrick reveals he is using social network sites to make contact with young people, "not to target them for sex!" he insists, "just for company!" He claims that by befriending lonely and depressed teenage boys, he is offering them support. The group is alarmed, despite his claims that he is doing only good, sending money to a vulnerable teenager and offering him a place to stay. "But he says he's over sixteen!", Patrick insists. Group members point out the sexual desires he disowns. Would he be doing all this for someone in whom he had no sexual interest, they ask. He is silenced. "You shouldn't be allowed the Internet," says James, "The terms of my SOPO (Sex Offences Prevention Order) do not allow me access."

Patrick bursts out, "I'm not like you lot! I would never touch a child!"

"But you don't mind photographing them, and exposing yourself! Don't you realise you're corrupting them?" Everyone is shouting. Patrick walks out. He stays away for three weeks. On the fourth week, the group write a letter expressing concern and encouraging him to return. On the fifth week there is an answer, in which Patrick explains he is in a psychiatric hospital, following a suicide attempt by means of an overdose. This had been triggered by his arrest for "grooming a young person for sexual relations". He is facing charges, and is terrified that he might go to prison. He adds that he felt too humiliated to face the group. The group respond with a letter saying that he is still a member of the group and that they want to help him through this.

At this point, Patrick's treatment required the intervention of the clinic's management structures (see Chapter Two). A case manager is better placed to liaise with local services, to maintain the link with the therapy, and to negotiate his return to the group, so that complex transference conflicts can remain with the therapist and contained in the sessions. Meanwhile, the group struggled with the difficult question of how much non-contact sexual offences are harmful, in comparison to contact offences, a burning question for many. The therapist discussed with colleagues whether he had allowed too much leeway to Patrick's perverse use of the group.

> On his return to the group from hospital, Patrick confesses he was hiding his suicide plans as well as his under-age contacts. "Even this group wouldn't understand," he said.
>
> "Sorry, mate," says someone, "But you didn't tell us because we would understand, only too well, and you'd have to give it up!" "I wish I had,"

he says, and describes his emotional collapse around the suicide attempt. Since discharge from hospital, however, he has felt stronger and is using support from his ex-wife, who has retained a caring role.

He describes a dream: "I was standing in a river trying very hard to pull up chains from under the water. There is a beautiful boy in the water and I am distracted by him. Suddenly a tidal wave comes, carries him off, and I am clinging to the chains to stop me from being swept away." He went on to say he felt terribly sad that he would never see that boy again. The group is fascinated by the image. Someone says, "But, what can the chains mean?"

Someone else says, "I think we know what the chains are." There is a thoughtful silence and someone else says, "They are the secrets and lies we live by. We try to pull them up, but we need them." And, after a thoughtful silence, "Glad to see you back, Patrick."

Patrick revealed more of his compulsive paedophilic fantasising to the group. Although he did not make physical contact with children, he would masturbate using the photos and had masturbated in front of children. It seemed there was no let-up in his sexual fantasy life. It could be linked to his traumatisation as a child: as well as pain and fear, there was also no experience of healthy separation or of becoming himself. The obsessive interest in finding his father was seen as an attempt to fill a painful hole in his life. The traumatised child was "father to the man". In his suicide attempt, he seemed to be enacting the death of his own childhood. Following this sequence, the group also seemed to have come through something relevant to all and was able to relate much more with each other. The metaphor provided by the dream of the chains they wanted to escape, but which then paradoxically became an anchor, was something that later recurred in group associations. There was an acknowledgement about the attachment to idealised and perverse fantasies, and a move eventually to the pain of giving them up. Over the months, Patrick used his experience of the ongoing legal process to think, rather than adopt once again the victim role. He calmed, and was more able to listen to others. This change seemed to go hand in hand with a change in the group. It is, perhaps, ultimately a mystery as to how people effect change in each other in a group. Nevertheless, it certainly is the case that the process of change in this very difficult group member brought changes in the perceptions and self perceptions of others.

Derek says to Patrick; "I'm sorry you had to go all through that, losing your job, family, going to prison, but I'm afraid I have to admit I can use it to stop myself looking at illegal images, to be aware of the consequences. I mean I already knew, but listening to you has made it more real. But it's not just the warning, I'm not sure if I could survive it as you have."

The case manager intervention in the above illustration when Patrick stays away from treatment is a good example of the "third element" (Welldon, 1996). Andrew Williams discusses in Chapter Two how a paternal function can be brought into play to compensate for the merged perverse transference with the group. As a response to acting out, the boundaries of the treatment can extend, enabling something having the function of a father to become a psychological reality. Thus, the treatment is vitally connected to the outside world and creates a triangle within which the patient is held and can resume work in the group. In the ensuing months, Patrick became less a victim to his sexual compulsions and more of an agent in his own life.

Conclusion: the therapeutic power of the group

At the most essential level, the group provides an experience of containment: an observation commonly made by group members is that "We speak here of things that may not be said anywhere else." Thus, the social isolation that can be so dangerous for the sex offender is decreased. Hostile and perverse projections, once contained, may then be understood, but the work is not primarily through interpretation by the therapist. Instead, interpretation becomes a group function, and is made less by referring to sophisticated psychoanalytical concepts and more through the understanding of meaning in each member's communications. The therapist comes to represent that function of finding meaning in experience. Manualisation of the group analytic method is problematic, because there is no predicting where the group will go in the spontaneous exploration of its own dynamics.

The group can be seen, therefore, as an arena for remembering rather than repeating, for relating rather than isolating. Reliability of the setting is a necessary, though not sufficient, prerequisite for a consistent contact with others. Within this protected space, change is possible. A child abuser benefits from being with others so that, instead of being ostracised or regarded with hatred and contempt, he becomes closer to his own emotional needs through the recognition of them in others. In a thoughtful environment, trauma can become accessible and, to an extent, bearable, or at least understood as part of the pattern of abuse that has persisted into adulthood. As shame is reduced, so a bond develops based on identification with each other's struggle. Even if there is, at times, scapegoating and judgement of each other, if properly managed there will arise concern, respect, and even affection for one another. All of this is despite, or because of, a recognition of the enduring nature of paedophilia, and the duty of each to ensure the safety of himself and others.

There may be something inherently healthy in any group, the "healthy group norm" (Foulkes, (1986[1975], p. 29). This may be seen as the sum total of the individual's need to get something good from others, in a life-giving rather than a destructive way. Access to healthy or healing processes might be more possible than for the individual therapist who has nothing but his or her own resources to bring against the powerful abuser–victim dichotomy. The group therapist holds on to an awareness of the power and value of the group, not so much as an article of faith, but as a guide, since sometimes the purpose of the treatment gets lost in the crosscurrents of transference–countertransference. A group therapist needs to be able to balance, at least in his or her own mind, the needs of members to find the help they need, as against the destructiveness of their psychopathology. The state of the group's functioning is, to that degree, a reflection of the therapist's faith in the potential of human nature to rise above all that has gone before.

Acknowledgement

This chapter was written with the generous help of Portman Clinic colleagues Dr Robert Hale and Dr Heather Wood, though the author takes responsibility for the views expressed.

References

Bentovim, A. (1988). *Trauma Organised Systems*. London: Karnac.
Bentovim, A. (1992). *The Trauma Organised System*. London: Karnac.

Bentovim, A., & Williams, B. (1992). Children and adolescent victims who become perpetrators. *Advances in Psychiatric Treatment, 4*: 101–107.

Brown, A., & Caddick, B. (1993). *Group Work with Offenders*. London: Whiting & Birch.

De Masi, F. (2007). The paedophile and his inner world. *International Journal of Psychoanalysis, 88*(1): 147–165.

Erooga, M., & Masson, H. (1999). *Children and Young People Who Sexually Abuse Others*. London: Routledge.

Fonagy, P. (1999). Male perpetrators of violence against women: an attachment theory perspective. *Journal of Applied Psychoanalytic Studies, 1*: 7–27. Kluwer Academic Publishers.

Fonagy, P., & Target, M. (1998). Towards understanding violence, the use of the body and the role of the father. In: R. Perelberg (Ed.), *The Psychoanalytic Understanding of Violence and Suicide* (pp. 51–72). London: Routledge.

Foulkes, S. H. (1975). *Group Analytic Psychotherapy*. London: Maresfield Reprints, 1986.

Garland, C. (1982). Taking the non-problem seriously. *Group Analysis, 15*(1): 4–14.

Garland, C. (Ed.) (2011). *The Groups Book*. London: Karnac.

Glaser, D. (2000). Child abuse and neglect and the brain: a review. *Journal of Child Psychiatry and Psychology, 41*(1): 97–116.

Glasser, M. (1964). Psychodynamic aspects of paedophilia. *Psychoanalytic Psychotherapy, 3*(2): 121–135.

Glasser, M. (1979.) Some aspects of the role of aggression in the perversions. In: I. Rosen (Ed.), *Sexual Deviation* (pp. 279–300). Oxford: Oxford University Press.

Hall, Z., & King, E. (1997). Group therapy within the NHS V: patients' views on the benefit of group therapy for women survivors of child sexual abuse. *Group Analysis, 30*(3): 409–427.

Hopper, E. (1997). Traumatic experience in the unconscious life of groups. *Group Analysis, 30*(4): 439–470.

Keogh, T. (2012). *The Internal World of the Juvenile Sex Offender*. London: Karnac.

McCarthy, B. (1988). Are incest victims hated? *Psychoanalytic Psychotherapy, 23*(2): 113–121.

Schaverien, J. (2011). Boarding school syndrome: broken attachments, a hidden trauma. *British Journal of Psychotherapy, 27*(2): 138–155.

Segal, H. (1957). Notes on symbol formation. *International Journal of Psycho-Analysis, 38*: 391–397.

Stoller, R. (1976). *Perversion: The Erotic Form of Hatred*. Brighton: Harvester.

Van der Kolk, B. A. (Ed.) (1987). *Psychological Trauma*. Washington, DC: American Psychiatric Press.
Welldon, E. (1988). *Mother, Madonna, Whore: The Idealization and Denigration of Motherhood*. London: Free Association Books.
Welldon, E. (1996). Group analytic psychotherapy in an out-patient setting. In: C. Cordess & M. Cox (Eds.), *Forensic Psychotherapy* (pp. 63–82). London: Jessica Kingsley Publishers.
Welldon, E. (2011). *Playing with Dynamite*. London: Karnac.
Welldon, E., & Van Velsen, C. (1997). *A Practical Guide to Forensic Psychotherapy*. London: Jessica Kingsley.
West, J. (1997). Caring for ourselves; the impact of working with abused children. *Child Abuse Review, 16*: 291–297
Wood, H. (2012). Applied analytic work in forensic settings: the understanding and treatment of paedophilia. In: A. Lemma & M. Patrick (Eds.), *Off the Couch: Contemporary Psychoanalytic Applications* (pp. 143–159). London: Routledge.
Wood, H. (2013). Internet offenders from a sense of guilt. In: A. Lemma & L. Caparotta (Eds.), *Psychoanalysis in the Technoculture Era* (pp. 114–128). Hove: Routledge.
Wood, H., & Hale, R. (2007). Portman lore on paedophilia. Unpublished.

CHAPTER SEVEN

The abused, the abuser, and the confusion of tongues

Alla Rubitel

In this chapter, I aim to demonstrate the various ways in which patients who have offended sexually can manifest their psychopathology within the context of a slow-open analytic group treatment. This is a reflection about a long and difficult journey, which not every group member managed to complete, but for those patients who did stay, I suggest that they successfully managed to establish meaningful changes within their lives.

I took the group over from a senior psychotherapist who had retired from the clinic. At that point, the group consisted of two subgroups: patients who had committed sexual offences against children involving bodily contact and those who reported histories of childhood sexual abuse as children, but who apparently were not perpetrators of abuse themselves. This constellation was in keeping with therapeutic work initiated at the Portman Clinic by Dr Estela Welldon, based on the idea that patients in a group comprising victims as well as perpetrators of sexual abuse can work effectively and benefit from this experience (Welldon, 1997).

From the very first day of my facilitating the group, I was struck by the high levels of arousal, concrete thinking, and extent of acting in of abuse between the group members within the group sessions. It felt as if there was a competition within the group for the title of champion: who had the most power to hurt and who was hurt the most in the group. It was as if the group was chained into a sadomasochistic enactment, where, as one group member put it, "there was no place for subtleties". Any semblance of a third position was strikingly absent. It seemed that I was faced with a self-traumatising abuser–abused group.

In *Beyond the Pleasure Principle* (1920g), Freud defined trauma as a failure of the protective shield to prevent the ego (mind) from flooding with excitations of stimuli. He considered that in the early years this protective function belongs to the infant's mother. Ferenzci (1994) draws attention to trauma as occurring within an interpersonal context, where a child had previously developed a trusting relationship with an adult, who later betrayed the child's trust. This paper, entitled "The confusion of tongues between the adults and the child", discusses the impact of the violence inherent in sexual abuse towards children in the "age of tenderness" when they do not have the sexual maturity of adults and, therefore, are not ready physically and psychologically for sexual intercourse. Rather than an expected defensive reaction to acts of abuse, the children

> feel physically and morally helpless, their personalities ... not sufficiently consolidated in order to be able to protest, even if only in thought, for the overpowering force and authority of the adult makes them dumb and and robs them of their senses. The same anxiety, however, if it reaches a certain maximum, compels them to subordinate themselves like automata to the will of the aggressor, to divine each one of his desires and to gratify these; completely oblivious of themselves they identify themselves with the aggressor. (Ferenczi, 1994, p. 162)

The guiltless child introjects the guilty feelings of the abuser, making him confused about the validity of his own feelings. "The misused child changes into a mechanical, obedient automaton or becomes defiant, but is unable to account for the reasons of his defiance. His sexual life remains underdeveloped or assumes perverted forms" (Ferenzci, 1994, p. 163). Balint defined such adults, who have a certain pre-existing intensity of relationship with a child and who are responsible for inflicting trauma on a child, as "traumatogenic objects" (Balint, 1969, p. 430). The process of identification in childhood is part of normal development, particularly in relation to the resolution of the oedipal situation. However, these identifications become more complex if the child is abused. Through the process of identification with the traumatogenic objects, the traumatising internal objects emerge as part of the intrapsychic life of the child.

Sexual abuse in childhood is known to be a powerful cause of trauma. One useful typology of sexual abuse differentiates "direct" (involving penetration of the body-boundary) from "indirect" (e.g. exposure the pornography) forms of abuse (OACPC, 1992). Our clinical experience has been that more direct forms of abuse result in more profound forms of psychological damage. Trauma results from the violation not only of a child's body, but also of his/her mind. Furthermore, if the child is not being helped to psychically digest this experience by an adult, or if the abuse is continuous, they become further traumatised. Such trauma has a powerful impact on the child's mind and its subsequent development.

> The adolescent who was abused as a child will be confused about his sexual identity, feel guilty about and ashamed of his pregenital fantasies and be ill-equipped for the tasks of adolescence. He feels a failure and is unable to identify with his peers. (Campbell, 1994)

It appears that the interplay of at least three variables determines the extent to which the effect of overwhelming stimuli on a child will become traumatic: the child's disposition, the nature of the overwhelming stimuli, and the capacity of the attachment figures to moderate the impact of such stimuli before, during, and after they occur.

To illustrate these processes, I shall introduce extracts of clinical material from group psychotherapy sessions. The patients' identities have been fictionalised and I have created composite characters to protect confidentiality but to preserve a meaningful sense of the dynamics in the group.

Defence against loss: intimacy and mourning vs. sadistic excitement

When I took over the group, it consisted of five patients: two women who had experienced incest as children and had committed acts of cruelty towards their children, and three men who were both victims and perpetrators of sexual abuse. I noticed that the group members were competing with each other and, ultimately, with me for the place of therapist, or at least for the place of my helper. I was also surprised that the previous therapist was not mentioned. However, my presence and my attempts to interpret this were ignored as if I were not there; they were compliantly "polite" towards me. In this way, the group members were warding off their unconscious feelings of abandonment in response to the retirement of their previous therapist and their anxiety about being with me, a new therapist, who was unknown to them. There was, perhaps, an unconscious anxiety that they might arouse envious retaliation or abuse from me. Through various interactions with each other and me, it seemed there was an unconscious phantasy of the lost object, a fusion of both their abusive childhood figures and the previous therapist as abandoning, demanding, and controlling. Sadomasochistic exchanges were predominant in the group and it felt impossible to find a third position outside this dyadic situation. It was unclear whether the group would fragment or remain fixed in sadomasochism, or whether it could transform into something like a three-dimensional space, where thinking might become possible in a third position.

The following sequences of material illustrate these dynamics. Some six months after I took over the group, one of the group members, Helen, announced that she had decided to leave the group as she had just completed a professional qualifying course, which, in her mind, she equated with qualifying from the group. On balance, she felt that she had achieved what she could with the help of the therapy. The group responded to this with fury. One of the group members, Jane, was particularly outraged, and claimed that she was going to leave as well, as if competing with Helen. It transpired that Jane's mother used to run away from home, leaving Jane and her siblings feeling abandoned and responsible for her abandoning them. There was no space for exploration of Helen's or Jane's feelings, and, as a result, the former withdrew into a superior position, inviting further attacks from the group. It was as if the group could not allow Helen to leave of her own accord; she had to be expelled by the group. She became a repository for the group's anxiety that they were not worthy of being "stayed with". They were afraid that Helen was breaking away and abandoning them, as she had abandoned her own children.

There was no place for a meaningful goodbye. Instead, sadistic exchanges between Helen and the group dealt with this painful separation. I noted that coming close to each other in a tender way was considered inconceivable by the group. I carried the sadness and pain of the situation, while the group was overwhelmed with the excitement of revenge. I interpreted that Helen became a repository for the group's feelings directed at the therapist who had left them, thus resurrecting their early experiences of abandonment and rejection by their parental figures. I took it as a warning for me, should I decide to leave. Somehow, it was easier to denigrate the leaving member than to risk knowing that each of them gave her something good and had helped her. To have something good and valuable inside meant for them to become vulnerable to abuse and exploitation. This left the group feeling robbed of all the goodness by Helen, whom they turned into the abuser.

Helen's departure gave rise in the group to an outburst of anger and suspicion about their former therapist, whom they feared had left the group because they were worthless and not deserving of his attention. They felt betrayed. The primitive part of the group was activated and found its identification in aggression. It became apparent to me later that tenderness is often viewed suspiciously by abused/tramatised patients, as if it is bound to be followed by cruelty and sadistic treatment.

Allowing the new analyst in: do we have the equipment to cope?

The group either behaved like hungry, bickering, and squabbling children or they were passively waiting for me to utter a word of wisdom. Initially, it was safer for the group to idealise me, hoping that I would never go on holiday and would never bring new patients into the group. Nevertheless, there was much curiosity in the group about who their new therapist really was. I was aware that I had to take ownership of the group and restore a more healthy dependency. I addressed their anxiety that I would offer nothing but yet another rejection. I tried to discriminate between the group's hungry demands and what I felt was needed from my point of view. I extended the length of the sessions. On the one hand, the group members were appreciative of these changes; on the other hand, they felt confused and excited, suspicious of me possibly setting them up for something bad. I interpreted the group's anxiety that they were not sure whether I had violated the boundaries set by the previous therapist, or whether I was making my own assessment of their needs and responding accordingly. I was a different experience for the group. I think, in this, I articulated something very important for the group about how a new structure could be negotiated in a benign way, in a slow transition.

New members, new conflicts

Anne, a new patient, joined the group. She was sensitive and imaginative. She provided dreams for the group and she became easily excited by hearing stories of abuse. Anne spoke about her abusers not as damaged and pathetic, but "omnipotent" and omnipresent. She idealised their power to destroy and seemed to see me as an omnipotent rescuer, who would undo the harm done by her abusers. However, Anne's extensive self-harm escalated and required involvement of other mental health services, thereby causing a confusing split between them and her perception of the psychotherapeutic treatment she was receiving at the clinic. Anne became mistrustful of me, since I failed to "rescue" her. She claimed that I had placed her in the group to be "tortured" by two group members, Zack and Phil, who had both been convicted of sexual assault on children. They became stand-ins for her family members who had sexually abused her when she was a child. In her mind, I did exactly what her mother had done: turned a blind eye to the abuse at home. My interpretations were taken concretely as a confirmation of Anne's anxieties. Getting close to me activated her complex identifications with her traumatising objects. On the one hand, she wanted me to prove that I was different and was not there to let abuse happen. On the other hand, this was too frightening for her to conceive, as then she would be faced with something she did not know and, therefore, it would be even more dangerous to take a leap of faith in trusting me. I felt that both the group and I became retraumatising objects for her, objects without remorse for their wrongdoing. Her capacity to think symbolically in an "as if" mode had broken down and she was struggling to think about the interpretations.

Anne reported a dream in which she was subjected to sadomasochistic sex. She associated this with her confused feelings about an adult who, on one hand, did some good, as he introduced her to the world of music which later influenced her career choice. On the other hand, he betrayed her trust and sexually abused her when she was a child. She was clearly overwhelmed by her proximity to me and to Zack in the group. I interpreted that Anne was expressing the group's mistrust about the care they received from me, and the fear that I disguised the abuse like the family members who abused her. Otherwise, why put them in the same group—this group of victims and abusers? At the same time, I brought to their attention how their excitement had become a solution to their ambivalence about my authority and their fear that I could abuse the power I had. Anne expressed acute mistrust of my motives, and in this way she was questioning my loyalties on behalf of the group.

At a point where some moments of apparent progress had been achieved, Zack, who had served a prison sentence for sexual assault of a child, reported that he had been traced by the police after he "unintentionally" downloaded indecent images of children. He claimed that he had never downloaded such images in his life. The group, while acting as if they cared about Zack, took up a position of judgemental authority over him. I put it to them that Zack was "downloading" a lot of excitement in the group, which they could not manage. Instead, the group had become a policeman, questioning Zack and accusing him, while claiming innocence, of setting himself up to be caught. I interpreted that I, like them, had to join in as a judge or a policeman to save them from the burden of their conflicting feelings towards Zack, and ultimately about themselves, caught in the revenge of righteousness. Temporarily, the group managed to recover from the flood of excitement. They now attended with sensitivity to Zack, who was reluctant to think about what he felt about his arrest.

When the group managed to find itself in a calmer place, yet another surge of excitement followed. Phil told the group how he had just established contact in a virtual Internet chat room with a child who had offered her friendship to him. Telling this story, Phil was noticeably aroused and sweaty, causing a lot of concern to other members of the group. He was excited and terrified that this encounter in the chat room could be a setup by the police. He told the group that he had withdrawn from the chat room completely, because he did not want to return to prison. However, he claimed with superiority that his sexual orientation was towards prepubescent girls and he could not see anything wrong with it. He was attempting to corrupt the group's mind with this propaganda: if he managed to convince and excite them, he would then manage to convince a confused part of his mind that befriending a child for sex was acceptable.

Triumph over empathy

This led Phil to tell a story of how, when he was a ten-year-old boy, on one occasion his supervisors found him masturbating other children at school. He was shamed by his teachers, but no explanations followed. He remembered being left feeling terribly confused about that incident. At this point in the session, he appeared vulnerable and lost. The group responded with empathic concern. Within a split second, Phil, a lost and confused "boy", transformed into an unreachable man glowing with excitement. He triumphantly rejected the empathy offered to him by the group. The group was thus pushed into the role of an abused child. In the next session, Phil informed the group that he had found a new job and had no time for the group any longer. This infuriated the group, who confronted him with making others feel played with, humiliated, and rejected, while he was enjoying watching their feeling of helplessness. This led to one of the group members telling Phil that he could not bear to be the "confused boy" in the group. Phil felt attacked by this comment and responded with a threatening gesture. I interpreted this as Phil's fear of being vulnerable in the group and feeling that he had to defend himself by attacking the group, which was safer than accepting their empathy. He and the group found themselves in a familiar place, the place of mutual rejection and abuse. By fleeing the group, Phil did not have to face the confusion within, which was brought to light by the group's concern about him. The group wanted to get to know a more vulnerable Phil rather than to submit to a destructive and perverse aspect of his personality. He could not bear to look at the vulnerable aspect of himself that he did not dare to acknowledge. He was experiencing the group in a way similar to the police, who wanted to catch him out rather than to help him. There was an anxiety in the group about Phil putting himself in danger and potentially endangering vulnerable children at large. The group also felt that I should have done something more to protect the group members from their feelings of being threatened by him, as well by what they felt about his leaving.

Action as the "solution"

Distressed as she was, Anne attacked Zack as if he were her abusive cousin. Zack retreated into masochistic grandiosity, claiming that he understood her anger, yet feeding on it by refusing to see a vulnerable boy inside himself, who had been abused by his neighbour when he was little. Instead, he set himself up as a martyr, as if saying to Anne, "My crime is beyond any repair. The more you chastise me with your anger, the more I suffer, the more I pay the price for the damage I did". Anne was increasingly disturbed by Zack seeing her as the abuser. It was as if she wanted to remain a victim, as if she had to make sure that her abusers would notice the extent of the damage they were doing to her, the damage that could not be repaired. In her phantasy, this would give her tremendous power over them by making them feel guilty. However, by assigning guilt to them in this way, she was unable to move on herself. Moving on meant that her abusers could move on as well and feel that, after all, they had not damaged her. She did not want to come close to a more active and destructive part of herself, which she acted out and drew group's attention to through self-harming behaviour. This was an expression of her identification with the aggressor. Feeling that the therapist and the group were powerless to help her think about what was going on, Anne left the group. It was as if she was re-enacting her early experience of not being able to mourn the loss of her cousin, who moved abroad after he stopped abusing her when she had become an adolescent; it was at this stage that she resorted to self-harm. On one hand, Anne felt compelled to follow the abuser Phil, who fled the group. On the other hand, it was her way of saying that she felt unsafe to stay in my "neglectful care" and that it would be safer to follow Phil. It looked as if I was being ascribed only an abusive role, that is, either I was an abusive mother/therapist to a vulnerable patient who was "abused" in the group, or I was allowing the abuser to go and abuse children outside the group. It felt that I was cruel either way.

More stories of incest emerged. It transpired that the group members who reported direct sexual abuse preferred to keep their abuse secret from other relatives. Although the patients felt like killing their abusers in fantasy, in reality they felt speechless and paralysed to confront them. They were holding on to a tantalising omnipotent fantasy of destroying both the abusers and the adults who did not protect the patients as children from abuse. The downside of this fantasy was a fear of humiliation at not being believed. They also expressed a wish that the adults who had failed them would show remorse. However, this gave rise to an anxiety that remorse will make these adults vulnerable and would stimulate a wish in the abused patients for a sadistic attack, leading to mutual destruction through complex identification with their traumatising objects. The group was able to think about the addictive quality of these exciting fantasies, which was preferred to the unbearable uncertainty of reality testing.

Although the group felt disappointed with me for not being able to stop Phil and Anne from leaving, they realised that something had shifted, and it was a frightened moment of change for all of them. The group was struggling with the questions of how much one can tolerate or has to get rid of things in order to survive and to move on. They felt both concerned and relieved when Phil left after three years. Having gone through an attack of anxiety that the group was fragmenting, there was also some recognition that I, as their "captain", could not stop the storm, yet I did not leave the "ship". The group members felt somewhat remorseful and uncertain about their part in what had happened. They asked me, in both a sarcastic and a concerned manner, "We did not make Phil run away; did we? Yes, we were frightened . . . but so was he. Who was more frightened after all? He was afraid of change." He either had to change or to leave the group. He chose the latter so that he could stay the same, feeling profoundly miserable, anxious, and inadequate.

Somatisation as a defence against fear of fragmentation

A temporary breakdown of the sadomasochistic structure unleashed the group's fear of fragmentation, which was followed by the members finding a retreat in physical conditions, as if the body of the group was in pain after having lost two of its members, Phil and

Anne. The hopelessness and helplessness became idealised and turned into a powerful weapon by Ronnie, one of the new patients, who claimed that he survived all his analysts, who had retired on him. The message to me and to the group was "You can't help me, you cannot fix me. You are now the powerless ones." He became another martyr competing with Zack, exerting a paralysing control, which temporarily obliterated the group's thinking. There was a sense of psychic murder in the group. The sexual fantasies were seen as dangerous, something to catch and imprison rather than to explore, and any new ideas were killed off.

Although Zack and Ronnie could recognise themselves in each other and could partially own their projections of psychic immobility, by the same token, these shared projections were protecting them against having to recognise the extent of their own damage. Both were in much psychic and somatic pain, including back and bowel problems. Both felt that they were beyond repair, blocked and stuck. I interpreted this as the group's need to hold on to their old pain to survive. If they were to let go of their pain, they would have lost their perceived omnipotent strength to endure this suffering; they would have become weak and eventually would collapse. It would have been like betraying the victims within. Zack and Ronnie left the group.

Clearing out the old

There was anxiety among the older members of the group that I was clearing the group bit by bit to bring in my new, more desirable patients. The name of the former analyst was mentioned by one patient in an idealised way, while I was denigrated in front of my new patients. There were ongoing squabbles among the group as if they were putting on a horror show for the newcomers to make them turn away. I interpreted this as their anger with me for bringing new patients, which echoed their previous feeling of abandonment by their old therapist and by the earlier experience of abandonment and neglect they suffered as children. They were receptive. It was as if, for a moment, they were unclear whether I would abuse them or take care of them at this juncture. They were testing out on me what they could and could not do to the new patients, which was an unconscious acknowledgment of a germ of trust in me.

The group members found it difficult to accept that I gave them some understanding and consistency, as it felt insufficient. Therefore, their concern for me had to be got rid of. It had to give way to grievances to avoid facing up to the anxiety that they could lose me to the new patients/siblings who they had to share me with, or that I would simply leave them as they felt their previous therapist did. They felt instantly worse than the newcomers. It was striking how Jane, one of the "oldies", felt that she ought to leave the group in order to balance out a new arrival, as if this meant that she would instantaneously lose her place in my mind to a new sibling/group member. This allowed us to explore the anxieties of both Jane and the group about me as their "mindless" therapist. Stories about their neglected childhood followed.

Climate change: from emotional tempests to drought

Some time later, I introduced several male offender patients into the group, who, in contrast to the established group members, had apparently not suffered direct physical or sexual abuse as children, and neither had they directly inflicted such abuse on others. They were convicted of downloading indecent images of children and had served prison sentences. The idea of sexually abusing a "real child" was abhorrent to them. Yet, they claimed that they could not understand that what they had done was a crime against children. They insisted that they could not see an obvious connection between acting out their fantasies through child pornography and the real children who were abused in order to produce these very images. Such lack of empathy in respect to the children they watched on the screen was astounding. Yet, every time they had looked at indecent images and felt the "buzz", they reported feeling disgusted with themselves afterwards. They appeared extremely self-doubting, anxious, sensitive, and fragile, yet at the same time they boasted of being told by the court and the newspapers that they were "dangerous and untreatable paedophiles", as undifferentiated emotional monsters, with no personal identity. Thus labelled, they became merely a statistic to the authorities. Just as they could not see the children in the computer images as real children, society could not see them as real people with feelings and their own problems. Their experience was of a world of mere transactions lacking in empathy, a world without relationships, feelings, or emotions. Initially, the new members had watched the group with a kind of arrogant curiosity and claimed that they did not feel that they were either insiders or outsiders in the group. Eventually, they began to see that they did indeed belong to this group.

It was striking how all of the newcomers, despite being unique individuals, apparently had a particular problem in common: that is, they had a major difficulty in identifying and putting their feelings into words, a phenomenon labelled as alexythymia by Sifneos (1973), and developed by Krystal (1979). McDougall (1982) also described this concept in patients suffering from perversions as a state of inner deadening employed by the patients against the emotional dangers of re-experiencing a traumatic state. It serves the function of warding off an underlying psychotic anxiety of becoming fragmented, as well as the confusion between feelings of love and hate. This defence is seen as more radical than denial (McDougall, 1982).

Thus, the group was both puzzled and intrigued by the newcomers, who claimed, "I do not know what I feel, I do not know what feelings are, I do not understand what you are talking about when you talk about feelings." An absence of the experience of being loved and seen as a separate individual by important others was a pervasive feature in their individual stories. Able to sense the deprivation, neglect, and emotional abuse that those men had suffered, the group was determined to explore this inability to articulate their feelings. The group was confronted with a new challenge of finding some liveliness in this apparently emotionally barren climate. There was a sense that both despair and hope were part of this illusion of lifelessness in them. It later became apparent during therapy that the newcomer patients had suffered emotional neglect and abuse over an extended period in their early life. According to the narratives of their personal histories, they had parents who failed to recognise, or were unable to attend to, the children's developmental needs. Instead, the parents used them as objects to gratify their own narcissistic needs. Their mothers were often described as controlling, judgemental, righteous, lacking sensitivity and warmth. Two of the new patients had been abandoned by their fathers and left to pacify their mothers' unconscious anxieties, having to be continuously alert so as not to provoke their intense anger, which alternated with withdrawal and detachment for which the patients, as children, felt responsible. A third patient recalled that, as a child, he was repeatedly made to watch his father disciplining his siblings by caning their upper legs in a sexually charged manner, which the patient grew to believe was normal, as his father claimed that he was caring for them. These confusing experiences instilled a lot of anxiety in the patients as children regarding their attachment figures as well as their sense of self, which they were not able to manage, and which resulted in cumulative traumas.

Their capacity to process and symbolise their traumatic experiences was hampered by the presence of their ongoing exposure to these demands and inhibition of healthy aggression. Khan (1963) hypothesised that such traumas come about as a result of the accumulation of breaches in the protective shield provided by attachment figures in the child's environment over a period of time, and may become apparent only in retrospect. Before treatment, however, these patients, exposed as they were as children to failures of a good enough holding environment, or "impingements", might have resorted to the kind of defensive organisation formulated by Winnicott (1948) as the "false self".

Gradually, the original members helped the newcomers to recognise that the latter also suffered a kind of abuse, although indirectly through accumulated emotional neglect. This indirectness was mirrored by symptomatic behaviour of seeing other children being abused. It was striking how the older members carried all the anger against the neglectful parents of the newcomers. The latter were becoming more anxious and were holding on to their addictive fantasies as a refuge from their dilemma: "If I lose my 'addiction' what will I have instead?" ". . . if I start thinking that after all my father did abuse me, I will start hating him and then I will lose him, I will be left without a father."

Ferenzci wrote about abused children who wish to recover a pre-existing state of tenderness (real or imagined) with an adult at all cost.

> Through the identification, or let us say, introjection of the aggressor, he (the aggressor) disappears as part of the external reality, and becomes intra- instead of extra-psychic; the intra-psychic is then subjected, in a dreamlike state as is the traumatic trance, to the primary process . . . the attack as a rigid external reality ceases to exist and in traumatic trance the child succeeds in maintaining the previous situation of tenderness. (Ferenzci, 1994, p. 162)

Although this "situation of tenderness" can never be recreated, it is the illusion of tenderness created by arousal, this dreamlike state, which temporarily eliminates the conflicting feelings about abuse. These patients who had not committed contact offences against children, but had engaged in viewing child pornography, had achieved this dreamlike state of sexual arousal free of any sense of guilt at their complicity with an abuser. Their masturbatory phantasies were reportedly focused around children who invariably survived their abuse. The child pornography downloaders felt falsely reassured by this, allowing them to normalise the pathology of abuse. It unveiled a confusion between fantasy and reality, which amounts to a denial of the psychic pain of knowing the destruction taking place within oneself as well as to these children. Although these are children whom the patients have never met, they are, nevertheless, being linked to the patients through the patients' identification with both aggressor and victim. The sense of immediate gratification, the connection with intense arousal, "buzz", and an illusion of never-ending excitement provide escape from a reality that contains real abuse. In fantasy, they can control both the abusers and the children who are being abused. Their addiction to pornography provided a way of retrieving an illusion that the patients were gaining control over both their internalised traumatising objects and the patients' violent impulses towards them. One patient was able to pretend in fantasy that the abused child on the screen was himself, now able to triumph over his own callous abusers. This masturbatory fantasy could relieve the sense of confusion about his violent state of mind by projecting on to the screen a "safe fantasy" of "non-real" victims and abusers.

Both subgroups of patients had experienced cumulative trauma, whether they had been subjected to repeated physical sexual contact, or subjected to abuse though the neglect of the wished-for proximity to their attachment figures. The cumulative effects of both direct and indirect traumas compromised the patients' ability to discern both real and imagined dangers, and inhibited their capacity for empathy. Gradually, the newcomers became able to articulate their feelings, rather than merely experiencing arousal and anger at times. It became possible for group members to see the "subtleties" of emotions, which had been painfully impossible until then, due to the overpowering arousal of acting in.

Discussion

The clinical material presented demonstrates how initially stark sadomasochistic dynamics prevailed within this group of victims and perpetrators of sexual abuse. This created a polarisation of "abuser–abused". Interactions within the group were typically charged with excitement and arousal. There was a call for the therapist to join in this drama and to become either an abuser or a rescuer for the group. These dynamics were particularly powerful in relation to losses, separations, and the arrival of new patients, when the group regressed to primitive states and operated in a paranoid–schizoid way. There was an addictive attachment to grievances and sadism, whose function was to ward off the task of mourning. The third position was occupied either by a superego, which voyeuristically observed a victim triumphing over an abuser, in metaphoric terms, a controlling policeman catching out a criminal, or by a neglectful and abusive parent or failing therapist. Some of the patients who had been sexually abused but were not sexual abusers themselves were unable to manage their "closeness" to both the perpetrators of contact offences and the therapist who had brought them close together. In a situation such as this, the "victim" experienced both group members and therapist as actual abusers. The "victims" became re-traumatised by this experience, as their capacity to think symbolically broke down.

During this work, it often seemed there had been an early failure of the "protective shield" in the patients' early history. At times, I found myself, as their therapist, in the position of a failing protective shield for the group, on occasions even becoming a traumatising transference object. Gradually, I realised that a rigid perverse sadomasochistic dynamic had been unconsciously employed by the group members to protect themselves from the emotional pain of hurt and shame. This also served the function of warding off a deeper unconscious anxiety about the threat of fragmentation within their fragile egos, the state of confusion resulting from complex identifications with their traumatising objects. At the times when the group experienced this threat as catastrophic and beyond the capacity of the therapist and/or the group to contain it, the group members would get locked into a highly arousing, rigid, two-dimensional structure of "victim and abuser", where thinking was not possible. At its height, the group would exclude certain members who were perceived as embodying unbearable projections of psychic immobility, bringing a momentary respite. In those situations, I shared an experience of the person who, as their therapist, was unable to stop this enactment, as my interpretations were apparently powerless. At these moments the group was acutely affected by the basic assumption of "fight/flight" (Bion, 1961). And, to draw further on Bion's ideas, a reversal of alpha-function took place, setting in a rigid beta screen (Bion, 1962a).

Working through of these failures allowed the group to have the experience of being *with* the therapist as an object who was able to think about such failures. This gave space for some mourning of the group losses and, ultimately, perhaps a partial reparation of their early traumas.

The dynamic changed when non-contact "paedophile" offenders, who had been compulsively downloading indecent images of children, were introduced into the group. It became apparent from their narratives that although they had not suffered direct sexual traumas, they had been exposed to continuous cumulative traumas of emotional neglect and abuse. Although they all were very different individuals, they seemed to have developed a similar defence against bombardments of overwhelming toxic stimuli from internal and external reality. Their paedophilic fantasies were projected from internal psychic reality into external reality, straight on to the computer screen. The confusing feelings from their own trauma met with pornographic images of children being abused. The unbearable horrendous feeling in internal reality met with the equivalent images in external reality, which, being externalised, were more bearable. The screen, therefore, became a reflection of the horror and confusion of what was going inside the patients minds, yet now it was also outside them. It temporarily provided them with relief that the horror of psychic torture was not inside them, but out there on the computer screen, while they were imagined to be safe.

This situation evoked in me an association to the myth of Perseus's battle with Medusa, whose lethal gaze turned the viewer into stone. Athena gave Perseus a shield to reflect Medusa's gaze, which allowed him to kill Medusa. "The head of Medusa is symbolic of the female generative or reproductive power having double significance of destruction and reproduction" (Miller, 1958). These patients, addicted to child pornography, were "looking" at something inside themselves that they could not manage. It seems that there was an unconscious sexual phantasy of a monster man/woman/child entangled in a frightening intercourse, which was psychologically indigestible, but sucked in the viewer and turned him into stone. The stone is without feelings, yet is alive stone, as patients with alexithymia report might describe themselves. In the story of Perseus, Athena is a kind of thinking mother who provides Perseus with a protective shield to help him deal with the intensity of the lethal/castrating gaze of Medusa. For her part, Medusa represents an archetypal imago of violent parental couple, which turns into a lethal combination when it meets with the unconscious incestuous wishes of the viewer. Athena provides Perseus with protection against this threat, as the mother will do for her child by helping him to accept his incestuous desires, the force of which he is not capable of withstanding in the presence of tantalising objects. As Bion saw it, this protection emanates from the mother's reverie (Bion, 1962b). The shield of Athena is a safe third position between Perseus and Medusa. Perseus now sees Medusa through his fearless and wise Athena's eyes, her shield. Perseus also receives a sword from Zeus, which represents male potency, so that aggression is permitted by Zeus, representing Perseus' father. The giving of the sword is in the service of survival and not sadism. Perseus is helped by a containing couple to defeat the Medusa, that is, the Perseus/child's unconscious phantasy of violent intercourse.

In contrast to the story of Perseus, people who feel compelled to view images of child sexual abuse cannot defeat psychic Medusa with their own resources; they are lacking an internal containing parental couple. Instead, through the use of these images and the instant gratification of sexual arousal, they reach a narcissistic self-regulation, a self-soothing in the absence/lack of an internal protective/empathic object relationship. Sadly, the shield, which was designed to protect the patient's mind, eventually compromises it and corrupts it even further. It has become a perverted shield. These patients disown their sadism and the knowledge that the children are real.

The introduction of the patients with this pathology to the group allowed for a one-step-removed position from the rest of the group members, who were, at times, locked into an overt victim–abuser arousal with each other. Instead, the patients who had not committed contact offences against children, but who were addicted to child pornography, displaced their arousal into a masturbatory fantasy away from the group, away from "real people". These "virtual paedophiles" introduced a perverse shield, yet this also provided the potential for introducing a third dimension in relation to the binary victim–abuser dynamic. This eventually allowed for a transitional space to emerge in the group, because of the increased awareness of difference. The group members were able to explore the destructive power of their individual perverse defences, and, working through the confusion between real and virtual abuse, they encountered the deeper confusion of victim and abuser. As therapy progressed, partial reparation was taking place through internalisation of the repeated experience of being understood, and, at the same time, the mourning of the loss of omnipotent defences. A possibility of creating a more functional protective shield became a reality.

Conclusion

In reviewing the overall progress within the group setting, it appears that the formation of a structured sadomasochistic defence was a response to the legacy of abuse, an intolerable experience of a "confusion of tongues", confusion of minds about external and internal reality, and about a complex system of identifications with traumatising objects. It became apparent in therapy that this confusion was hidden by sadomasochistic arousal and excitement in the group. The therapist might have to struggle to find a third position, because the binary dynamic might, at times, be so powerful that it is beyond the group's and therapist's capacity to contain and to modify the propensity to enacting abuse within the group. The learning process is a slow and painful one in order to manage the ongoing breakdown in the capacity to think when the group is in a situation of extreme arousal.

The introduction of patients who had apparently not suffered direct sexual trauma, but instead had been exposed to cumulative psychological trauma, allowed for the emergence of a new group constellation. It became possible to stand back from the "confusion of tongues" state of mind, which might previously have been highly defended against in the group by relentless acting in of abuse and high levels of arousal. The group members who stayed with the treatment experienced change as a major psychic event. They developed a sense of trust in each other and in the therapist, in a context of empathy that was previously lacking in their lives. This enabled them to recognise and to name different feelings and aspects of themselves, as well as to identify themselves with a group that was functioning as a whole. The process of therapy allowed a shift from confusion towards symbolic exploration.

Acknowledgements

The author would like to acknowledge the kind help of Ms Valerie Charles for her editorial assistance, and also the valuable support of David Morgan, Don Campbell, Edna O'Shaughnessy, and Judy Hoskins.

References

Balint, M. (1969). Trauma and object relationship. *International Journal of Psychoanalysis, 50*: 429–435.
Bion, W. R. (1961). *Experiences in Groups and Other Papers*. London: Tavistock.
Bion, W. R. (1962a). Learning from experience. In: *Seven Servants* (pp. 24–30). New York: Jason Aronson.
Bion, W. R. (1962b). Learning from experience. In: *Seven Servants* (pp. 31–37). New York: Jason Aronson.
Campbell, D. (1994). Breaching the shame shield: thoughts on the assessment of adolescent child sexual abusers. *Journal of Child Psychotherapy, 20*(3): 309–326.
Ferenzci, S. (1994). Confusion of Tongues between the adults and the child. In: *Final Contributions to the Problems and Methods of Psychoanalysis* (pp. 156–167). London: Karnac [Classics series 1994, reprinted 2002].
Freud, S. (1920g). *Beyond the Pleasure Principle*. S.E., 18: 7–64. London: Hogarth.
Khan, M. R. (1963). The concept of cumulative trauma. *Psychoanalytic. Study of the Child, 18*: 286–306.
Krystal, H. (1979). Alexithymia and psychotherapy. *American Journal of Psychotherapy, 33*: 17–31.
McDougall, J. (1982). Alexithymia: a psychoanalytic viewpoint. *Psychotherapy and Psychosomatics, 38*: 81–90.

Miller, A. A. (1958). An interpretation of the symbolism of Medusa. *American Imago*, 15: 389–399.
OACPC (Oxfordshire Area Child Protection Committee) (1992). *Child Protection Procedures*. Oxford: Oxfordshire Social Services Department.
Sifneos, P. E. (1973). The prevalence of 'alexethymic' characteristics in psychosomatic patients. *Psychotherapy and Psychosomatics*, 22: 255–262.
Welldon, E. (1997). Let the treatment fit the crime. *Group Analysis*, 30: 9–26.
Winnicott, D. W. (1948). *Paediatrics and Psychiatry: Collected Papers of D. W.Winnicott*. New York: Basic Books, 1958.

CHAPTER EIGHT

Mentalization-based group treatment for antisocial personality disorder

Jessica Yakeley

Almost eighty years after it was founded, the Portman Clinic continues to thrive as a unique institution of which the core clinical activity consists of psychoanalytic therapies for a patient population—the perverse, violent, antisocial, and delinquent— whom others, including many psychoanalysts, believed were untreatable, or did not wish to treat. The clinic's longevity and ability to survive the many challenges it has faced, both internally and externally, depends on a small dedicated staff group, who remain united in a commitment to the basic principles of a psychoanalytic understanding of violent and antisocial behaviour. However, there is also a need to be able to adapt to changing circumstance and opportunity without losing their core psychoanalytic identity, ensuring that therapeutic technique continues to evolve and is tailored to the specifics of current patient need. Estela Welldon describes the resistances she encountered when she introduced group analytic therapy in the early 1970s to the Clinic, where, until that time, individual psychoanalytic psychotherapy was the only treatment offered (Welldon, 2011). Despite the considerable reservations, and even outright hostility, expressed by her colleagues from within the Portman, as well as from the Group Analytic Society and Institute of Group Analysis about why such disturbed patients should not be put together in a group, Welldon persisted in her endeavour. The result is that group analytic therapy is now not only the main modality for at least half of all patients in treatment at the Portman, but has become an established form of treatment within forensic psychotherapy as a whole for perverse and violent patients, underpinned by sound and well-articulated theoretical principles which remain loyal to their psychoanalytical origins.

It is in this spirit of adaptation and innovation, while not abandoning the Clinic's core therapeutic principles or ignoring the considerable clinical expertise that has consolidated from its long tradition and history of treating violent and perverse patients, that I and a small group of colleagues (in particular, my co-therapist, Dr Andrew Williams, whose support and expertise in this project have been invaluable) have introduced another modification of psychoanalytic technique to the Portman Clinic in the form of a mentalization-based treatment (MBT) programme for a very specific patient group: violent men with a diagnosis of antisocial personality disorder (ASPD). In this chapter, I describe the recent background and some of the contextual complexities of this new service, and introduce the conceptualisation of ASPD as a disorder of attachment. I then focus on describing the treatment programme, and, more specifically, the technical aspects of adapting MBT in a group therapy setting to patients with ASPD, highlighting points of convergence and difference in technique from more traditional group analytic therapy. Although I briefly outline the main principles of MBT, I do not here provide a comprehensive description of its technique, which the interested reader can find elsewhere (Bateman & Fonagy, 2004, 2006).

A new service

The idea to develop a specific service at the Portman Clinic for patients with a diagnosis of ASPD arose in early 2009 out of discussions among various clinicians treating patients with personality disorder within the Tavistock and Portman NHS Foundation Trust, against the backdrop of the wider mental health arena in which several important developments were occurring in the diagnosis of, and treatment for, individuals with ASPD. In brief, we identified a "gap in the market" in service provision, and an associated research opportunity, for certain violent individuals who were diagnosed with ASPD, but could not find a service to treat them. At the Portman, we had recognised for a while that the relative ratio of referrals for patients with paraphilias and illegal sexual behaviours, particularly individuals who accessed child pornography through the Internet, compared to patients referred for violent behaviour, was increasing. This reflected the increasing numbers of people arrested for downloading illegal pornography and seeking help to understand or limit their behaviour. This gradual shift in the demography of our patient population towards seeing fewer violent patients than before could not be explained by a corresponding decrease in the incidence of violent behaviour in society, which, if anything, has remained stable, or slightly increased in the last decade (Ministry of Justice, 2008). In recent years, as the political emphasis in the management of offenders has veered heavily towards punishment and away from therapeutics, antisocial and violent individuals are less likely to be offered treatment, or if they are, this is likely to be in the form of short-term cognitive–behavioural interventions such as anger management delivered within the criminal justice system. Violent individuals seldom come to the attention of mental health services unless their violence is the result of a psychotic illness, although abnormal personality traits such as impulsiveness and emotional instability are a much more common cause of violent behaviour than psychosis. However, many psychiatrists remain ambivalent about treating individuals with personality disorder who present with violent or antisocial behaviour but who do not also present with mental illness. This phenomenon persists despite influential government documents such as the Department of Health's *Personality Disorder – No Longer a Diagnosis of Exclusion* (Department of Health, 2003), and more recent National Institute for Health and Clinical Excellence's guidelines for the treatment of borderline personality disorder (BPD) (NICE, 2009a) and antisocial personality disorder (NICE, 2009b). While community services for patients with a diagnosis of BPD have significantly increased throughout England and Wales, those who present with violent behaviour, many of whom may have a diagnosis or significant traits of ASPD, are either not recognised as suffering from the disorder, or, even if they are accurately diagnosed, cannot find a service to treat them. The situation for people with ASPD is not helped by the individuals themselves, who often find it difficult to accept responsibility for their antisocial actions, let alone accept a traditional sick role (Parsons, 1951), and tend to reject or fail to engage with any treatment that might be offered. This leaves clinicians feeling consciously or unconsciously demoralised and rejected themselves, and, therefore, less likely to persist in offering treatment, resulting in a vicious circle of disengagement and despair and the continued marginalisation of a group of people who are desperately in need of help.

ASPD: prevalence and aetiology

Although often not recognised by professionals, ASPD is a relatively common disorder, with most studies reporting a prevalence of between 2% and 3% in the general population (Gibbon et al., 2010), and a much higher prevalence of up to 50% in the prison population (NICE, 2009b). The recent NICE guidelines for ASPD were welcomed in raising awareness of this disorder and also in challenging the widespread belief that it is untreatable. Although their emphasis on prevention, by focusing on interventions aimed at children (e.g., those with conduct disorder) and families at risk of developing the disorder, is important, the guidelines were limited in their recommendations for the treatment of adults with ASPD. This is a reflection of the dearth of methodologically sound treatment studies of ASPD, which has been due not only to the significant difficulties in engaging patients with ASPD in treatment at all, let alone in research trials, but is also a result of diagnostic confusion and controversy, linked to disagreements among researchers regarding the aetiology of ASPD. The current psychiatric diagnostic classification systems—the American Psychiatric Association's *Diagnostic and Statistical Manual of Mental Disorders* (*DSM-IV*; American Psychiatric Association, 1994), and the World Health Organization's *International Classification of Mental and Behavioural Disorders, Tenth Edition* (*ICD-10*; World Health Organization, 1992)—are based on descriptive phenomenology and use a categorical approach to classify disorders on the basis of observable behaviours and symptoms, rather than theories of causation. The main features of both the *DSM-IV* diagnosis of ASPD and the equivalent diagnosis of "dissocial personality disorder" in *ICD-10* centre on antisocial behaviours and features of criminality, such as violation of the rights of others, deceitfulness, impulsivity or failure to plan ahead, irritability and aggressiveness, reckless disregard for safety of self and others, consistent irresponsibility, and lack of remorse, but say nothing about the aetiology or development of these unpleasant behaviours and personality traits. There is substantial evidence to suggest that the current ASPD *DSM-IV* category describes a broad and heterogeneous population containing several different subgroups of the disorder which are the outcome of different aetiological and developmental pathways and which show different responses to treatment. Although early onset antisocial behaviour that starts in childhood tends to remain stable over the lifetime, different aetiological factors contribute to produce different adult phenotypes or manifestations of ASPD. Studies show that such aetiological factors include genetic vulnerability (Viding, Larsson, & Jones, 2008), malnutrition, smoking in pregnancy, and, most importantly, harsh parenting practices (Hodgins, Kratzer, & McNeil, 2001), including parental abuse (Caspi et al., 2002). This empirical data resonates with the everyday clinical experience of working with people with ASPD, who often give histories not only of childhood abuse, but also of neglect, parental mental illness and alcoholism, poverty, unemployment, domestic violence, family breakdown, and periods of time in care, all of which might interfere with the process of attachment.

There is, therefore, increasing evidence that both biological and environmental factors can interact in complex ways and to varying degrees to produce different forms of ASPD. The measurement of psychopathy, a term that is frequently but erroneously equated with the disorder itself, can be usefully applied to differentiate between these different subgroups. Psychopathy, exhibited in callousness towards others, a disregard of emotional attachments, and lack of remorse or shame, is, in fact, just one of the personality dimensions or traits that make up the antisocial syndrome, and which differs in severity in different forms of the disorder and should, therefore, be measured independently by an accredited instrument such as the Pyschopathy Check List-Revised (PCL-R) (Hare & Wong, 2003). In fact, only one out of three patients with ASPD has severe psychopathy, and this latter group has a significantly poorer treatment prognosis than patients with mild to moderately psychopathic antisocial personality disorder (Hare 1991; Hare & Wong, 2003), which reflects a more severe form of personality disorder that is likely to have a considerable genetic and biological basis (Felthous & Sass, 2007; Meloy, 2007).

We are interested in a different subgroup of people with ASPD, whose psychopathology is determined less by genetics than by early environmental adversity that has affected their psychological development via disruption to the attachment process. This group comprises individuals who have lower levels of psychopathy, but proportionally higher levels of anxiety, the presence of which may also be used to differentiate different subtypes of ASPD. Studies of children and adults show that around a half of the ASPD population is characterised by anxiety as well as persistent antisocial behaviour. These individuals have low levels of callous/unemotional traits (a predictor of adult psychopathy) as children and low levels of psychopathic traits as adults (De Brito & Hodgins, 2009). This group is more likely to have experienced physical abuse as children and resort to violence as a compensatory response to underlying emotional conflict and distress. Psychoanalysts such as Bowlby (1944), with his description of "affectionless psychopaths", and Winnicott (1956, 1986), with his concept of the "antisocial tendency", recognised early on that certain children's apparent indifference to others, or their anger, resentment, and violence, represented defences against underlying feelings of anxiety and despair which stemmed from earlier experiences of environmental adversity, trauma, and loss. As adults, unlike those categorised as more psychopathic under the broad diagnostic umbrella of ASPD, these individuals are more prone to experiencing anxiety and depression, which might become more prominent as their antisocial defences break down. At this point, they might present to their GPs or be referred to mental health services with depression. However, when their violent and criminal history becomes known, or a diagnosis of ASPD is made, professionals become less willing or able to treat them, and they end up being referred from service to service without being accepted for treatment, an experience which is often an unfortunate but not coincidental repetition of their early disrupted attachment history.

Attachment and mentalization in ASPD

There is increasing evidence that certain forms of ASPD are the outcome of a developmental disorder of attachment in which the capacity for mentalization is impaired. Mentalization is the capacity to reflect and to think about one's mental states, including thoughts, beliefs, desires, and affects, to be able to distinguish one's own mental states from others, and to be able to interpret the actions and behaviour of oneself and others as meaningful and based on intentional mental states (Allen, Fonagy, & Bateman, 2008). Put simply, mentalization means "holding mind in mind", or thinking about one's own mental states and those of other people. Mentalization is not a new concept, but includes a variety of meta-level operations of mind such as empathy, theory-of-mind, mindfulness, emotional recognition, meta-cognition, and self-reflective function. However, influenced by Winnicott and Bowlby, Fonagy and his colleagues have been foremost in extending the concept of mentalization by synthesising psychoanalytic with attachment theory and developmental psychopathology to provide a coherent and convincing theory of personality development, including the development of pathological aggression and violent behaviour in individuals with ASPD. An increasing body of empirical evidence to support the hypothesis that ASPD is a developmental disorder rooted in attachment comes from studies showing abnormal attachment patterns in forensic patients and prisoners diagnosed with ASPD (Frodi, Dernevik, Sepa, Philipson & Bragesjo, 2001; Levinson & Fonagy, 2004; van IJzendoorn et al., 1997).

Mentalization develops within the context of a secure attachment relationship. Secure attachment in childhood is associated with the development of enhanced mentalization processes, which, in turn, contribute to the homeostatic regulation of negative affect and arousal regulation (Sarkar & Adshead, 2006; Schore, 1996, 2001). The normal development of mentalization is dependent on the intersubjective process of emerging psychological awareness between the securely attached child and his primary care-givers. The child becomes increasingly aware of his own mind through his growing awareness of the mind of his mother via her capacity to demonstrate to him that she thinks of him as a separate person with his own distinct intentions, beliefs, and desires. This is akin to Winnicott's (1971) role for the "good enough mother", who, in her mirroring, or containment and reverie (Bion, 1970), facilitates the infant in developing a healthy capacity to find his own mind in the mind of the object. If, however, the mother's, or primary care-giver's, thoughts are frequently malevolent or fail to view the child as a separate being, he cannot develop a capacity to feel safe about what others think of him, which might lead to a more generalised failure to see others as thinking beings at all. In such abused or neglected infants, aggression arises as a defensive response to protect the fragile emerging self from the hostility of the object. If the abuse or neglect is ongoing, a fusion will occur between the aggression and self-expression of the child. The mother who is not attuned to her baby's experience will provide inadequate mirroring of the infant's behaviour (Winnicott, 1956), so that the child is unable to develop a representation of his own experience, and instead internalises the image of the care-giver. Where the mother or primary care-giver has been neglectful or abusive, as in many individuals with ASPD, this internalised representation will be experienced as foreign or bad, and will never be fully integrated into his overall schema of self-representations. Bateman and Fonagy (2008) have called this discontinuity within the self the "alien self", and suggest that this internalised self-representation is continually subject to the pressure of projection into others to maintain the illusion of a self that does not contain unacceptable aspects.

As adults, people with ASPD are dependent on relationships with others into whom they can project these alien aspects of themselves in order to stabilise their minds and feel a sense of self-coherence. Relationships in individuals with ASPD tend to be rigid, hierarchical, and controlling, as exemplified in dismissive attitudes towards women who are viewed as inferior, or in the "gang culture" of organised crime. Notions of recognition and respect assume a special importance in their interpersonal relationships. If, however, such relationships are challenged by the other person refusing to be the recipient of malign projections, as in the subjugated wife who talks back to her abusive husband, the return of the alien self threatens the person's fragile stability of mind, leading to unbearable feelings of shame and humiliation which could trigger violence in an attempt to regain control and sense of integrity. Fonagy's theory here draws on that of Gilligan (1996), who proposes that violence is precipitated by feelings of shame and humiliation. Gilligan describes the devastating effects of a poor development of self, sense of identity, and agency that results from early trauma and parental abuse in his work with high-security violent inmates in the USA. These offenders' early experiences of being rejected, ostracised, abused, or made to feel as if they did not exist, predisposed them as adults to be sensitised to feeling ostracised, bullied, or ignored, leading to unbearable feelings of shame and humiliation which need to be defended against by violent means. Gilligan also reminds us that words alone can constitute trauma, that the violent person might not have been the victim of actual violence, but of verbal and emotional abuse that can equally damage the developing mind.

Fonagy and Target (1996, 2000, 2007; Target & Fonagy, 1996) have identified several different primitive modes of thinking that predate the emergence of mentalization, which they call "psychic equivalence", "pretend mode", and "teleological thinking". These pre-mentalistic modes of organising subjective experience are normal in the early childhood development of all of us, but persist and predominate in people with certain personality disorders, notably BPD and ASPD, whose capacity for mentalization has not developed normally due to disruptions in the attachment process. Psychic equivalence, sometimes referred to as concrete thinking, is where the person experiences internal and external reality as isomorphic, there is no tolerance of differing points of view, and thoughts cannot be symbolised. In pretend mode, thoughts and feelings are dissociated from reality to the point of meaninglessness, so that a person might appear to be talking about important internal experiences, but these are disconnected from any meaningful context. Teleological mode refers to a mode of thinking in which the motivations of others are interpreted according to the presence of physical actions. Here, changes in mental states are felt to be real only when confirmed by physically observable action. An example of teleological mode demonstrated by one of our ASPD patients was his belief that others would find him threatening only if he was physically violent, and he could not understand why his family might be frightened of him at other times. Another example is of the patient who was convinced he had been "disrespected" by the therapist, whom he thought had "winked" at him, and could not accept any alternative explanation for whatever facial expression the patient had apparently observed in the therapist. These three modes of pre-mentalistic, or non-mentalizing, thinking will inevitably become evident in the patients' discourse in therapy, and one of the fundamental tasks of the MBT therapist is to identify these as non-mentalizing and to facilitate mentalizing modes in their place.

Violence can be understood in particular relation to such primitive thinking. Bateman and Fonagy (2008) propose that reactive or affective violence arises where there is a failure or inhibition of the capacity for mentalization. The person with ASPD experiences psychic stability so long as projection of the alien self remains successful, but when this fails, pre-mentalistic types of thinking emerge, especially teleological thinking. A person with a limited capacity to mentalize struggles to manage negative emotions such as normal anger, hatred, and wishes to hurt, and instead might become highly aroused very quickly and experience themselves as unable to think, overwhelmed with negative affects. The person with ASPD, who is already highly sensitive to threats to his self-worth or "respect", cannot tolerate internal emotional states of shame and humiliation at all, which are experienced as threatening to his very psychic survival. These unbearable feelings cannot be managed by representational means within his mind, but are experienced very concretely in psychic equivalence mode as feelings that the person needs to expel in violent action or teleogically. The expression of aggression is further potentiated by the reduced capacity of the individual to mentalize; if he is unable to see others as having mental states as different from himself, this will reduce the inhibition of his aggression and violence towards others, since he is unable to empathise or appreciate another person's suffering. Moreover, the onset of pretend mode creates an illusory sense of safety in which the violent person is detached from reality and, hence, the danger and consequences of his actions. Mentalization, therefore, protects against violence and individuals whose capacity for mentalization is reduced are more likely to be violent. It is also important to note that Bateman and Fonagy are describing "reactive" or "affective" violence (Meloy, 1992) (equivalent to Glasser's (1998) self-preservative violence) that is primarily defensive in origin, as opposed to the more cold, calculated, and planned psychopathic (Meloy, 1992) or sadomasochistic (Glasser, 1998) violence seen in psychopathic or perverse individuals.

The treatment programme and patients

Our MBT ASPD treatment programme is modelled on that developed by Anthony Bateman (Bateman & Fonagy, 2011), to whom we are indebted for his invaluable supervision and close involvement in this project. The structure of treatment comprises hour-long weekly MBT group therapy sessions in a slow-open group run by two therapists, both of whom are consultant psychiatrists in forensic psychotherapy, and monthly fifty-minute individual sessions with one of the two therapists. Each patient is offered eighteen months of treatment. Additional sessions for crisis review and risk management may be offered by another consultant psychiatrist in the clinic, although this has been rarely necessary (see below). In the monthly individual sessions, the therapist continues to use an MBT approach, but his or her main function is to support the patient's engagement with the group, which is seen as the primary vehicle of treatment. To encourage engagement in the group, individual sessions are only available if the patient is regularly attending the group. The content of the group therapy sessions is steered by the therapists towards encouraging the patients to talk about recent violent or highly emotive incidents, although exploring other relevant issues in their lives is not discouraged if these can become mentalizing topics. However, most of the patients find it more difficult to talk in front of the other members of the group about the inevitable relationship difficulties they experience in their external lives, and will often use the individual sessions to do this. Here, we encourage them to articulate the thoughts and feelings they have about these difficulties (i.e., to mentalize) and to talk about them in the group. Invariably, difficult states of mind, such as shame and impotence, that they might feel in relation to their girlfriends or relatives will be linked to how they perceive other people in general make them feel, which might then lead to acting out their aggressive and violent behaviour.

Before starting the programme, the patients are assessed by one of the two therapists over several assessment appointments. These meetings are used to take a history, establish a clinical diagnosis of ASPD, assess the patient's risk, and ascertain his ability to engage in the treatment process, particularly assessing whether he will tolerate a group setting. Patients are not accepted for treatment if they have a history of a major psychotic illness, such as schizophrenia, or if they are currently showing frank dependence on alcohol or drugs. However, as substance misuse is a frequent problem in patients with a diagnosis of ASPD, we do not insist that the patient is completely abstinent, as is the policy in many psychotherapy services, including the Portman in general, as this would limit the engagement of many patients with ASPD who view their substance misuse as a way of life. In practice, our own discouragement of these patients' addictions is far outweighed by the disapproval and intolerance of other ASPD group members who have had serious alcohol or drug addictions in the past but are now religiously abstinent through attending twelve-step groups such as Alcoholics Anonymous or Narcotics Anonymous.

We are also excluding patients with evidence of severe psychopathy (a score greater than thirty, as measured by the PCL-R), since these patients are less likely to engage in treatment or benefit from a mentalizing approach. Most of the patients have been referred by their GPs or general mental health services, having originally presented with depression, although some have sought help directly for their aggression. In accordance with the NICE guidelines for ASPD, we discourage psychotropic medication prescribed for the primary traits of the personality disorder, such as impulsivity and aggression, but will encourage patients to take antidepressant medication if we feel that they are also suffering from depression.

The assessment sessions contain some elements of psycho-education aimed at introducing the patient to basic principles of MBT, and discussion of the diagnosis if necessary. During the assessment, the therapist will also explain some of the parameters of group treatment, such as the need to maintain confidentiality, discouragement of meeting other patients outside of the group, and our stance of not writing reports on individual patients for external agencies such as the courts, housing departments, or probation services. The rationale for not providing such reports is that to do so might interfere with the patient's motivation for treatment. Individuals who are currently involved with legal proceedings might (consciously or unconsciously) frequently wish to present themselves in a better light by agreeing to enter treatment to impress a prison parole board in order to be released from prison, a criminal court judge to obtain a more lenient sentence, or a family court in order to gain access to their children, rather than possessing any real motivation for therapeutic change.

Once they have completed the assessment and agreed to participate in treatment, the patient will then meet with our assistant psychologist over two or three appointments to complete various diagnostic tools and outcome measures and to consent to participating in treatment, which is part of a pilot outcome research project. These meetings include being video-recorded for the Structured Clinical Interviews for *DSM-IV* I and II (SCID-I and SCID-II) (First, Spitzer, Gibbon, & Williams, 1997a,b), which are semi-structured diagnostic instruments providing a profile of *DSM-IV* diagnoses, necessary to confirm that the patient has a diagnosis of ASPD as well as establishing whether the patient is suffering from other personality disorders or concurrent mental illnesses such as depression. Most of the patients will meet diagnostic criteria for other personality disorders in addition to ASPD, the most common being narcissistic, borderline, and paranoid. Meeting the assistant psychologist in a one-to-one setting prior to starting the group can prove to be a useful transition period in which some patients may express their anxieties about starting treatment that they had not dared voice to the assessing psychiatrists. It also tests the patient's tolerance of being video-recorded, an experience they must accept as the group sessions are all recorded for our own supervisory and learning purposes. Although recording psychotherapy sessions is often thought of as an unhelpful intrusion into the therapeutic space, in practice, to our surprise, given the high levels of paranoia in many of these patients, we have found that most quickly get used to the camera and forget its presence.

Following the initial assessment meetings, the assistant psychologist will arrange to meet with the patients at three monthly intervals during treatment to administer a battery of outcome measures covering various domains, including emotional states, social functioning, aggression, and drug and alcohol use. The primary outcome measure, however, is the Overt Aggression Scale-Modified (OAS-M) (Coccaro, Harvey, Kupsaw-Lawrence, Herbert, & Bernstein, 1991), which is a brief self-report measure that the patients fill in fortnightly after the group session. The OAS-M asks about violent acts and thoughts towards self and others, as well as feelings of irritability and suicidality that the patient has experienced in the previous two weeks.

The patients who enter treatment are all men who fulfil the diagnosis of ASPD, but also accept that they have a problem with their aggression, for which they are seeking help. All have a history of violence and most have previous criminal convictions for violent acts, including patients who have been convicted of murder and are serving the end of their life sentence in the community. The majority continue to be involved in more minor incidents of aggressive behaviour in their everyday life such as disputes with neighbours, pub fights, and road rage. The majority of the patients come from deprived working-class backgrounds, and all have experienced various forms of serious abuse and neglect from their parents and parental figures, some spending time in care. All of the patients also report difficulties in their close interpersonal relationships with partners and family. Those with children are also often subject to the involvement of social services and the family courts, and might have limited access to their children due to the risk of their violence. We have found that, in general, younger patients who have been referred have found it more difficult to accept responsibility for their aggression or the long-term nature of their difficulties and have tended to drop out of treatment early on, citing that they no longer need it. We have, therefore, ended up with a cohort of men aged between their mid-thirties and mid-fifties, most of whom have presented to health services with depression and anxiety, the diagnosis of ASPD emerging later.

Establishing a group process

One of the most important elements of our treatment programme is the group setting. This specifically resonates with the thinking of Estela Welldon (1996), who felt that group therapy was very often the treatment of choice for violent patients, rather than individual therapy. In individual therapy, the intensity of the relationship with the therapist might feel overwhelming, and the violent person could feel terrified of his own capacity to be violent towards the therapist. By contrast, in group therapy, violent patients might feel more contained as the multiple transferences available offer more than one target for their aggressive impulses. Interestingly, we find that many of the ASPD patients attend the group more regularly than the individual sessions, particularly those offered with the female therapist.

Welldon also emphasised the fact that as many people who resort to violence, including those with a diagnosis of ASPD, have grown up in dysfunctional families in which anger and violence characterised the communication between family members, the therapy group can act as what she called "a socio-familial microcosm" in which the violent person's interactions with other group members can be understood as reflecting the pathological dynamics of their original familial experiences. As such individuals inevitably have difficulty in forming intimate adult relationships based on mutual respect and trust, the group experience may offer the opportunity of learning more healthy and mature ways of relating to others. The triggers to potential violent behaviour might also be more easily recognised and confronted in a group setting than in individual treatment, and, from a mentalization viewpoint, the more minds that are present in the room, the more opportunities there are to mentalize.

However, before any specific mentalizing techniques will be effective, a group process needs to be established in which there is a sense of connection and trust between the group members. This is very difficult for patients with ASPD, whose long-standing interpersonal difficulties, suspicion, and lack of trust of others will inevitably enter into their relationships with each other in the group. When patients first start in the group, they tend not to engage with, or show genuine interest in, each other, and the group discourse is comprised of a series of disconnected monologues from each patient about his own particular difficulties, aimed primarily at the therapists for individual responses. This calls for the therapists to actively intervene in making explicit links between the discourses of individual patients, asking patients what they think of what another patient just said, and in general fostering a group discussion in which they may begin to relate to each other. Ironically, a common view of the world that they often express early on, and on which they all unite, is that no one is to be trusted! The patients' paranoia and narcissistic intolerance of others receiving too much attention from the therapists, especially in the early stages of their treatment, has led us to limit the active membership of the group to a maximum of six, rather than the customary eight, patients in treatment at any one time, although, in practice, fewer patients will attend each session due to their difficulties with engagement.

Engaging the patients in treatment has been one of the major challenges that we continue to encounter. This is perhaps to be expected in any attempt to treat individuals with ASPD, given that the majority of such patients do not accept that they have mental health difficulties and do not accept a traditional sick role (Parsons, 1951), let alone that of a psychotherapy patient (Norton & McGauley, 1998). Referral to mental health services might be associated with shame and stigma, and the assessor should be sensitive to this. In our experience, many patients do not attend the initial assessment following referral, or drop out during the assessment phase, let alone engage in treatment. Although we have taken an assertive approach to encourage patients to attend, including telephoning the patient after missed sessions, the treatment programme has been slow to establish. At the time of writing, we started the group two years ago with four patients, and more patients have joined since then. However, to date, only one patient has completed the eighteen-month programme and, of a total of twelve patients who completed the assessment, including the interviews with the assistant psychologist, only six have remained in treatment, the other six dropping out after several months and not responding to follow-up. One patient stopped attending after only two sessions, but then re-presented a year later and has subsequently engaged well, reporting that when he first started in the group he felt anxious talking in front of others and also did not accept the seriousness of his difficulties.

Although we can only speculate as to the reasons for the disengagement of the other patients, these appear to include anxieties about joining a new group, reluctance to acknowledge psychological difficulties and associated feelings of vulnerability, and difficulties in managing confrontations and conflicts between members within the group. Some patients, who have missed several sessions then returned to the group following our contacting them, have reported feeling too depressed to attend and not wanting other group members to see them in what they perceive as a weak and vulnerable state. Other, often younger, patients might stop attending after they perceive themselves to be better and no longer in need of treatment. Yet others appear to lose track of time and miss sessions, or arrive late, despite professing that they wish to come, due to the general chaos of their lives and their inability to organise themselves. The patients' erratic attendance also makes it difficult to maintain themes that arise from one session to the next. Because of these challenges of engagement, a closed, fixed-term group is not viable, and so the group has an ongoing, slow-open format with new patients being introduced following patients dropping out or being discharged. Although the unexpected disappearance of patients might be disconcerting and demoralising for the remaining members of the group, and new members might feel anxious coming into a group in which people know each other already, we have found the slow-open process helpful for newer members to see the progress that some of the more established group patients have made after a few months of treatment. With time, a slow but gradual development of solidarity emerges between group members, so that the group atmosphere begins to feel more supportive. The essence of treatment is to stimulate affiliative bonds without simultaneously provoking the threat of shame and humiliation, while at the same time nurturing feelings of trust, honesty, and openness within the context of the attachment process (Bateman & Fonagy, 2011).

Mentalizing principles: techniques in encouraging mentalization

Bateman and Fonagy (2006) emphasise two basic principles underpinning MBT for personality disorder, and this remains true for MBT for ASPD. First, there needs to be a focus on techniques that facilitate the development of mentalizing, and second, there must be a concomitant avoidance of interactions that either maintain non-mentalizing or decrease it. This necessitates the therapists taking a more active and focused approach than in more traditional psychotherapy, intervening when the patients deviate into non-mentalizing modes. For example, discussions in the group might quickly move away from the current personal experiences of the patients into a wider philosophical–political discussion about the problems with the world, which is, in fact, a form of pretend mode.

Because individuals with ASPD find it very difficult to empathise with other people's affective states, or feel another person's emotional pain, interventions aimed at consideration of their effects on others, or "victim empathy", are likely to be counterproductive and should be avoided, at least in the early stages of treatment. This is especially relevant to patients with ASPD, who seem to quickly feel that encouragement to mentalize others' states of mind is a sign of neglect of their own experiences.

In the following fragment of a group session, a patient has been complaining how hurt he is because his daughter never visits him, and refuses to allow him contact with his grandchildren.

Therapist: Why do you think she does not visit you?

Patient: Because she's always been no good—it's her mother's influence.

Therapist: Do you think she is frightened of you?

Patient: Why should she be frightened of me? I've never hit her.

Therapist: How do you think she felt when you went to prison after assaulting her friend?

Patient: I have no idea and I don't care. She never visited me there. Her friend deserved to be hit, as he swore at me, and showed me no respect in my own property.

Another patient to the therapist: Why are you going on about her? It's us you should be focusing on, how *we* feel when we are badly treated.

In this interchange, the therapist has erroneously focused on trying to get the patient to think about the emotional impact of his violence on his daughter. The other patient rightly points out that the primary task is to help the patient understand what is going on in his own mind, to focus on what the patient feels or has been made to feel, not ask him to consider the feelings or motives of the other person. To begin with, therefore, the therapist encourages the patients to reflect on their own mental states and affective experiences, especially those leading up to the violent act. Interventions focusing on improving self-regard and promoting social and interpersonal success are also emphasised, with the aim of creating a positive and hopeful atmosphere in the group (Bateman & Fonagy, 2011).

However, the patient with ASPD whose habitual mode of operating is by acting, not thinking, finds it very difficult to identify his internal state of mind or know what he is feeling, particularly when those feelings are associated with states of vulnerability and weakness. A seemingly simple question from the therapist such as "What are you feeling about that?" can be experienced as very threatening for the patient with ASPD, who finds it hard to put his feelings into words and will fear that he will be made to look stupid and humiliated in front of others in the group if he is unable to do so. Therapists must be sensitive to the patient's narcissistic fragility in that they are hypersensitive to being criticised or corrected, which, in itself, might trigger aggression within the group if the patient becomes more aroused and less able to mentalize. This calls for technical sensitivity in inviting the patients to think about their minds in a manner that is not experienced as demanding. One way of gently introducing patients to their internal states, so that they can begin to monitor how they feel and identify their reactions to others, is for the therapist to model his or her own state of mind in hypothetical situations, without inappropriate personal disclosures, as in the following example:

A black patient, Mike, who finds it difficult to think of himself as a violent person, despite getting into frequent violent altercations in which he believes he is "rescuing" others whom he perceives have been attacked, is describing how he is often seemingly randomly stopped and searched by the police.

Therapist: I wonder how being stopped and searched makes you feel?

Mike: (appears slightly agitated) I can understand why they might stop me in an area where they don't know me, but I don't think it's fair when they do it in my area, where I'm known and I just want to keep my head down and cause no trouble.

Therapist: If I was stopped and searched with no apparent reason, I think I'd feel quite upset, angry or humiliated.

Another patient, Kevin: Well, you are unlikely to be stopped and searched, Doc, as you are white and middle class! But yes, it makes you feel disrespected, which makes me feel very angry. You can't trust the police in this country.

Mike: Actually, some of the police officers I know are OK. But others seem to think because I'm black, have dreadlocks and wear this woolly hat that I must be carrying knives or something, which is unfair and makes me angry.

Therapist: Perhaps the feeling of being disrespected, or seeing others that you are believe are being treated unfairly, contributes to you getting into the fights you often find yourself in unwittingly.

In this interchange, Mike is initially unable to describe his feelings about being stopped and searched when put on the spot by the therapist, and his visible agitation might be due to feeling somewhat embarrassed or humiliated in not being able to articulate his internal mental state. Instead, he attempts to provide a rationalisation of the motivations of the police officers. The therapist then offers his own example of how he might feel if put in a similar situation to Mike. This facilitates another group member to mentalize how he and Mike might feel disrespected, which in turn frees Mike to admit that he feels angry. The therapist then highlights the feeling of being "disrespected" as a key feeling state that might trigger Mike's violence in general. The therapist does not take up the transference, as one might in psychoanalytic therapy (e.g., commenting that perhaps Mike feels humiliated by the therapist, or responding to the "jest" from Kevin about being middle class), as that would risk making the patient feel more humiliated.

In the group, the patients are encouraged to reflect on how they feel about recent violent incidents they have been involved in, or interpersonal situations that made them feel angry or upset. However, anger in the group is easily activated when a patient is attempting to describe an emotive topic, and the person might quickly become emotionally aroused and, not uncommonly or consciously, starts acting out the situation he is talking about in his bodily movements. The patient's emotional state has now shifted to bodily action, mentalization has temporarily ceased, and the therapist needs to intervene actively to shift the patients' attention back to focusing on internal states of mind by encouraging "step back" or "rewind" types of interventions. If the patient is too aroused, attention may be temporarily deflected away from him until he calms down by asking the other patients what they think, the therapists reflecting themselves on the situation, or, if the patient appears very angry or distressed, by changing the subject altogether until the group's affective temperature has lowered enough for some reflective capacity to be regained. The monthly individual sessions could also be useful in allowing the patients to air any difficulties that they are experiencing within the group, including tensions with other group members.

The stance of the therapist is an important component of MBT. This is generally more active than in traditional psychodynamic therapy, not only in that the MBT therapist will tend to say more, but also needs to actively convey a non-judgemental attitude. Although all therapists of every modality should be authentic, honest, respectful, and courteous with their patients, when working with patients with ASPD who exhibit extreme narcissistic sensitivity to perceived criticisms and disapproval, it is important for the therapist to actively avoid appearing opaque, hesitant, or secretive, which can make these patients feel more paranoid. Conventional psychoanalytic technical interventions, such as allowing silences, encouraging free association, and delivering transference interpretations, might make the patient with ASPD feel confused or humiliated and should be avoided (as in the above example of Mike). The therapist's basic default position is in trying to understand what is happening in the patient's mind while maintaining a "not-knowing" stance with a positive attitude. This is important, as it models a basic mentalization principle: that while we might think we have a good idea, we can never know for certain what is in another person's mind. This is challenging for individuals with

ASPD, who, when thinking in psychic equivalence mode, very often assume that they do know exactly what the other person is thinking, often in a paranoid way: for example, that they "know" that the other person hates them or looks down on them. The fact that there are two therapists running the group, who at times might express different ideas or opinions without leading to a confrontation, is also helpful in modelling another principle of mentalization, that of generating and tolerating different perspectives.

Power, control, and boundaries

Patients with ASPD experience relationships with others according to a paradigm of power and control, domination and submission, predator and prey, and any notion of intimate attachment to another person in which both partners are equal and make compromises according to the other's needs is alien. This paradigm will inevitably influence their relationship with the therapist, who might be experienced as an authority figure to be rebelled against. Many individuals with ASPD distrust parental figures and institutions of authority, often based on their earlier experiences of being unfairly treated by their own caregivers, but, at the same time, often belong to groups such as gangs or organised criminal syndicates which are in opposition to societal authority but have their own strict internal hierarchical structures, codes of honour, and leaders. Although the antisocial person will defy the laws of society with no apparent compunction, breaking their own internal code of conduct might induce feelings of shame and wrongdoing in the individual.

Developing a code of conduct, with appropriate rules and boundaries in relation to each other, is a key task of any therapeutic group in order for its members to function together effectively, but can become a central feature in groups for ASPD. It is important that the therapists do not impose their own code of conduct on the group, but first establish the patients' moral values, sense of responsibility, and fairness. Although the overt reason for each patient's referral has been for acts of violence that have been deemed problematic, the therapist must appear neither to condemn nor condone his offences, but instead maintain a benign attitude of attempting to understand the patient's internal state of mind and mental precursors of violence. This is, of course, consistent with one of the fundamental principles of forensic psychotherapy, which is not to condone the crime or excuse the criminal, but to gradually help the offender understand his internal motivations and accept responsibility for his acts (Welldon, 2011).

The group therapists must set the group rules in order for the group to feel safe, but must also permit the expression of anti-authoritarian attitudes without these becoming destructive to the group, as the person with ASPD will inevitably react against whatever rules he feels are imposed upon him. If the therapists are identified as agents of social control, arbitrarily imposing "socially acceptable" rules and regulations, the patients will inevitably oppose this and therapeutic work becomes impossible. The therapists should be able to explain the rationale behind the group's structure and boundaries, and make clear that these are recommendations made for their benefit from our experience of running groups, rather than rules that we are enforcing for no good reason. For example, while most of the patients readily accept the rule that there should be no violence in the group or clinic, they find it more difficult to accept the recommendation that group members should not meet up outside of sessions. Although we give them a variety of explanations as to why this is discouraged, such as the formation of sub-groups of patients from which others might feel excluded, the dilution of therapeutic efficacy within the group, and the risk that patients might disagree and have a confrontation externally without the possibility of any intervention from the therapists and containment of the group, which might lead to patients not wishing to return to the group, patients often do not accept these intellectual rationalisations until they have experienced the deleterious effects themselves. In practice, we have adopted a flexible stance in which we allow the patients to congregate on the porch of the clinic to have a cigarette and brief chat after the group session finishes, but discourage more extensive contact with each other outside of the group.

A critical role for the therapists is to carry a patient's alien self, that is, all the aspects of the patient associated with weakness and vulnerability that he abhors, disavows, and projects into others. The therapists might need to accept being perceived as weak or ineffectual for a long time until the patient feels safe and contained and these projected aspects can be talked about. All of the patients in our group readily identify threats to their self-esteem, being "disrespected" by others, and the resulting unbearable feeling of shame, as common triggers to their violence. As noted above, transference interpretations should be avoided, as these can also stimulate feelings of humiliation where the therapist is perceived as elevating himself to a position of importance in relation to the patient. Instead, the therapist should readily apologise for perceived errors and accept criticism to counteract the patient's expectations that the therapists hold all the power. Here, differences in the ways in which the patients relate to the male and female therapists could reveal gender prejudices that inform the power differential in their relationships and the construction of their codes of honour, such as the prohibition against violence towards women. Our patients appear to experience the female therapist as more vulnerable and less authoritative than her male counterpart, and have even discussed how they would protect her should she be attacked! At the same time, they appear less comfortable at having individual sessions with her than with the male therapist, which might be a manifestation of their unconscious anger and ambivalence towards women and maternal figures, based on earlier personal experience.

Managing risks and anxieties

The most obvious risk to be managed in offering a service to patients with ASPD is that of violence. During the assessment phase, we conduct a careful risk assessment, including a full consideration of their forensic history and criminal record, as well as a formal assessment of their risk of violence using the HCR-20 (Historical Clinical Risk-20; Webster, Douglas, Eaves, & Hart, 1997), which includes a measure of psychopathy with the PCL-R (Psychopathy Checklist-Revised; Hare & Wong, 2003). As noted above, patients with very high psychopathy scores, which are associated with an increased risk of violence towards others, are excluded from treatment. At the assessment stage, the therapists will make contact with the patient's GP and other mental health services involved with the patient, such as the patient's community mental health team or forensic psychiatric service, to establish where the patient may be referred to in an emergency if his mental state breaks down, given that the Portman Clinic is not an inpatient facility. It is helpful if external psychiatric support can be ongoing, even if the patient is seen infrequently, to provide external support not only for the overall containment of the patient and the risks that he poses, but also to manage the anxieties of the therapists working directly with these patients. However, this model of care is no longer so tenable with the fragmentation of mental health services in recent years, and we are finding that we are often the only mental health service willing to have active involvement with the ASPD patients. For this reason, there is another consultant psychiatrist in the Portman Clinic who is available to see the patients individually for crisis review, the prescribing of medication, and risk management where necessary, although to date, the patients have not needed to see her.

Some of the patients will also be managed by criminal justice agencies, such as the probation service or Multi-Agency Public Protection Arrangements (MAPPA), that we may be required to liaise with while respecting the patient's confidentiality. We have found that the ASPD patients appear reassured by our policy of not reporting the content of sessions to external agencies unless we consider there to be a current and serious risk of harm to themselves or others (which has not occurred to date). This allows them to feel freer in discussing their violent fantasies and actions in the group without the risk of routine disclosure, but to feel contained by knowing that we will impose a boundary if necessary. This is also again consistent with a basic mentalizing stance in which the therapist does not condone or collude with the patient's violent state of mind in a mode of psychic equivalence, but can offer a different viewpoint, which might occasionally necessitate acting by informing others of the patient's risk.

Ongoing assessment of risk is monitored in the content of each group session, as well as in the monthly individual sessions, and also with the Overt Aggression Scale (OAS) measure which the patients complete fortnightly at the end of the group session, reporting thoughts and acts of violence towards others and self over the past two weeks. The OAS is very useful in also being able to monitor the patients' suicide risk, a risk that is often overlooked in relation to the more obvious risk of violence towards others, but one that might be very serious. As we have seen, patients with ASPD often find it shameful to admit to feelings of depression, let alone suicidality, in front of others, instead often maintaining a front of aggressive bravado within the group. Preliminary results using the OAS as an outcome measure show that the patients' reported levels of violence externally decrease quite quickly within several months of starting treatment, while their feelings of irritability remain more constant. This suggests that the patients appear to be fairly quickly contained by entering therapy and able to control their violence more, but that the process of mentalization and encouraging them to reflect on their internal states, particularly negative feelings, is arduous and makes them feel more internally agitated. In our experience, new members are initially wary of disagreeing with other patients in the group, and any irritability (often expressed in their voiced dissatisfaction with some element of the treatment programme, for example, that an hour is too short for the group session) is directed towards the therapists, who are unconsciously perceived as safer targets for their aggression. As the group members get to know each other, however, they begin to feel safer in challenging each other, which has led at times to verbal disputes and patients storming out, but returning to subsequent sessions in which the antecedents to the patients' anger can be examined.

To date, we have had only one violent episode in a group session, when a patient became agitated, stood up, and kicked a piece of furniture before leaving the session and the building in anger. It appears that the patients are more likely not to attend the group, rather than become violent within the treatment setting. If a patient does become aroused and angry within a group session, the therapists may intervene in a variety of ways to avert the threat of violence. If possible, the therapists should employ a "stop, rewind, explore" mentalizing intervention (Bateman & Fonagy, 2006) in which the therapist stops the discussion, takes control of the group, and insists that the session rewinds to the point at which constructive interaction was taking place, and then to trace exactly what happened to trigger the aggressive reaction. Attention may be deflected from the aroused patient to asking the other patients to comment on what they think happened in the group discussion that upset their fellow group member, or if the atmosphere is too heated, temporarily changing the subject altogether until the patient or group calms down sufficiently to be able to reflect on what made him so angry. Although, at the time, changing the subject might be felt by the therapist to be an avoidance of dealing with a difficult issue, on some occasions it is important to do this quickly to allow space for the patients' level of arousal to decrease so that they are later able to revisit the more emotive topic of discussion later in the session. If the patient attempts to leave the session, he should be allowed to do so rather than be persuaded to stay, as he might be anxious that if he is forced to stay he will become violent within the group, and his leaving therefore protects the group from his aggression.

The decision to have two therapists in the group was partially based on considerations of risk, particularly the risk to a single female therapist in a group of violent men, but represents a departure from the Portman tradition of single therapist groups. As described in Chapter Five, this tradition is based on Welldon's experience of the pre-oedipal level of functioning of perverse and violent patients which manifests itself in the group's unconscious envious attack on any notion of an oedipal couple enacted in their attempt to split the two therapists apart. She describes how such patients recreate the primal scene in a very concrete way in their fantasy of the relationship that exists between the co-therapists, whose skills at containing the group's primitive anxieties, intense envy, and destructive impulses might not withstand the patients' own skills in splitting the two therapists (Welldon, 2011). In the ASPD group, perhaps because we are constantly vigilant to the potential for the patients' destruction of co-therapeutic functioning and thus strive to work together constructively while being respectful of differences in our opinions and therapeutic style, working together has proved effective to date. The patients' perceptions of the male therapist as being more forthright and in charge, and the female therapist as gentler and more maternal, yet correspondingly less effectual, reflects a conscious model of a parental couple that can be tolerated and protects them from more unconscious fears of an omnipotent, controlling, and non-caring maternal object (based on their early historical experiences) which might be more evident, with a corresponding increased risk of violent enactment, were there to be a sole female therapist.

Breaks in treatment are particularly sensitive times for these patients and are associated with an increased risk of acting out. The potential impact of the therapists' absence on patients with ASPD might be underestimated due to the erratic attendance of the patients themselves and their denial of attachment needs. However, it is important not to collude with the patient's conscious rejection of his need for treatment, and be alert to the patient becoming more disturbed during breaks in treatment, which he might not be able to acknowledge consciously. This is another example of the usefulness in having two therapists in the group, one of whom can still be present when the other takes leave, so that overall breaks in the treatment programme are minimised.

Finally, the importance of the containment provided by the institutional setting of the wider clinic and its host trust should be stressed as being an essential structural element of managing the risks and anxieties of both patients and staff. Although MBT is a new model of therapy that we have introduced to the Portman Clinic, the success of its implementation is dependent upon its integration within an older, wider psychoanalytic model of containment influenced by Winnicott and Bion, from which it derives (Yakeley, 2012). This is a model of containment in which the totality of the treatment setting has within it reflective spaces at many levels, where the patients' violent actions and their underlying affects, defences, and fantasies, and the corresponding complex and disturbing countertransference reactions in the therapists may be thought about and processed. The group therapists themselves constitute the first layer of containment by their mentalizing functions, providing an intermediary or transitional space where violent actions can be thought about, and feelings and thoughts can be played with. At the same time, they act as containers of the patients' unmanageable affects until these can be processed and fed back to the patient in a more manageable form. A second critical layer of mentalization and containment is provided by other minds external to the immediacy of the therapeutic encounter: for the patients, this is available in access to their case manager within the clinic, or to their psychiatrists and health workers externally; for the therapists, this is provided in the help of an external supervisor who can objectively review the video-recordings of the sessions, as well as the many different reflective meetings that exist at the Portman Clinic to support all of the therapeutic work, and which are invaluable in aiding the therapists in processing their countertransferential responses. These alternative perspectives offered by other people and forums act to triangulate the therapeutic experience by providing what might be thought of as a paternal function, in conjunction with the maternal aspects of the therapy (which include the experienced and thoughtful administrative staff and receptionists who greet the patients, as well as the physical building itself—"the brick mother"—

experienced by the patients as a concretisation of their wish for care and protection) to create a more healthy parental couple that can think together constructively about the patients, an experience that most have never had.

Conclusion

The introduction of MBT to the Portman Clinic exposed some tensions and anxieties within the staff group. For some, the MBT ASPD programme seemed like a radical departure from the traditional psychoanalytic psychotherapy practised at the Portman Clinic (even the word "programme" was anathema for those who oppose any structured, time-limited intervention). These criticisms and anxieties appeared more due to a fear of change than based on any rigorous analysis of the theory and technique of MBT, in which there are, in fact, many points of convergence with psychoanalytic psychotherapy, not surprisingly, perhaps, given that MBT emerged firmly out of a psychoanalytic model. Fonagy and Bateman (2010) describe the history of MBT and its roots in psychoanalytic theory and practice, and how the model has been influenced by the writings of psychoanalysts working with borderline and narcissistic pathology, such as Bion, Glasser, Green, Kernberg, Mahler, Racker, Rosenfeld, and Winnicott, as well as developmental work with children carried out at the Anna Freud Centre. As we have seen, although there are some marked differences in specific technique between MBT group therapy and more traditional group analytic therapy, the fact that the main vehicle for treatment is the group setting is consistent with Welldon's ideas that violent patients are best treated within a group.

It should also be emphasised that MBT has been developed specifically for patients with BPD, and that we aim to adapt the model for another specific group of patients, those with ASPD, whose psychopathology is similarly based in a disorder of attachment, and who are widely thought not to be treatable with traditional psychoanalytic psychotherapy (Meloy & Yakeley, 2010). Our treatment programme in which the core treatment of MBT is embedded within a wider psychoanalytic model of containment can be thought of as akin to a therapeutic community in which different modalities of treatment are delivered (e.g., CBT, MBT, art therapy, etc.) within the overall democratic and group orientated therapeutic community setting, which is also based on a psychoanalytic model.

Although the ASPD service at the Portman is still in the early stages of development, patients who are thought to be too risky to be seen by general community mental health services, or who have a diagnosis that other clinicians do not wish to treat, are attending the group regularly and are reporting benefit. The words of one group member, a "lifer" on parole for the murder of a man many years previously, conveys the containment that the treatment offers: "The clinic is the one place I feel safe to vent my feelings, I can get things off my chest here which I can't talk about to anyone outside, which makes me better."

References

Allen, J. G., Fonagy, P., & Bateman, A. (2008). *Mentalizing in Clinical Practice*. Washington, DC: American Psychiatric Press.

American Psychiatric Association (APA) (1994). *Diagnostic and Statistical Manual of Mental Disorders, 4th edition, Text Revision*. Washington, DC: American Psychiatric Association, 2000.

Bateman, A., & Fonagy, P. (2004). *Psychotherapy for Borderline Personality Disorder: Mentalization-based Treatment*. Oxford: Oxford University Press.

Bateman, A., & Fonagy, P. (2006). *Mentalization-based Treatment for Borderline Personality Disorder: A Practical Guide*. Oxford: Oxford University Press.

Bateman, A., & Fonagy, P. (2008). Co-morbid antisocial and borderline personality disorders: mentalization-based treatment. *Journal of Clinical Psychology*, 64(2): 181–194.

Bateman, A., & Fonagy, P. (2011). Antisocial personality disorder. In: A. Bateman & P. Fonagy (Eds.), *Mentalizing in Mental Health Practice* (pp. 357–378). Washington, DC: APPI.

Bion, W. R. (1970). *Attention and Interpretation*. London: Karnac.

Bowlby, J. (1944). Forty-four juvenile thieves: their characters and home life. *International Journal of Psychoanalysis*, 25: 1–57, 207–228.

Caspi, A., McClay, J., Moffitt, T., Mill, J., Martin, J., Craig, I. W., Taylor, A., & Poulton, R. (2002). Role of genotype in the cycle of violence in maltreated children. *Science*, 297: 851–854.

Coccaro, E. F., Harvey, P. D., Kupsaw-Lawrence, E., Herbert, J. L., & Bernstein, D. P. (1991). Development of neuropharmacologically based behavioral assessments of impulsive aggressive behaviour. *Journal of Neuropsychiatry & Clinical Neurosciences, 3*(2): S44–51.

De Brito, S. A., & Hodgins, S. (2009). Antisocial personality disorder. In: M. McMurran & R. Howard (Eds.), *Personality, Personality Disorder and Violence* (pp. 133–155). Chichester: Wiley.

Department of Health (2003). *Personality Disorder – No Longer a Diagnosis of Exclusion*. London: Department of Health.

Felthous, A., & Sass, H. (2007). *International Handbook on Psychopathic Disorders and the Law*. New York: Wiley.

First, M. B., Spitzer, R. L., Gibbon, M., & Williams, J. B. W. (1997a). *Structured Clinical Interview for DSM-IV Axis II Personality Disorders (SCID-II)*. Washington, DC: American Psychiatric Press.

First, M. B., Spitzer, R. L., Gibbon, M., & Williams, J. B. W. (1997b). *Structured Clinical Interview for DSM -IV Axis I Disorders—Clinician Version (SCID-I)*. Washington, DC: American Psychiatric Press.

Fonagy, P., & Bateman, A. (2010). A brief history of mentalization-based treatment and its roots in psychoanalytic theory and practice. In: M. B. Heller & S. Pollett (Eds.), *The Work of Psychoanalysts in the Public Health Sector* (pp. 156–176). London: Routledge.

Fonagy, P., & Target, M. (1996). Playing with reality: I. Theory of mind and the normal development of psychic reality. *International Journal of Psychoanalysis, 77*: 217–233.

Fonagy, P., & Target, M. (2000). Playing with reality: III. The persistence of dual psychic reality in borderline patients. *International Journal of Psychoanalysis, 81*(5): 853–874.

Fonagy, P., & Target, M. (2007). Playing with reality: IV. A theory of external reality rooted in intersubjectivity. *International Journal of Psychoanalysis, 88*(4): 917–937.

Frodi, A., Dernevik, M., Sepa, A., Philipson, J., & Bragesjo, M. (2001). Current attachment representations of incarcerated offenders varying in degree of psychopathy. *Attachment and Human Development, 3*(3): 269–283.

Gibbon, S., Duggan, C., Stoffers, J., Huband, N., Völlm, B. A., Ferriter, M., & Lieb, K. (2010). Psychological interventions for antisocial personality disorder (review). *The Cochrane Collaboration*. The Cochrane Library, www.thecochranelibrary.com/view/0/index.html.

Gilligan, J. (1996). *Violence: Our Deadliest Epidemic and Its Causes*. New York: Grosset/Putnam.

Glasser, M. (1998). On violence: a preliminary communication. *International Journal of Psychoanalysis, 79*: 887–902.

Hare, R. (1991). *Manual of the Revised Psychopathy Checklist* (Toronto: Multi Health Systems).

Hare, R. D., & Wong, S. (2003). *Program Guidelines for the Institutional Treatment of Psychopaths*. Toronto: Multi-Health Systems.

Hodgins, S., Kratzer, L., & McNeil, T. F. (2001). Obstetric complications, parenting and risk of criminal behaviour. *Archives of General Psychiatry, 58*: 746–52.

Levinson, A., & Fonagy, P. (2004). Offending and attachment: the relationship between interpersonal awareness and offending in a prison population with psychiatric disorder. *Canadian Journal of Psychoanalysis, 12*: 225–251.

Meloy, J. R. (1992). *Violent Attachments*. Northvale, NJ: Jason Aronson.

Meloy, J. R. (2007). Antisocial personality disorder. In: G. O. Gabbard (Ed.), *Treatments of Psychiatric Disorders, Vol 2* (3rd edn) (pp. 775–790). Washington, DC: American Psychiatric Press.

Meloy, J. R., & Yakeley, J. (2010). Treatment of cluster B disorders: antisocial personality disorder. In: J. Clarkin, P. Fonagy, & G. Gabbard (Eds.), *Psychodynamic Psychotherapy for Personality Disorders: A Clinical Handbook* (pp. 349–378). Washington, DC: American Psychiatric Press.

Ministry of Justice (2008). *Arrests for Recorded Crime (Notifiable Offences) and the Operation of Certain Police Powers under PACE England and Wales 2006/07*. www.justice.gov.uk/docs/arrests-recorded-crime-engl-wales-2006-07.pdf.

National Institute for Health and Clinical Excellence (2009a). *Borderline Personality Disorder: Treatment, Management and Prevention. NICE Clinical Guideline 78*. London: NICE.

National Institute for Health and Clinical Excellence (2009b). *Antisocial Personality Disorder: Treatment, Management and Prevention. NICE Clinical Guideline 77*. London: NICE.

Norton, K., & McGauley, G. A. (1998). The counselling transaction. In: K. Norton & G. A. McGauley (Eds.), *Counselling Difficult Clients* (pp. 1–15). London: Sage.

Parsons, T. (1951). *The Social System*. Glencoe: Free Press.

Sarkar, J., & Adshead, G. (2006). Personality disorders as disorganization of attachment and affect regulation. *Advances in Psychiatric Treatment, 12*: 297–305.

Schore, A. (1996). Experience dependent maturation of a regulatory system in the orbital pre-frontal cortex and the origin of developmental psychopathology. *Development and Psychopathology, 8*: 59–87.

Schore, A. (2001). The effect of early relational trauma on right brain development, affect regulation and infant mental health. *Infant Mental Health Journal, 22*: 201–249.

Target, M., & Fonagy, P. (1996). Playing with reality: II. The development of psychic reality from a developmental perspective. *International Journal of Psychoanalysis, 77*: 459–479.

Van IJzendoorn, M. H., Feldbrugge, J. T. T. M., Derks, F. C. H., de Ruiter, C., Verhagen, M. F. M., Philipse, M. W. G., van der Staak, C. P. F., & Riksen-Walraven, J. M. A. (1997). Attachment representations of personality-disordered criminal offenders. *American Journal of Orthopsychiatry, 67*: 449–459.

Viding, E., Larsson, H., & Jones, A. P. (2008). Review. Quantitative genetic studies of antisocial behaviour. *Philosophical Transactions of the Royal Society of London B: Biological Sciences, 363*: 2519–2527.

Webster, C. D., Douglas, K. S., Eaves, D., & Hart, S. T. (1997). *HCR-20: Assessing Risk for Violence*, Version 2. Vancouver: Mental Health, Law and Policy Institute, Simon Fraser University.

Welldon, E. (1996). Group-analytic psychotherapy in an out-patient setting. In: C. Cordess & M. Cox (Eds.), *Forensic Psychotherapy: Crime, Psychodynamics and the Offender Patient* (pp. 63–82). London: Jessica Kingsley.

Welldon, E. (2011). *Playing with Dynamite*. London: Karnac.

Winnicott, D. W. (1956). The anti-social tendency. In: D. W. Winnicott (Ed.), *Through Paediatrics to Psychoanalysis* (pp. 306–315). London: Hogarth Press [reprinted London: Karnac, 1992].

Winnicott, D. W. (1971). *Playing and Reality*. London: Tavistock.

Winnicott, D. W. (1986). *Deprivation and Delinquency*. London: Tavistock.

World Health Organization (WHO) (1992). *International Classification of Mental and Behavioural Disorders, Tenth Edition (ICD-10)*. Geneva: WHO.

Yakeley, J. (2012). Treating the untreatable: the evolution of a psychoanalytically-informed service for antisocial personality disorder. In: A. Lemma (Ed.), *Contemporary Developments in Adult and Young Adult Therapy. The Work of the Tavistock and Portman Clinics, Volume 1* (pp. 179–204). London: Karnac.

CHAPTER NINE

The invisible men: forensic group therapy with people with intellectual disabilities

Alan Corbett

Introduction

This chapter seeks to illustrate the particular use made of a forensic psychoanalytic group by people with intellectual disabilities. I contextualise "disability therapy" within the psychodynamic frame, and examine some of the reasons why psychoanalysis with patients with disabilities has rarely been addressed within psychoanalytic history. I use material from the life of a forensic group for men with intellectual disabilities to examine some key clinical themes that accompany work with people with cognitive deficits, and conclude with some thoughts about the future of forensic group analysis with such patients. The material I examine in this chapter comes from a four-year group I conducted under the clinical supervision of Earl Hopper. Dr Hopper's understanding of group and social unconscious processes (Hopper, 2003) became key to my ability to hold in mind experiences of disability, trauma, and abuse that, at times, felt unbearably painful.

History of disability therapy

The birth of psychologically informed assessment and treatment of people with intellectual disabilities can be traced to the "wild boy of Aveyron" (Itard, 1932, Seguin, 1856), an early case that should have presaged the blossoming of psychotherapy for patients with disabilities. Instead, however, it stands in isolation within a history of psychotherapy in which patients with disabilities have been strikingly absent. We could argue that Freud's (1904a) dictum that "a certain measure of natural intelligence" was required of patients entering psychoanalysis provided his followers with a reason to exclude those without this certain measure from their consulting rooms. The dearth of clinical writing on intellectual disability throughout the twentieth century (certainly when compared with most other patient groups) should give us pause to consider how far their invisibility is due not so much to their intellectual failings as to our own. To encounter someone with an intellectual disability might evoke primitive fantasies about the contagion of disability—fears of close encounters with minds that do not work well enough. The world of psychoanalysis has tended to be one in which intelligence is prized extremely highly. Small surprise, then, if we, as a profession, have sought to shut the door on those who we fear might do something annihilatory to our capacity to think (Corbett, 2011).

As well as reflecting on the reasons for psychoanalytic psychotherapy with patients with intellectual disabilities being viewed with suspicion and fear, we must also remember that it has not been an entirely untried experiment. Alongside the other founding mothers of "disability therapy" (Corbett, 2009; Kahr, 2000), such as Dr Pat Frankish (Frankish, 1992; Frankish & Terry, 2003) and Baroness Hollins (Hollins & Esterhuyzen, 1997; Hollins & Sinason, 2000), Dr Valerie Sinason stands tall as the clinician who has done most to pioneer the use of psychoanalytic psychotherapy with patients with intellectual disabilities (Sinason, 1986, 1988a,b, 1990, 1991, 1992, 1995, 1996, 1997a,b, 2002). Her psychoanalytically informed—but broadly pluralistic—work enabled the formation of the Institute of Psychotherapy and Disability in 2000, a UKCP recognised organisation that exists to move psychotherapy with patients with intellectual disabilities from the margins to the centre of clinical practice.

What, then, of group analysis and intellectual disability? Like Freud before him, Foulkes appeared to view intellectual ability as a prerequisite for entry into group analytic treatment. In his four criteria for assessment, he specified "... intelligence not below average – preferably high" (Foulkes, 1964, p. 44), while also privileging the "potential social value of individual". When faced with these strictures, it is not difficult to see why men with intellectual disabilities who have committed sexual crime present a number of challenges to traditional thinking about the indications and contra-indications for group analysis.

In order to examine the use made by forensic patients of group analysis, I shall discuss aspects of a group conducted over a period of four years within a clinic providing specialised psychoanalytic treatment to intellectually disabled victims and perpetrators of sexual crime. I have disguised and altered all aspects of the group and its individual members in order to protect their confidentiality.

The men presented with a range of communication levels, levels of intellectual disability, and forensic history. This history included sexual abuse of children, suspected involvement in organised abuse, indecent assault, stalking of women, gross indecency, and the abuse of other male clients in respite, home, and day settings. The men referred had their own histories as victims of sexual abuse, a fact that should not be surprising when working with a forensic as well as a disabled population, both of whom present disproportionately high levels of childhood abuse, deprivation, and other significant trauma (Brown, Stein, & Turk, 1995; McCormack, Kavanagh, Caffrey, & Power, 2005; Sobsey, 1994).

Assessing the container

In assessing people with intellectual disabilities for group analysis, some key differences from mainstream analytic practice emerge. In common with forensic as opposed to mainstream group analytic practice (Doctor, 2003), one is assessing not only the internal world of the potential patient, but also analysing their external world to ensure it has the potential to contain and hold the patient through the lifetime of the group. This is particularly apposite with people with intellectual disabilities, many of whom live tightly regulated lives, often in group homes or other institutions, where they rely on the care of staff to facilitate their daily lives. We are, thus, considering the impact on forensic work of engaging with patients at the centre of often complex matrices of social and psychological support.

Just as the world of child psychotherapy has had to engage with parents and families of patients on a practical as well as a psychodynamic level, the world of disability therapy has to build a strong bridge into the residential and day care worlds of our patients. This ensures that those caring for the patient are briefed on the forensic work being undertaken, and given a parallel space in which the unconscious processes evoked in them through such close engagement with disability and sexual aggression are attended to. They will then be better prepared to think about the nature of analytic work, its engagement with the unconscious, and the ways in which defences might be strained and acting out might re-emerge through the course of therapy. Foulkes (1975) has already stressed the importance of solid therapeutic administration, a point further developed by Woods (2003) in his examination of group therapy for adolescents who have abused.

In order to attend to the frame in which the men lived, my colleagues and I conducted assessment sessions with professionals such as their social workers, and the residential key workers involved in their daily care. In addition to ascertaining the level of support available to the men during their time in the group, the assessment sessions with their carers took on a therapeutic hue, with a key question being posed: "How does this person make you feel?" The answers given revealed strongly polarised reactions of hatred and love, denigration, minimisation, fear, and envy. Envy of the men would sometimes be couched in terms such as, "They're getting so much—a place to live, this therapy. What about us as workers—what do we ever get given?" More frequently, direct criticism of the men would be contained within a more acceptable hatred of their abusive actions. The assessing team formed a judgement as to whether it was wisest to accept such statements at face value (hating the sin rather than the sinner), or to attempt to drill down beneath them, to wonder about the murderous rage felt towards the man himself, and not just at his actions. These judgements were predicated on an assessment of the ego strength of the individual worker and, importantly, of their holding environment. In those with sufficient ego strength, the statement "Perhaps you sometimes feel strong feelings of hate towards the man you're paid to care for?" could be responded to with an open acknowledgement and, indeed, with relief. Without it, the response was a shutting down, a disavowal, and a sense of outrage that such a presumption could be made. Such a failure to think, to reflect, or to dare to look at the deep ambivalence that is inevitably evoked by working with men who embody damage and destruction is an important indicator of a lack of reflective functioning. Splitting and the concretisation of murderous rage into murderous actions were issues to be tackled not only in the primary patient's therapy, but also in the work done with the staff in their circles of support, who could so easily oscillate between objectifying their clients, and feeling objectified by them.

Assessing the three core conflicts

Assessing the men themselves took many months, due not only to the poor levels of verbal communication and comprehension exhibited by some of them, but also, more importantly, because of our desire to gain insight into what Hollins and Sinason (2000) have described as the three core conflicts at the heart of psychotherapy with patients with intellectual disabilities:

1. Disability
2. Sexuality
3. Mortality.

With each man, we were seeking to think with them about their relationship with their disability and what it meant to them to be different from most of the rest of the world, sexuality, not just in relation to their forensic enactments, but also how possible it was for them to think about sex as a creative, non-destructive force, and mortality: how able were they to think about their life and their eventual death, how symbolically could they think about their place in the world?

When asked to reflect on the reasons he thought he had been referred to the group, one man said, "I think it [the group] will be special ... I'm coming because I'm a slow learner. Well, I'm really a quick learner but I think it takes me a long time to respond." He then talked about one of his victims as having Down's Syndrome, and seemed to struggle with understanding why he was sexually attracted to a condition that also filled him with revulsion and fear. There was a point at which his insight appeared to run out, and he fell back on a more familiar projection of his hatred of his disability into his victim: "I hope there won't be any spastics in this group. I don't want to be anywhere near them." This man oscillated between a desire to enter the group and a paralysing fear of what further disabilities it might uncover in him. This raised the knotty question of consent when working with forensic patients, and the need to be mindful of the imbalance of power between a clinician and a patient who occupies the lowest rung of society's ladder. The traditional markers of consent (explaining the proposed treatment, outlining alternatives, and explaining the risks and benefits) are, of course, more difficult to negotiate when assessing people with intellectual disabilities, and tend to dictate a much slower, more thoughtful and gradual assessment process (Appelbaum, 1997; Arscott, Dagnan, & Stenfert Kroese, 1999; Goddard, Murray, & Simpson, 2007; Murphy & O'Callaghan, 2004; O'Neill, 1998).

Early phases

The first phase of the group's life was preoccupied with who all the men were and what they had done. The men found it difficult to stay with any exploration of their history of abusing, and there was much more heat generated by a group disclosure of their experiences as victims of sexual and physical abuse. This led to a discussion about who in the group had ever been locked up or been in prison, with a fiercely competitive edge to this discussion, prefiguring a wider theme of competition and envy that ran throughout the life of the group. This led to a discussion about birth, with the following exchange serving to illustrate the men's difficulties with symbolisation and concrete thinking:

A: I was in my mum's womb.

B: So was I.

A: No, it was just me.

Given the large number of group members (it began with ten members, and three therapists. A year later this had become a core group of six, with one therapist), it is unsurprising that some of the men were quiet, almost invisible, in this first session. What was also striking was the tendency of the men to transmute their experiences of sexual abuse and abusing into other events. One man began to talk about his myriad experiences of being anally raped as a child by neighbours. Early on, he substituted the word "burglary" for "buggery", gradually convincing the group that as a child he had been burgled repeatedly. This confused some of the men, although others seemed to hear it in as symbolic a way as the therapists did, and understood him to be describing shattering experiences of being entered into against his will and being stolen from emotionally, physically, and sexually. Another man talked about his experiences of abusing children using the language of fire setting, using another crime to diffuse some of the shame he felt at what he had done to children. With this man, it became important for the therapists to intrude upon this, as the symbolic became concrete and he seemed to be seeking to delude the rest of the group into thinking he was an arsonist and not a child abuser. This was a difficult moment to manage therapeutically, mindful as the therapists were of the need to give space to the symbolic and also the need for the group to know that reality had a pivotal place here, too, particularly in relation to the first voicing of their crimes to each other.

Another man regaled the group with accounts of his sexual experiences that seemed designed to titillate and frustrate the rest of the group. As the group progressed, he appeared to only really engage when there was an opportunity to be sadistic to other group members. Some of the men talked about the power they exercised over women, and it was noted how rare this feeling must be, how fleetingly must they ever feel a real sense of power in any other part of their lives. The denigration of women in this group was often painful to hear, with women sometimes being described as sexual terrorists, wearing miniskirts as an invitation to rape. Another man spoke about his hatred of children for, in his view, provoking him with their youthful bodies. He spoke about wanting to wire his front door bell so that it gave them electric shocks when they rang at his door, and spoke of this in a gleeful, aroused state, betraying the sadomasochism that underpinned his connections with the world.

One man, who was at the more severe end of the disability spectrum, brought in many child-like props, toys and children's annuals, inviting the other men to admire them. An early sign of group cohesion was another man's refusal to collude in this dynamic, saying instead he thought it was wrong that a grown man was so interested in children's things. This presented the group with an immensely difficult and painful dilemma. To agree with this man's accuser would be to split off a child-like, regressed part of themselves. The speed with which the group approached this level of material should be noted, alongside an extremely accelerated process of group disclosure. In the third session, one of the men talked about two of his experiences of suicide attempts, prompting many of the group members to list their own various attempts to kill themselves. At the end of this, one man showed the group newspaper cuttings he had collected during the week about a heart transplant, as if unconsciously asking whether the group has a heart that works. The heart, in its various manifestations, became a recurring motif throughout the group's life, one that was rich in symbolic value.

I wish now to present a disguised account of one session that occurred in the third year of the group's life in order to provide a sense of the often chaotic and fragmented nature of this group's functioning, and the pockets of insight and integration that were able to emerge.

Group excerpt

The group began with just three men. They spoke about a documentary one of them had seen about the ambulance service. The part of London in which the clinic was located was shown on the programme, and some of the programme was about ambulance staff going on strike. I linked this to the coming break, the unconscious fantasy being that I was myself going on strike for a while. This triggered some discussion about the break, the talk becoming more concrete as dates were exchanged and queried. One man wrote the date of the last session before the break in his diary, saying he would most certainly be there for that. A discussion followed about what this final group would be like. I commented on this, wondering how possible it might be to talk about what the break itself might be like. As some of the men began to talk about this, a latecomer arrived, followed by two more, who were greeted with a round of applause from the rest of the group. One of the late comers announced that he was in love with a man outside the group, and they might move in together. The group lapsed into an awkward silence. I said that he seemed to have brought up something that had always been hard for the men to talk or think about—homosexuality. Another man asked the man to repeat what he had said, as he did not think he had heard it correctly. The man did. The other man said that the thought of men having sex together made him feel sick, and that he did not understand "queer people". I said how I was struck by this, and remembered how he had talked in the past about wanting to have sex with a fourteen-year-old boy. This provoked an argument between two of the men about this, an argument that lasted some time.

The man who had earlier disclosed his romantic relationship then said that he had been thinking about coming to the group in drag in the session before the break, but had decided instead to enter the group as a famous racing driver. Another man said he had a great surprise for the group that he would bring to the session preceding the break. This provoked a torrent of excited questions from the group, with the man finally saying that he planned to come into the group dressed as a woman. He then took a Barbie doll from his bag. The doll was passed around the group. I commented on the notion of femininity coming into this men's group. The man who had talked about wearing drag for the pre-break group looked immensely emotional at this point. Another man said he thought this conversation was disgusting. This provoked a loud outcry from the remainder of the group, with people saying they were sick of hearing this man. I found it difficult to make myself heard amid this outcry and, as the clamour subsided, said I was struck by how easy it was for the group to gang up on this man. A tremendously protective countertransference response was evoked in me, and it felt as if I were witnessing an act of abuse being perpetrated by a mob. Unfortunately, the scapegoated man had a tendency to elicit aggression, and he began to shout the word "Sex!" loudly, thus incurring yet more disdain from his peers. "Shut your cakehole!" yelled one of them as his shouts grew louder.

One man asked me what I was going to do about the man shouting "Sex!" Would I expel him? Some of the other group members echoed this question, saying they were sick of him. I struggled to keep alive in the group mind an understanding that the scapegoating of the shouting man was partly to do with wanting to expel sex from the group—he was actually articulating the main reason why the group existed. I found myself growing angry at this point, and, triggered partly by my wish to defend the scapegoated man, I went into a kind of lecture mode, pointing out to the men they were here because they had been in trouble, and now they were trying to put into someone else the bad, unacceptable parts of themselves.

A quieter, more reflective man (who had brought in the Barbie doll) said that no one actually knew why the man who had shouted was in the group. Another group member asked the man who had shouted to say explicitly why he was here. He refused at first, before gradually disclosing that he was here for having sex with a child. The group appeared much relieved at this disclosure, with one man shouting "Hallelujah!" I said I thought the group had worked extremely hard, and the man himself had been working hard for many weeks by shouting the word sex as a way of really bringing it, and what he had done, into the group. Another man nodded slowly, saying that he found this hard to listen to. He then said that he himself had struggled with terrible sexual feelings during the week. Another man agreed, saying he had not slept since the last group meeting because of his thoughts about children.

I spoke here about the fact that we were hearing more about the reality of people's lives. There had been much excitement about the pre-break group, much talk about dressing up as someone else, and perhaps this had disguised the deep worries the men were holding about the break, and how frightened they were about their sexual feelings.

One man said that he was worried, as he had been thinking about the naughty children who had got him into trouble. The children had rung his doorbell at 8 p.m., midnight, and 5 a.m. Rather than taking up the concrete reality (I knew that this man actually did not have a doorbell), I wondered aloud about the symbolism of what he was saying—perhaps it was similar to what others had been saying about being troubled by sexual thoughts about children almost constantly.

A man said that the previous weekend he had been very upset and had absconded from his home. He was vague about how long he had been gone and said he had eventually been found by the police with fifty pairs of gloves and a tube of KY jelly. When he finished saying this, he put his head in his hands and sighed heavily. I commented on his bravery in sharing this with the group. Another man asked what the gloves were for. There were a few moments of tension after this. Another man broke the silence with "Well, I was abused last night. I was. Some man abused me, he did." This was followed by a group silence, in which I was aware of my own scepticism about this story, as this man often seemed to bring in dramatic stories which turned out to be fantasy. As I was reflecting on this, I noticed, for the first time, a look of terrible sadness on this man's face at the lack of any response from the group. I then said, "That sounds terrible." He nodded in a detached, hopeless kind of way.

Someone had brought in a letter addressed to me from their key worker. I read it out to the group: "To whom it may concern—please get X to talk re: sexual behaviours". There was a brief silence, and conversation returned to what the gloves were for. The man then explained he liked to wear gloves while he masturbated. As he said this, he pulled his jumper up over his head, like a kind of glove, or condom, hiding him from view.

Another man suddenly said to me, "You've got a wife." This provoked much laughter in the group. Before I could make any kind of interpretation, another man said he thought it would be good for the group to talk about light bulbs and how they flash whenever you had a naughty thought. Another man stuck his thumb in the air at that point, and then started to tap at his chest, saying that he often got heart pains. Many of the men in the group said at this point that they also got pains in their heart. One man grabbed a large sheet of paper and drew the outline of a heart. He said he wanted to write his name on the drawing but did not know how to spell it. Some of the group members offered to help him with this, leading to the group eventually having all of their names written inside the outline of the heart. As we all sat looking at the finished piece of work lying in the centre of the room, the men said they wanted to write other words on the sheet. As the group ended we looked again at the sheet with its drawing of a heart, its list of the men's names (rather scruffily written, with much scribbling out and many corrections) and, around them, words such as Feelings, Sad, Scared, Lonely, Worried. The group ended with silence, a rare occurrence for this group of men who so often filled the room with movement, laughter, shouting, and the white noise of anxiety. This silence felt somehow more of a silence of processing, an acknowledgement of the enormous symbolic task they had begun through their use of the picture of the heart.

Discussion

This vignette serves to illustrate, among other things, the ways in which forensic patients with intellectual disabilities can access deeply unconscious material that touches on their core experiences of fear of annihilation, sexual aggression as a defence against loss and pain, and the perverse search for attachment through acts of sexual abuse. In seeking to facilitate a process by which these men could gradually give voice to their pain rather than inflict it on their victims, a complex group transference had to be played out in which the ability to think, feel, and mourn could emerge from their defences of concrete thinking and perverse sexualities. I came to think that this could most authentically happen through a painful process of projection into me as the container of the group's fury, envy, hatred, and, crucially, disability. It was through my work with this group that the notion of the Disability Transference (Corbett, 2009, 2011) first began to develop. This concept refers to the ways in which the therapist's countertransference can hold intensely powerful projections of disability. On occasion within this session, I found myself relating to the material in ways that meant it was impossible to think, form words, understand what people were saying, and hold a true sense of time and space. The men's experiences of early trauma and of having minds that did not function in conventional ways conflated to form a powerful projective experience that threatened not only to place me in the position of powerless abused victim, but also that of traumatised, non-thinking, disabled other. This transferential response can also be experienced with a vivid power in individual analytic work but appears to be more intense in a group context.

A core countertransferential phenomenon was one of hysterical and barely suppressed laughter. These dangerous, vulnerable, damaged, and damaging men often spoke in surreal twists, voicing childlike views of the world alongside worryingly adult sexualised and perverse stances. Each of the therapists involved in the first year of the group reported terrible fears that they might laugh out loud at something absurd said by the men, thus humiliating and belittling them. Laughter served so many evolving functions through the life of the group: sometimes a manic defence when fears of castration and annihilation became too unbearable, at other times a more congruent glue between the men, particularly towards the end of the group, where a process of mentalization (Fonagy, Gergely, Jurist, & Target, 2004) could more clearly be seen to have occurred, and where pain, love, and failed dependency were easier for the men to withstand and survive.

The group member shouting "sex" had assumed the voice of polarity many months before this session. He tended to place his chair nearer the wall than nearer his group colleagues, and he interacted minimally with them. He voiced a paranoid–schizoid (Klein, 1946) view of his offences, saying repeatedly "it was wrong", and that he would never do it again, and rarely stopping to reflect on any of the complexities of his forensic history. He was also, through his frequent accusatory shouting of "sex", the most forthright in the group in claiming that sex itself was wrong, and dirty. He was a vivid reminder of Sinason's (1992) development of Wolfensberger's (1987) notion of "death-making". In this, Sinason explores people with disabilities' unconscious sense of sex as something that can result in the creation of something damaged and abnormal. Thus, sex becomes more about death and damage than life and joy. Throughout the life of the group, this man found it impossible not to place himself in a position that invited ridicule, aggression, and hatred. He would bring in a cassette, asking to tape-record the group, or an empty sheet, saying "Can we put sex on to this?" This request seemed to baffle the group until one of the therapists interpreted it as a question about whether the group is allowed to be a sexual place, where sex can be thought about and spoken of. Is it possible to talk about and wonder about sex in the group? His anti-group (Nitsun, 1996) valency became something that could be used for the benefit of the group.

What simmers underneath this session (and is expressed more explicitly in later sessions) was the men's rage at having to be escorted everywhere, of having to have twenty-four-hour supervision. This violation of their human rights is too often seen in the lives of people with intellectual disabilities; we are talking here about a patient population upon whom forms of incarceration can be imposed without any due legal process. This was related to by some of the men alongside their fears of being in the outside world, full, as it was for them, of the temptation of men, women, and children. At the heart of this was a deep ambivalence about attachment coming from these men who so often thought of themselves as unloved and unloving, men whom someone would only wish to be close to if they were being paid.

From early on, the group voiced its anxieties as to whether the group would be a safe place in comparison with the outside, threatening world. Glasser's (1979) concept of the core complex became a useful notion with which to understand the men's constant wondering as to whether it is ever possible to be safe when enjoying intimacy. This oscillation between a longing for and a fear of intimacy was felt most acutely in transferential terms, and in the countertransference, too. As the sole therapist left after the first year of treatment, I sometimes found myself wanting to run away from the barbarity of the men's histories, behaviours, and disabilities, while also feeling drawn in by a strong sense of curiosity and fascination.

One can see from the closing moments of this session that a strong heart was needed for and by the group. For much of the group's life, any absences or lateness seemed to throw the men into a state of confusion and bafflement, as if the group's heart could very easily stop beating, revealing how tightly gripped they were by annihilation anxieties (Freud, 1926d). Bomb threats in London occupied many groups, with absences in the group being ascribed to terrorist outrages, revealing the group terror of the outside world as a place of attack and death. When one man missed a session, the group immediately presumed something catastrophic had happened to him, with someone seeming to remember (wrongly) that this missing man had complained of pains in his chest, before moving on to remember that in the previous week's session he had talked openly about his sexual attraction towards children, and that this could be his reason for not returning. The group's anxiety intensified as his absence grew by another week, with the group debating whether he had committed suicide. This also led them to wonder who would take his place in the group, with an increasing fantasy existing that he was, in fact, the leader of the group, and a new one was now needed. An inordinate amount of time would be spent trying to work out which of the men were missing, with names getting forgotten and, in more than one session, a non-existent (missing) member of the group being invented. This invisible man seemed to fascinate the group, with several of the men ascribing to him all sorts of qualities that were highly prized—an ability to talk articulately, as well as an ability to be very honest about his feelings, and about things he had done. He became, over the life of the group, an object of yearning for the men (if they could only be like him, their disabilities and their perversions would fall away), while also being an object of fear. If they were to become him, they would no longer need the group and they would have to leave, to become invisible again.

Conclusion

The focus of this paper has been upon forensic group therapy with men, which has allowed little space for the consideration of forensic group therapy with women. This should not be read as a denial of the capacity of women to enact sexually perverse and aggressive acts upon others, or as a statement about women's capacity to engage in forensic group analysis (Motz, 2001; Welldon, 1988; Welldon, 2011). It is my hope and expectation that future clinical papers will examine the development of group analysis with all forensic patients, regardless of gender.

Forensic group work with people with intellectual disabilities operates within a matrix of modalities. Central to this matrix is the therapeutic space in which the material is processed. This will, as the material outlined above indicates, be a space suffused with the pain of disability itself, alongside the agony of being abused and abusing others. The work, then, has much more in common with pure trauma work than it does with other forms of psychoanalytic group process. The psychopathology of the patients I have described can only be addressed through the treatment matrix being a co-ordinated one. Once this particular group was under way, the need for a parallel process was identified, in which the support systems for the men with disabilities could be attended to. This took the form of a weekly group comprising some education and training on areas such as risk management, sexual aggression, and the role of learning disability in psychopathology, alongside a process space in which the group's emotional response to the men they were working with could be analysed. The level at which such a group could be worked with varied. Only with long-term engagement could the deeper level process work be attempted. This would typically involve some examination of countertransference issues and workers' responses to both sexual aggression and disability itself.

The examples of group process described in this chapter seek to convey some of the nature of forensic work with people with intellectual disabilities, while also illustrating the need for such work to take place within the context of a containing and facilitative environment. There are, of course, myriad practical reasons for this. People with intellectual disabilities live largely in settings where they are dependent on others for their care. Therapy will not happen unless care is taken to communicate well with those around them. I argue further that the need for the environment to be a containing one is also rooted in the unconscious weight of the clinical material itself, and the powerful nature of the disability transference. When working with forensic patients who have intellectual disabilities, one is entering a territory of deep pain, of unprocessed thought, confusion, and trauma. Unless the environment is sturdy enough to allow the therapist's own responses to this level of trauma to be processed, it is fundamentally impossible to engage in meaningful therapeutic work. When the environment is nourished and nourishing, the potential for therapeutic growth is huge. Hope is a concept that was experienced more and more by the men in the group and, indeed, by me. This increased as I came to see the group's growing ability to tolerate pain and to process loss in a way that was about connection and relatedness rather than about the defensive acting out that the men had previously been consumed within. Above all else, the group, over a period of four years, created a space in which it became possible to think about not just the agonies of being abused and becoming an abuser, but also the paradox of one's emotional intelligence far outweighing one's cognitive abilities.

References

Appelbaum, P. S. (1997). Informed consent to psychotherapy: recent developments. *Psychiatric Services, 48*: 445–446.

Arscott, K., Dagnan, D., & Stenfert Kroese, B. (1999). Assessing the ability of people with a learning disability to give informed consent to treatment. *Psychological Medicine, 29*: 1367–1375.

Brown, H., Stein, J., & Turk, V. (1995). The sexual abuse of adults with learning disabilities: report of a second two year incidence survey. *Mental Handicap Research, 8*: 22–24.

Corbett, A. (2009). Words as a second language: the psychotherapeutic challenge of severe disability. In: T. Cottis (Ed.), *Intellectual Disability, Trauma and Psychotherapy*. London, Routledge.

Corbett, A. (2011). Silk purses and sows' ears: the social and clinical exclusion of people with intellectual disabilities. *Psychodynamic Practice*, 17(3): 273–289.

Doctor, R. (2003). *Dangerous Patients: A Psychodynamic Approach to Risk Assessment and Management*. London: Karnac.

Fonagy, P., Gergely, G., Jurist, E., & Target, M. (2004). *Affect Regulation, Mentalization, and the Development of the Self*. London: Karnac.

Foulkes, S. H. (1964). *Therapeutic Group Analysis*. London: George Allen & Unwin.

Foulkes, S. H. (1975). *Group Analytic Psychotherapy*. London: Gordon and Breach.

Frankish, P. (1992). A psychodynamic approach to emotional difficulties within a social framework. *Journal of Intellectual Disability Research*, 36(6): 559–567.

Frankish, P., & Terry, S. (2003). Modern therapeutic approaches in learning disability services. *Tizard Learning Disability Review*, 8: 3–10.

Freud, S. (1904a). Freud's psycho-analytic procedure. *S.E.*, 7: 249–256. London: Hogarth.

Freud, S. (1926d). Inhibitions, Symptoms and Anxiety. *S.E.*, 20: 77–174. London: Hogarth.

Glasser, M. (1979). Some aspects of the role of aggression in the perversions. In: I. Rosen (Ed.), *Sexual Deviation* (pp. 278–305). Oxford: Oxford University Press.

Goddard, A., Murray, C., & Simpson, J. (2007). Informed consent and psychotherapy: an interpretative phenomenological analysis of therapists' views. *Journal of Psychology and Psychotherapy*, 81: 278–305.

Hollins, S. & Esterhuyzen, A. (1997). Bereavement and grief in adults with learning disabilities. *British Journal of Psychiatry*, 170: 497–501.

Hollins, S., & Sinason, V. (2000). Psychotherapy, learning disabilities and trauma: new perspectives. *British Journal of Psychiatry*, 176: 32–36.

Hopper, E. (2003). *Traumatic Experience in the Unconscious Life of Groups: The Fourth Basic Assumption: Incohesion: Aggregation/massification or (ba) I:A/M*. London: Jessica Kingsley.

Itard, J.-M. (1932). *The Wild Boy of Aveyron*. New York: Century.

Kahr, B. (2000). A new breed of clinicians: disability psychotherapists. *Psychotherapy Review*, 2: 193–194.

Klein, M. (1946). Notes on some schizoid mechanisms. *International Journal of Psychoanalysis*, 27: 99–110.

McCormack, B., Kavanagh, D., Caffrey, S., & Power, A. (2005). Investigating sexual abuse: findings of a 15-year longitudinal study. *Journal of Applied Research in Intellectual Disabilities*, 18: 217–227.

Motz, A. (2001). *The Psychology of Female Violence: Crimes Against The Body*. Hove & New York: Brunner-Routledge.

Murphy, G., & O'Callaghan, A. (2004). Capacity of adults with intellectual disabilities to consent to sexual relationships. *Psychological Medicine, 34*.

Nitsun, M. (1996). *The Anti-group: Destructive Forces in the Group and Their Creative Potential*. London: Routledge.

O'Neill, P. (1998). *Negotiating Consent in Psychotherapy*. New York: New York University Press.

Seguin, E. (1856). Origin of the treatment and training of idiots. *American Journal of Education*, 2: 145–152.

Sinason, V. (1986). Secondary mental handicap and its relationship to trauma. *Psychoanalytic Psychotherapy*, 2: 131–154.

Sinason, V. (1988a). Richard III, Hephaestus and Echo: sexuality and mental/multiple handicap. *Journal of Child Psychotherapy*, 14(2): 93–106.

Sinason, V. (1988b). Smiling, swallowing, sickening and stupefying: the effect of sexual abuse on the child. *Psychoanalytic Psychotherapy*, 3(2): 97–112.

Sinason, V. (1990). Passionate lethal attachments. *British Journal of Psychotherapy*, 7(1): 66–76.

Sinason, V. (1991). Psychoanalytical psychotherapy with the severely, profoundly, and multiply handicapped. In: R. Szur & S. Miller (Eds.), *Extending Horizons: Psychoanalytic Psychotherapy with Children, Adolescents and Families* (pp. 225–242). London: Karnac.

Sinason, V. (1992). *Mental Handicap and the Human Condition: New Approaches from the Tavistock*. London: Free Association Books.

Sinason, V. (1995). Revenge and learning disability. *Self & Society*, 23(1): 16–19.

Sinason, V. (1996). From abused to abuser. In: C. Cordess & M. Cox (Eds.), *Forensic Psychotherapy: Crime, Psychodynamics and the Offender Patient. Mainly Practice* (pp. 371–382). London, Jessica Kingsley.

Sinason, V. (1997a). Gender-linked issues in psychotherapy with abused and learning disabled female patients. In: J. Raphael-Leff, & R. J. Perelberg (Eds.), *Female Experience: Three Generations of British Women Psychoanalysts on Work with Women* (pp. 266–280). London: Routledge.

Sinason, V. (1997b). Stress in the therapist and the Bagshaw syndrome. In: V. P. Varma (Ed.), *Stress in Psychotherapists* (pp. 101–113). London: Routledge.

Sinason, V. (2002). *Attachment, Trauma and Multiplicity: Working with Dissociative Identity Disorder*. Hove: Brunner-Routledge.

Sobsey, D. (1994). *Violence and Abuse in the Lives of People With Disabilities: The End of Silent Acceptance?* Baltimore, MD: Paul H Brookes.

Welldon, E. V. (1988). *Mother, Madonna, Whore. The Idealisation and Denigration of Motherhood*. London: Karnac.

Welldon, E. V. (2011). *Playing with Dynamite: A Personal Approach to the Psychoanalytic Understanding of Perversions, Violence, and Criminality*. London: Karnac.

Wolfensberger, W. (1987). *The New Genocide of Handicapped and Afflicted People*. New York: Syracuse.

Woods, J. (2003). *Boys Who Have Abused: Psychoanalytic Psychotherapy with Victims/Perpetrators of Sexual Abuse*. London: Jessica Kingsley.

INDEX

absence, 20, 24, 26, 42–43, 65, 91, 97, 102, 141, 146, 176, 196
abuse (*passim*)
   child, xxiii, 4, 13, 21, 83–85, 107, 109, 111–112, 114–116, 118, 120, 124, 129, 131, 136–138, 142–143, 145, 155, 158, 185, 189
   cycle of, 109
   emotional, 109, 141, 145, 159
   parental, 155, 158
   pathology of, 143
   pattern of, 124
   physical, 156, 188
   sexual, xv, xxiii, 3, 6, 9, 15, 17, 23, 45, 83, 90, 107, 109–110, 112, 114, 117–118, 121, 129–132, 134–135, 138, 140, 144, 146, 185, 188–189, 194
   verbal, 159
   virtual, 147
acting out, xvi, xxiii, 13, 18–19, 24, 34, 44, 46, 53–54, 60–61, 65, 99–102, 124, 140, 161, 170, 176, 186

catastrophic, 61
dangerous, 89
defensive, 198
sexual, 55, 57, 64–65
violent, 89
Adshead, G., 157
affect(ive), 71, 77, 94, 145, 157, 170, 177
   atmosphere, 70
   difficult, 38
   experience, 87, 168
   negative, 157, 160
   painful, 17, 28
   state, 167
   unmanageable, 177
   violence, 159–160
aggression, 10–11, 20, 28, 36, 60, 63, 72, 81–83, 85–87, 89, 101, 103, 130, 133, 137, 142–143, 146, 155, 158, 160–164, 168, 175–176, 191, 195, 197
behaviour, 83–85, 163
bravado, 174

destructive, 86
direct, 86
excessive, 85
female, 84
healthy, 142
impulse, 164
infant, 61
passive-, 76
pathological, 157
reaction, 86, 175
response, 82, 85
sexual, 33, 86, 110, 114, 186, 194, 197
tendencies, 50
Alcoholics Anonymous, 162
Allen, J. G., 157
Altman, N., 6
Alvarez, A., 16
American Psychiatric Association (APA), 154
Anderson, L., 95
Andrews, P., 14
anger, 14, 17, 24–26, 33, 38, 75, 89–90, 96–97, 99, 102, 119, 121, 133, 137, 139, 141–143, 153, 156, 160, 164, 169–170, 173, 175, 192 *see also*: unconscious(ness)
anxiety, xxii, 4, 18–19, 23–24, 36–37, 54, 57, 62–64, 70, 72, 75, 78, 85–86, 90, 98, 100–101, 109, 130, 132–134, 136, 138–140, 142, 156, 163–164, 166, 174, 176–178, 193, 196 *see also*: unconscious(ness)
  abandonment, 91, 95
  annihilation, 10, 85, 95, 196
  castration, 87
  complex, 96, 100, 103
  high, 44
  infantile, 93
  initial, 69
  intense, 96
  pervasive, 85
  pre-oedipal, 85, 87, 92
  primitive, 82–83, 89, 92, 95, 176
  psychotic, 44, 46, 54, 95, 141
  separation, 89, 99
  symptoms of, 45

Appelbaum, P. S., 188
Appleby, L., xiv
Arscott, K., 188
Athena, 145–146
attachment, 28, 36, 86, 96, 99–101, 123, 152, 155–156, 178, 194–195
  see also: disorder
  addictive, 144
  disrupted, xxii
  emotional, 155
  figures, 131, 142–143
  history, 156–157
  intimate, 171
  needs, 176
  patterns, 111, 157
  process, 156, 159, 167
  relationships, 28, 157
  robust, 36
  secure, 157
  theory, 28

Balint, M., 130
basic assumption (ba), xi, 8, 89
  fight/flight, 145
  Incohesion:
    Aggregation/Massification
    (I:A/M), xi, 8
  theory of, 120
Bassen, C. R., 93
Bateman, A., 152, 157–160, 167–168, 175, 178
behaviour, ix, xiv–xvi, xix–xx, 4, 12, 26, 36, 42, 44, 53–55, 58–59, 61, 81, 84, 88–89, 100, 107, 116, 133, 153, 155, 157, 196 *see also*: aggression
  abusive, 24
  acceptable, 9
  antisocial, 151, 153–156
  cognitive-, xxiv, 153
  correct, 5
  destructive, xiv, 8
  deviant, xix, 60
  disturbing, xv, 101, 103
  exhibitionist, 90
  infant, 158

observable, 154
offending, xxiv, 76, 108, 118
patterns, 112
perverse, 13, 85–87
problematic, 5, 36, 63, 96–97
repetitive, 54
self-harming, 137
sexual, x, xxiii, 56, 69, 83, 84–85, 92, 117–118, 153, 193
symptomatic, 142
transgressive, xiii
violent, 53, 80, 83, 86, 111, 153, 157, 161, 164–165
Behr, H. L., xxi
Bentovim, A., 109, 116, 118
Bernstein, D. P., 163
Bion, W. R., xxii, xxiv, 6, 8, 12, 17, 42, 50, 57, 89, 95, 120, 145–146, 157, 177–178
  alpha function, 42, 145
  concept of containment, 50
Blackmore, C., 3
Bowlby, J., 156–157
Bowman, D., 80
Bragesjo, M., 157
Breen, D., 94–96
Brown, A., 107
Brown, D., 15
Brown, H., 185
Brown, S., 5
Burlingame, G. M., 3

Caddick, B., 107
Caffrey, S., 185
Campbell, D., 131
Caper, R., 77
Carnes, P., 24
Caspi, A., 155
Catina, A., 14
Chambers, E., 3
Chasseguet-Smirgel, J., 20, 60, 103
clinical vignettes
  Chapter One
    Derek, 22
    Frank, 21–22
    Fred, 26–27
    Geoff, 25–27
    Graham, 18
    Jim, 18, 25–27
    Joe, 16–17
    Larry, 14
    Leslie, 19
    Mark, 16, 25–27
    Martin, 11, 13
    Michael, 14, 20, 22
    Mick, 17
    Nigel, 24
    Patrick, 11
    Phil, 15
    Roger, 9
    Ron, 15
    Steve, 19
    Timothy, 13
  Chapter Two
    Alan, 38
    Brendan, 46–49
    Colin, 46–48
    George, 40–41
    Mark, 45
    Stephen, 42–43
  Chapter Three
    Adrian, 58–59
    Derek, 61–65
    Jonathan, 56–58
  Chapter Five
    Andy, 96–101
    Bill, 97
    Darren, 97, 99–100
    Dr L, 96–102, 104
    Dr S, 98–99, 101, 104
    John, 90
    Martin, 99
    Matt, 90
    Richard, 97–102
    Simon, 90
    Toby, 89
    Tony, 90
  Chapter Six
    Adrian, 119–120
    Derek, 124
    Fred, 113
    George, 113, 121

James, 113–114, 122
Martin, 113–114, 119
Patrick, 121–124
Roger, 117
Chapter Seven
   Anne, 134–135, 137–139
   Helen, 132–133
   Jane, 132, 140
   Phil, 134–138
   Ronnie, 139
   Zack, 134–135, 137, 139
Chapter Eight
   Kevin, 169
   Mike, 168–170
Chapter Nine
   group excerpt, 190–193
Coccaro, E. F., 163
Coles, P., 10
compulsion, x, 6, 9, 19, 21, 24, 45, 54–55, 76
   repetition, 55, 57, 65
   sexual, 124
conflict, xiii–xv, xx, xxiii, 4, 6–7, 9–10, 14, 60, 65, 73–75, 93, 110, 112, 120, 166
   core, 187
   emotional, 4, 156
   existential, 10
   feelings, 88, 91, 135, 143
   fundamental, 85
   inner, 27, 65, 113
   intense, 119
   interpersonal, 114
   oedipal, 10
   sexual, 22
   transference, 122
   underlying, 54
Conlan, I., 82, 92
conscious(ness), 6–7, 43, 88, 91, 112, 154, 162, 170, 176–177 *see also*: unconscious(ness)
   rejection, 176
containment, xvi, xxiii, 14, 34, 39–40, 50, 104, 124, 157, 172, 174, 177, 179 *see also*: Bion, W. R.
   maternal, 111

   multi-layered, xvi
   psychoanalytic model of, 178
   supplementary, xvi
Cooper, A. M., 87
Corbett, A., xxiii, 184, 194
countertransference, xxi, 56, 117, 125, 177, 194, 196 *see also*: transference
   issues, 197
   reaction, 177
   response, 82, 191
Craig, I. W., 155

Dagnan, D., 188
Davis, M., 33
death, 10, 61, 70, 73, 102, 104, 123, 187, 195–196
   instinct, 55, 57, 65
   living, 120
   -making, 195
De Brito, S. A., 156
delinquency, ix, xiii, xix, 9, 11, 34, 60, 151
De Masi, F., 114–115
Department of Health, xiii, 35, 153
dependence, 16, 18, 57, 85, 89, 91, 95, 97, 111, 115, 157–158, 161, 177, 198
   absolute, 96
   failed, 195
   fears of, 88
   healthy, 133
   heightened, 115
   hostile, 4
   infantile, 82
   needs, 99
   relationship, 57
depression, 4, 14, 41, 45, 54, 56, 61–64, 70, 75, 122, 156, 162–164, 166, 174
   clinical, 44
   episode, 42
   position, 57, 61, 102
   stance, 82
   state, 42–43
Derks, F. C. H., 157
Dernevik, M., 157

de Ruiter, C., 157
development(al), xvi, 18, 23, 27–28,
    57, 74, 87, 95, 109–110, 131, 155,
    157–158, 166–167, 178–179
  achievement, 21
  child, 33, 141, 159
  disorder, 156–157
  experience, 96
  individual, 10
  lack, 109
  narcissistic, 86
  normal, 130
  of thinking, 28
  pathway, 155
  personality, 10, 157
  psychological, 156
  psychopathology, 157
  psychosexual, ix
  stage, 86
  therapeutic, 40
disability, 183–184, 186–188, 194, 197
    see also: transference
  intellectual, 184–185
  learning, xxiii, 197
  spectrum, 189
  therapy, 183–184, 186
disorder, 18, 153–155 *see also*:
    development(al)
  conduct, 154
  eating, 83
  of attachment, 86, 152, 178
  personality, xiii, 152–153, 155, 159,
      162–163, 167
    antisocial (ASPD), xi, xiii–xv,
        152–165, 167–168, 170–174,
        176, 178
    borderline (BPD), 90, 178, 153
  dissocial, 154
distress, xiii–xiv, xix, 43, 62, 116, 137,
    156, 170
disturbance, xiii–xv, 33–34, 46, 53,
    80
Doctor, R., 185
Dolan, B. M., 3
Douglas, K. S., 173
Duggan, C., 154

Eaves, D., 173
empathy, 76, 101, 136, 140–141, 143,
    146–147, 157, 160, 167
envy, 8, 55, 57–58, 60, 62, 65, 94, 102,
    110–111, 186, 188, 194 *see also*:
    unconscious(ness)
  attack, 103
  intense, 92, 176
  primitive, 103
  retaliation, 132
Erooga, M., 114
Esterhuyzen, A., 184
Etchegoyen, A., 93

fantasy, 8, 86–87, 92, 110–111, 138,
    143, 146, 176, 193, 196 *see also*:
    unconscious(ness)
  omnipotent, 99, 138
  perverse, 11
  safe, 143
  sexual, 59, 91, 113, 123
fear, xiv, xxi, 16–17, 21, 23, 27–28, 39,
    61, 77, 85, 97–98, 103, 120, 123,
    133, 135–136, 184, 186, 188,
    194–195, 197 *see also*:
    unconscious(ness)
  of abandonment, 20
  of annihilation, ix, 20, 194
  of breakdown, 96
  of castration, 194
  of change, 178
  of dependence, 88
  of destruction, 8
  of exposure, xxi
  of fragmentation, 100, 138
  of humiliation, 138
  of intimacy, 196
  of loss, 20, 86
  of punishment, 75
  of retribution, 10
Feldbrugge, J. T. T. M., 157
Feldman, M., 55
Felthous, A., 155
Fenster, S., 94
Ferenzci, S., 130, 142
Ferriter, M., 154

First, M. B., 162
Fishman, A., 3
Flora, D. B., 4
Floyd, M., 80
Fonagy, P., 21–23, 120, 152, 157–160, 167–168, 175, 178, 195
Foulkes, S. H., xxi–xxiii, 6–8, 14, 17–18, 92, 125, 184–186
Frankish, P., 184
Freud, A., 53–54
    Centre, 178
Freud, S., 10, 20, 28, 54–55, 57–58, 61, 87, 130, 184, 196
Friedman, M. E., 93
Frodi, A., 157

Garland, C., 6, 8, 12, 112, 121
Gavin, B., 95
Gergely, G., 195
Gibbon, M., 162
Gibbon, S., 154
Gilligan, J., xxiv, 23, 158–159
Glaser, D., 120
Glasser, M., x, xxiii, 20, 33, 85–86, 108, 110, 160, 178, 196
Glenn, L., 28
Glover, E., x, xix
Goddard, A., 188
Goldberg, J., 81
Gould, L. J., 82
Greenson, R. R., 23, 95
Group Analytic Society, 151
Groves, J. E., xiv
guilt, 10–11, 37–38, 59, 61, 75, 114, 118, 121, 130–131, 137, 143

Hale, R., 108
Hall, Z., 3, 112
Hare, R. D., 155, 173
Hart, S. T., 173
Harvey, P. D., 163
Heavey, C. L., 81
Herbert, J. L., 163
Hinshelwood, R. D., xvi, xxii, 6
Hitler, A., 10
Hodgins, S., 155–156

Hollins, S., 184, 187
Holmes, J., 6
Hopper, E., xi, 8, 120, 183
Huband, N., 154
Hume, F., 6

identity, xxii, 7, 27, 76, 85, 94, 116, 131, 158 *see also*: self
    gender, ix
    individual, 6
    masculine, 23
    personal, 140
    psychoanalytic, 151
    separate, 85
    sexual, ix, 93, 100, 131
Institute of Group Analysis, 151
Institute of Psychotherapy and Disability, 184
International Association of Forensic Psychotherapy, x, xx
intervention, 44, 73, 77, 107, 114, 122, 124, 153–154, 167–168, 170, 172, 175, 178
    active, 113
    collaborative, 44
    practical, 121
    therapeutic, xiii, 13, 36
Itard, J.-M., 184

Jones, A. P., 155
Joseph, B., 57
Joyce, A., 10
Jurist, E., 195

Kahr, B., 184
Kavanagh, D., 185
Keogh, T., 111
Khan, M. R., 142
King, E., 112
Klein, M., 10, 57, 61, 195
Kratzer, L., 155
Krystal, H., 141
Kupsaw-Lawrence, E., 163

Lacan, J., 10
Larsson, H., 155

Lax, R. F., 94–95
Leibing, E., 3
Leichsenring, F., 3
Levinson, A., 157
Lewis, G., xiv
Lieb, K., 154
Limentani, A., x, xix, 60
Lloyd-Owen, D., 83
Lorentzen, S., 3

Malcolm, R., 56
Martin, J., 155
Masson, H., 114
McCarthy, B., 111, 114
McClay, J., 155
McCormack, B., 185
McDougall, J., 141
McGarty, M., 93
McGauley, G. A., 165
McKendree-Smith, N., 80
McKinnon, D., 81
McNeil, T. F., 155
McWilliams, N., 93
Medusa, 145–146
Meloy, J. R., 155, 160, 178
Meltzer, D., 56
mentalization, 156–157, 159–160, 165, 170–171, 175, 177
 -based treatment (MBT), xi, xxii, 152, 160–162, 167, 170, 177–178
 principle, 170
 process, 157, 195
Menzies, D., 3
Mill, J., 155
Miller, A. A., 145
Mills, T. M., 81
Ministry of Justice, 153
Mitchell, J., 10
Moffitt, T., 155
Morgan, D., xix
Morgan, G., xiv
Morgan, R. D., 4
Mosier, J., 3
Motz, A., 197
Mullee, M., 3
Multi Agency Protection Panel, 25

Multi Agency Public Protection Arrangements Panel (MAPPA), 4, 174
Murphy, G., 188
Murray, C., 188

narcissistic, 10, 12, 21, 96, 108, 163
 see also: development(al), self
 extension, 84
 fragility, 168
 intolerance, 165
 mortification, 95
 needs, 85, 141
 pathology, 178
 relating, 111
 self-regulation, 146
 sensitivity, 170
 state, 86
 withdrawal, 20
Narcotics Anonymous, 162
National Health Service, xi, xxiv, 4
National Institute for Health and Clinical Excellence (NICE), 153–154, 162
Nitsun, M., 195
Norton, K., 3, 165

object, 11, 20, 57, 84, 86, 103, 110, 120, 141, 145–146, 157–158, 196
 see also: sexual, transference
 bad, 61
 choice, 21, 115
 early, 65
 gender-, ix
 good, 57, 61
 internal, 57, 70, 73, 103, 130
 lost, 132
 maternal, 20, 82–83, 85–87, 91, 100–101, 176
 of desire, xx
 of fear, 196
 of hate, 77
 part, 18, 111
 paternal, 87
 persecuting, 46
 primary, 61

relations, 20, 86, 146
    traumatising, 134, 138, 143–144, 147
    traumatogenic, 130–131
    unattainable, 24
O'Callaghan, A., 188
O'Dowd, T. C., xiv
oedipal, 95, 110 see also: anxiety, conflict
    couple, 92, 94, 176
    desires, 101
    level, xxiii
    pattern, 27
    pre-, 11, 82, 86–87, 89, 92, 95–96, 101, 103, 110–111, 176
    situation, 131
    themes, 101
Oedipus complex, xx
Ogden, T., 56
O'Neill, P., 188
Overt Aggression Scale (OAS), 174
Overt Aggression Scale-Modified (OAS-M), 163
Oxford English Dictionary, 5
Oxfordshire Area Child Protection Committee (OACPC), 131

paedophilia, xv, 21, 84, 107–109, 115, 125
paranoid, 163, 165, 170
    –schizoid position, 144, 171
    solutions, 75
Parry, G., 3
Parsons, M., 59–60
Parsons, T., 154, 165
Pedder, J., 15
Perelberg, R., xxiii, 23, 87
Perlman, L., 81, 88
Perseus, 145–146
perversion, ix, xix, 14, 19–20, 53–55, 60, 65, 83–85, 87, 90–91, 103, 116, 141, 196
    female, 83
    sexual, 5, 11, 20, 112, 116, 118, 121
Philipse, M. W. G., 157
Philipson, J., 157

Phillips, S., 94
Pikus, C. F., 81
Pines, M., 15
pornography, 17, 20–21, 24, 61–62, 118, 131, 143
    child, 38, 140, 143, 145–146, 153
    cinematographic, 101
    illegal, 38, 153
    images, 145
    Internet, 61
Portman Clinic, x–xi, xiv, xix, xxiv, 3, 5, 8, 20, 24, 34, 36, 54, 60, 69, 73, 77–78, 80, 83, 92–93, 95, 99, 102, 108, 129, 151–152, 173–174, 177–178
Poulton, R., 155
Power, A., 185
Probation Service, 5, 93, 162, 174
projection, xiv–xv, 34, 43, 46, 77, 82, 86–87, 91, 110, 114, 139, 143, 158, 160, 188, 194
    malign, 158
    mutual, 121
    of hostility, 23
    perverse, 124
    powerful, 194
    shared, 139
    unbearable, 145
projective
    experience, 194
    identification, 86–87
    processes, 39
Psychopathy Check List-Revised (PCL-R), 155
psychotic, 46, 111 see also: anxiety
    episodes, 44–45
    illness, 153, 161
    intensity, 95, 100
    processes, 6
    symptoms, 46

Raphael-Leff, J., 95
Rapoport, E., 94
reactions, xvi, 17, 60, 71, 83, 88, 94, 100, 168, 186 see also: aggression, countertransference

counterphobic, 96
defensive, 77, 130
primitive, 89
visceral, 114
reality, xxi, 14, 20, 34, 55, 63, 75, 77, 86, 100–101, 103, 109, 115–116, 138, 143, 147, 159–160, 189, 192
   concrete, 192
   external, xxi, 21–22, 46, 75, 142, 145, 159
   internal, 145, 147
   painful, 114
   paradoxical, 59
   present, 7
   psychic, 145
   psychological, 124
   symbolic, 22
   testing, 138
   visual, 93
Reid, S., 18
Reiss, D., xix
Rey, H., 34
Riksen-Walraven, J. M. A., 157
Rogers, C., 95
Rosen, I., xix
Rosenfeld, H., 61, 178
Rubitel, A., xix, xxiii
Ruszczynski, S., xix

sadistic, 20, 22, 86, 112, 144, 146, 189
   anal-, 103
   attack, 138
   control, 86
   exchanges, 133
   excitement, 131
   parental, 10
   punishment, 110
   treatment, 133
sadomasochistic, 74, 132, 189
   arousal, 147
   behaviour, 92
   defence, 147
   dynamic, 76, 92, 144
   enactment, 130
   exchanges, 47, 132

opportunity, 49
pleasure, 47
practices, 86
relationship, 110–111, 118
sex(uality), ix, 135
structure, 138
violence, 160
Sarkar, J., 157
Sass, H., 155
Saunders, D. G., 3
Schaverien, J., 109
Schore, A., 157
Scogin, F., 80
Segal, H., 24, 111
Seguin, E., 184
self, 5, 10, 14, 19, 82, 86, 118–119, 142, 155, 158, 163, 174 *see also*: behaviour
   alien, 158, 160, 172
   -awareness, 114
   bodily, 120
   -centred, 18
   child, 111
   -coherence, 158
   -deception, xxi, 19
   -destructive, 12–13, 116
   -doubt, 140
   -esteem, 23, 173
   -exploration, xxi
   -expression, 158
   false, 142
   -feeding, 57
   -harming, xxi, 13, 43, 134, 137
   -help, 18
   -identity, 6
   innermost, 16
   -justification, 116
   -knowledge, 7, 17, 112
   -less, 87
   narcissistic, 146
   -perception, 123
   -preservative, 86, 160
   -reflective, 157
   -regard, 168
   -regulation, 146
   -report, 163

-representation, 158
sense of, 109
-soothing, 146
-traumatising, 130
-understanding, 12
-worth, 160
Sepa, A., 157
Sex Addicts Anonymous (SAA), 24, 63, 88
Sex Offences Prevention Order (SOPO), 122
Sex Offenders Treatment Programme, 5
sexual, ix, 20, 57, 59, 75 *see also*: abuse, aggression, behaviour, compulsion, conflict, development, fantasy, identity, perversion, sadomasochistic
  acting out, 55, 57, 64–65
  addiction, 24
  anonymous, 8, 146
  arousal, 20, 112, 143
  assault, 37, 134–135
  attraction, 96, 98, 100, 187, 196
  body, 96
  compulsion, 124
  conflict, 22
  contact, 114, 143
  crime, 185
  desire, 122
  deviant, xix, 24
  differences, 80, 103
  encounter, 14, 61, 75
  excitement, 86, 91, 101
  experience, 96, 189
  exploitation, 8, 117
  feelings, 192
  foreplay, 97
  function, 21
  gratification, 19
  intercourse, 130
  interest, 19, 107, 115, 122
  Internet, 63
  liaison, 88
  life, 130
  matters, 99

maturity, 130
motivation, 86
object, 118
  choice, 115
objectification, 75
offenders, x, xxiv, 107–108, 110, 112, 116, 118, 129
orientation, 19, 107–108, 115, 136
partner, 110
phantasy, 146
place, 195
pleasure, 90
predators, 90
promiscuity, 88, 91
provocative, 99
psycho-, 107
relationship, 8, 20, 24–25, 88, 122
roles, 79
seductive, 88
terrorists, 189
thoughts, 113, 192
threat, 94
trauma, 145, 147
violence, xiii, 69
sexuality, ix, 60, 76, 79–80, 89, 92–94, 109, 187
  adult, 109
  bi-, ix
  deviant, 21
  hetero-, ix, 59
  homo-, ix, 20, 94–96, 98, 100, 191
  infantile, 87, 110
  paedo-, 21
Shepherd, R., 33
Sifneos, P. E., 141
Simpson, J., 188
Sinason, V., 184, 187, 195
Sobsey, D., 185
Spitzer, R. L., 162
splitting, xx, 5, 36, 42, 61, 82, 85–88, 91–92, 114, 187, 190
Spoto, G. F., xxi
Stein, J., 185
Steiner, J., 16
Stenfert Kroese, B., 188
Stoffers, J., 154

Stoller, R. J., xxiii, 95, 118
Strauss, J., 92
symbol(-ic), xx, 23–24, 27–28, 100, 104, 111, 115, 134, 142, 144–145, 159, 187–190, 192–193
    exploration, 148
    formation, 116
    order, 10–11
    reality, 22
    representation, 120

Tantum, D., 3
Target, M., 21–23, 120, 152, 159, 195
Tavistock
    and Portman Trust, xi, xix, 152
    Centre, 34
Taylor, A., 155
Taylor, R., 3
Terry, S., 184
Thunnissen, M., 95
Trampuz, D., 95
transference, xxi, 18, 55–56, 70, 77, 82, 91, 93–94, 103, 125, 169 *see also*: conflict, countertransference, unconscious(ness)
    ambivalent, xxiii
    content, 15
    disability, 198
    group, 194
    idealised, 81
    implications, 74
    interpretations, 170, 173
    issues, 94, 102
    maternal, 11, 79
    multiple, xv, 164
    negative, 61, 81, 88
    object, 144
    paedophile, 115
    perverse, 124
    relationship, 54, 56, 87
    sibling, 10
    stimulus, 93
    vertical, 10
    violent, xv
Tschuschke, V., 14
Turk, V., 185

unconscious(ness), xxi–xxii, 7–8, 84, 86, 89, 91, 94, 99, 101–103, 118–119, 144–145, 154, 162, 175, 186, 190, 195, 198 *see also*: conscious(ness)
    acknowledgment, 139
    agenda, 84
    anger, 173
    anxiety, 82, 132, 141, 144
    attack, 87, 176
    communication, 14, 103
    content, 15
    determinants, 13
    dynamics, 82
    envy, 92
    fantasy, 79, 82, 87, 93, 100–101, 190
    fears, 176
    feelings, 132
    material, 194
    phantasy, 132, 146
    process, xxi, 39, 183, 186
    purpose, xiv
    recognition, 48
    transference, 84
    wish, 92, 101, 146

Van der Kolk, B. A., 120
van der Staak, C. P. F., 157
Van IJzendoorn, M. H., 157
Van Velsen, C., xx, 5, 114
Verhagen, M. F. M., 157
Viding, E., 155
Völlm, B. A., 154

Warren, F. M., 3
Watts, D., xiv
Webster, C. D., 173
Welldon, E., x, xiv, xix–xx, xxiii–xxiv, 3–5, 8, 10–11, 19, 21, 27, 36, 39, 79, 83–84, 89, 92, 108, 112, 114, 124, 129, 151–152, 164, 172, 176, 178, 197
Wellendorf, E., 10
West, J., 114–115
Whyte, N., 95
Williams, B., 109

Williams, J. B. W., 162
Winnicott, D. W., xx, 33–34, 39, 50, 59, 142, 156–158, 177–178
  concept of holding, 50
Wolfensberger, W., 195
Wong, S., 155, 173
Wood, H., 21, 107–109, 112, 116, 118
Woods, J., x, 13, 186

World Health Organization (WHO), 154
Wright, F., 82

Yakeley, J., xxiii, 11, 177–178
Yalom, I., 4

Zeus, 146